The
Last
Patriot

A novel

Michael Hilliard

*An invisible, highly-skilled terrorist faction
has declared war on the United States.*

*They have no conscience.
They have all the time in the world.*

© *2005 Michael Hilliard. All Rights Reserved.*

No part of this book may be reproduced, stored in a retrieval system, or transmitted by any means without the written permission of the author.

First published by AuthorHouse 11/08/05

ISBN: 1-4208-9634-2 (sc)
ISBN: 1-4208-9635-0 (dj)

Library of Congress Control Number: 2005909759

Printed in the United States of America
Bloomington, Indiana

This book is printed on acid-free paper.

Cover design by Bridgette Swab

For Kimberly and Chase
My home team

The
Last
Patriot

Prologue

December 1978
Oval Office
The White House

IT WAS JUST AFTER MIDNIGHT when the president gave the order.

Standing with his back to the director of the CIA, the weary leader stared through the south window of the Oval office; stroking his chin and wondering just how many other chief executives had stood where he was at such odd hours in thoughtful contemplation.

With a wall of darkness just outside the thick glass, he was barely able to see the expansive lawn; further challenged to detect anything specific. Still, he tried to discern the odd shapes and jagged shadows, more an attempt at distraction than deliberation. He didn't like making such decisions, and the one he was approving bothered him perhaps more than any other.

The president felt the penetrating stare at his back, the pointed gaze of the director of the CIA, and with a smooth twist of his waist the president nodded to the man, a silent approval of the operation that had been over a year in the making. The Patriot Operation.

The director regarded the signal without emotion, though his mind was reeling with the substantial and far-reaching implications.

"Are you sure, sir?" he asked, the words breaking the stale silence.

The president cast a cool look at the man. "Yes I am."

But then empty moments passed and the president's look softened. "But explain it to me again. Tell me why it's the right thing to do."

The director was expecting the query. He eyed the president keenly, but spoke casually, nonchalantly.

"Sir, the Cold War is over. There are no more beaches to land on and no more strategic hills to take. The days of sending troops to a distant land to fight a war are gone. The front lines of the future will be invisible, ambiguous, and exponential; encompassing the backyards of the American populace. We are moving to a world economy and the enemies of the future will most likely be terrorist factions or loose governments that our satellites simply cannot track effectively."

The director slowly rose and walked to the president, who stood unmoved, his back turned as if trying to dismiss the idea altogether. The director's demeanor was relaxed but engaging, and a look of concern was evident as he searched for an emphatic end to the message he was so careful in communicating.

"Mr. President," he began slowly. "We need operators on the inside -- human intelligence -- if we are to eliminate or even reduce the threat."

The president squared himself against the director, his words almost accusatory.

"And who are these men who will so eagerly relinquish their freedoms, their lives?"

"We've code named them 'Patriots,' sir. And they will operate without any support or recognition from the United States, entrenching themselves in the most dangerous of places, attacking these threats from the inside. They are making the ultimate sacrifice to their country and are true examples of the word."

The president studied the director. Hearing the words flow so easily, he was struck with a harsh reality. He was creating an elite group of fighting men -- committing twenty in all -- to a lifetime mission that would most likely end in their deaths. Their duty and ultimate demise would go unnoticed, their gravesites likely shallow and unmarked. Unceremonious at best; uncolorful and without honor for sure.

And although it was something he knew was necessary, the operation's design had been orchestrated by others within the Defense Department; its plans known only to a few and based upon intelligence that he couldn't validate.

"Tell me about them," The president said, now walking the room slowly, his eyes focused on the floor.

"They are the most highly trained, battle-proven, and mentally equipped operators we have; perfectly able to melt into any culture or scenario and personally handpicked from the deepest extensions of the Special Forces community. They are each an island to themselves -- one-man war machines -- and they will be moving independently from one another."

"And they will kill 'innocents' to achieve their ultimate goal?"

"If it is necessary to gain a foothold into an organization, they will fully participate in terrorist actions, perhaps against our interests. But we figure any short-term casualties can be absorbed at the prospect of long term stability."

"And I assume no one will know of this?'"

"No one but the men themselves and a very small contingency that I control. Everything dies with us and them, and this conversation never took place."

The president walked back to the window, resuming his deliberate stare into the darkness. The meeting over and the order delivered, the director of the CIA exited the Oval office without further discussion.

When alone, the president spoke to himself in a hushed whisper, barely audible for even him to hear.

"May God forgive me for what I've just done."

The Patriot Operation was born.

Chapter 1

Present Day
October
Eastern Afghanistan
White Mountains

THE TERRORIST STRIKES were only day's away, so the most
wanted man in the world took refuge in the White Mountains of
eastern Afghanistan. Alone with his thoughts; alone to pray.

Almedi Hahn Sahn knew they couldn't find him but also that
they'd never stop looking. The old man moved often and in very
small groups, using body doubles and contingency plans, but most
importantly exploiting every safe harbor he knew.

He was the spiritual leader of al Assad -- the most dangerous
terrorist faction in the world -- but it hadn't always been that way.
He was from a respected Saudi oil family worth billions, educated
in universities in both London and Saudi Arabia, and was once a
legitimate and well-regarded owner of several businesses in the oil
industry.

But that was before Egypt and Israel had signed a peace treaty
that acknowledged a Jewish state on Islamic land, before the Soviets
occupied Afghanistan and defiled Islamic territory, and before he

turned to Islamic fundamentalism with an unchecked hatred for the West. After openly financing terrorist activity for over twenty years, most of his assets had been frozen and were now reportedly reduced to only *tens* of millions of dollars, scattered across hundreds of institutions around the globe.

Now in his seventies, he was a tiny man with thinning white hair and a long, stray beard. He was, however, surprisingly agile and alert; completely at ease with a nomadic lifestyle of dishevelment and volatility. The effects of time, it seemed, were unable to reduce his energy or dull his resolve.

Perhaps that's why he felt so comfortable in the mountainous Pashtun tribal land near the Pakistan border. He knew there was a sizeable bounty on his head, but also that he would find no safer refuge than among the Pashtun culture and specifically their time-tested code of honor, the Pashtunwali.

The system was based on revenge, hospitality, and sanctuary. It was something he knew the West would never understand and their ignorance only aided him further. Because of his earlier dealings with the Pashtun people, their traditions offered him sanctuary forever. And because several U.S-led bombing raids -- like Qulaye Niazi in late 2001 -- had killed Afghan civilians; the Pashtunwali granted an *inherited* duty to take revenge. As such, many Pashtuns resented the West and he found sanctuary throughout the Afghan villages.

He was here to pray for his mujahideen; the holy warriors he had sent to strike at the American infidels. The attacks were just days away and he knew that his four top lieutenants -- Yamir, Simon, Hortence, and most importantly Falby -- were working at their duties with fervor.

He glanced at his communications bag and smiled. It held a satellite phone and computer hardware that made any translation or tracking of his location impossible. Just minutes prior, he had contacted Yamir in London and provided the final details of the man's mission.

For now though, he stared up and into the night, regarding the bright stars against the vast sky. With no hint of any real technology for almost a hundred miles, the darkness wasn't tainted by unnatural illumination and the complete and total silence left him in awe. In a moment's time he saw hundreds of thousands of stars, but then the tiny dots became more defined as several constellations appeared.

He stared at Leo -- the lion -- with its ninety-five stars shining magnificently. Then he looked to the brightest star on the ecliptic which marked its heart and another on the mane named al Giebha. The Exaltation.

In a way, he and the constellation were related. He had founded and financed al Assad -- The Lion -- and was about to strike at the heart of the United States of America.

He thought of the specific strikes and smiled: The Golden Gate Bridge, Madison Square Garden, and the Sears Tower, among others. And then there was the ultimate prize that no one would see coming.

And there was nothing anyone could do to stop it.

Chapter 2

YAMIR RAN FOR HIS LIFE -- sprinting through the streets of London's West End -- looking ahead as much as behind. Dodging random groupings of people and tearing through untested alleys, he dashed between moving cars and curious onlookers; his eyes darting in all directions in search of the enemy that was surely tracking him. *They* were finally on to him and wouldn't stop until he was dead. *They* were everywhere.

But the envelope had to be delivered.

Athletic by nature and toned by years of dedication, he was accustomed to running several miles per day. But this was different. The city streets, ranging from cobblestone, brick, and modern concrete and asphalt, were clearly not homogeneous and the flow of people in his hurried path tested his even strides. Exhausted from the day's events and half-expecting to be shot dead at anytime, he couldn't concentrate on his breathing, which burdened him further. Still, he ran until his breaths erupted into short heaves and his body shook for more air.

Abandoning the sleek form he had maintained for several miles, he allowed his arms to flail wildly as he clumsily threw his legs in front of him. But even as his hurried gasps injected an intolerable hotness into his chest, and the air he swallowed dried his throat even more, he ran harder.

The information he carried *had* to make it to the U.S. embassy where it *had* to reach the CIA. Only then would his mission be satisfied and thousands of innocent lives could be saved, though probably not his own.

He was a "Patriot," one of the forgotten clandestine operators who were tasked to disappear forever and align with the most evil of intentions. And Yamir had done just that until he had come into specific information of terrorist activity, including dates and targets.

He had broke from the faction -- had even killed a man in doing so -- and thus had exposed himself as a traitor to al Assad. And now the best equipped and most focused terrorist faction in the world was hunting him. So he ran.

He was heavily armed and unafraid of the confrontation that was sure to come, but *they* were anywhere and everywhere, practically invisible, and he was completely exposed. The path he took was unplanned and not secure, and he was grossly outnumbered by a faceless enemy, most of whom he'd never even known.

Exhausted, he turned the corner onto North Adlee and then crossed Upper Brook Street, as the United States embassy finally drew near. He paused at the statue of Dwight D. Eisenhower, allowing a few moments of rest before pressing on.

Then, with only a few hundred yards to go, he sprinted to Upper Grovesner Street and to the long cement barricades and high barbed-wire fencing that encircled the U.S. embassy. Uniformed guards stood at select corners and well-positioned video cameras kept a silent, detached eye on the happenings at the perimeter.

Removing the envelope from the inner workings of his jacket, he started toward the fencing as a United States Marine, and several others, moved to meet him.

"Sir, you must move on," the Marine ordered, and Yamir studied the man as his breathing leveled.

The soldier's finger was directly on the trigger of his M-16, though the barrel was pointed a few feet to the right and down. And although young, the Marine's clean look, muscular frame, and dignified uniform spoke of authority; his alert but calm demeanor gave Yamir little doubt that the man was poised to take any action necessary.

The guard quickly looked Yamir over, searching the man's intentions for any possible threat. His eyes traded focus between the envelope and the man's hands, which to Yamir's credit, were kept in plain view.

Yamir extended the envelope through the fencing and toward the Marine, who took a step back.

"Take it," Yamir directed. "I cannot explain the agency I'm with, but it is very important that it gets to Steve McCallister of the CIA. All of the routing information is on the envelope."

"Sir, I can't accept anything that…"

"Just take it!" Yamir shouted. "Thousands of lives are at stake!"

"Sir, the proper channels to deliver a…"

"I don't have time for procedure. Deliver it or thousands will die."

"Throw it through the fencing," the young guard conceded. Then he turned to the others. "Bring me a dog."

Yamir did as he was told as a German Shepherd was brought to the area. After checking the envelope with several quick and uneventful sniffs, it was verified as non-threatening and some of the tension lifted.

The Marine picked up the envelope and read it aloud. "Steve McCallister, huh?"

Yamir nodded and watched as the guard walked the stairs that led to the embassy, finally disappearing inside and around a corner. Then his line of sight floated upward to the impressive gold lettering of "The United States of America" in the lobby.

He had completed his mission and in doing so compromised his life. The immediate burden lifted, he looked around expectantly, placed both hands in his windbreaker and onto the two fully loaded 9 millimeter handguns in his pockets. He stepped into an uncertain future, but with his confidence rebuilding, it was one he was certain he could control.

He was after all a 'Patriot' and fully capable of handling anything the enemy had in mind.

Dodging the man's glance, Simon emerged from the convenient shelter of a town home across the street. He witnessed Yamir's exchange with the Marines and the envelope trading hands, silently cursing himself for letting it happen. Still, Yamir had never seen Simon, and this was a formidable advantage.

After following him for a couple blocks, Simon was about seven feet behind Yamir as they both crossed South Adlee Street and walked along the road.

Chapter 3

THE COFFEE WAS STRONG; hitting his taste buds hard and washing over his heavy tongue. The caffeine charged his system immediately and a comfortable warmth coated his stomach, emphasizing the large breakfast he'd just enjoyed. He walked onto his deck and into the morning air, regarding the expansive tree line before sitting at a large plastic table.

It was early on a crisp October Sunday morning and Steve McCallister was very much looking forward to reading the Washington D.C. newspapers and enjoying the colors of the season. Opening the first of three, he sat and wrapped his hands around the hot mug, bringing it to his lips once more.

His home in Great Falls, Virginia was located in the small community of Potomac Overlook. Located just off the D.C. Beltway, it was pitted at the northeast extremity of Potomac River Road, a winding offshoot that rose and fell as it descended from Georgetown Pike.

The trees were centuries old and rose high, offering the extra degree of anonymity he sought. It had not been a major consideration when the government had moved him into the area, and in fact the coverage could work against him just as easily, but with his current ties to the CIA, the ex-military man favored the added barrier.

The topography of the land fell dramatically behind his home, allowing a high and splendid view into the woods from his deck. The hickory's, oaks, spruces, and sugar maples hosted an array of spectacular colors, especially this time of year, and Steve had recently been carving out time to enjoy the scenery.

With all the craziness he'd seen, he found no better comfort or solitude than when drinking a cup of good coffee and admiring the colors of nature. The view allowed his mind to wander and to think of things much less arduous than what he had specialized in for over thirty years. Soldiering, and indeed the whole practice of war, was not glamorous and he was rarely allowed repose -- especially at his level -- even in supposed peacetime.

He hoped to someday *truly* retire and seek refuge in the beautiful landscape of Colorado, breathing the clean air and spending entire days doing mundane tasks, household duties, and watching old movies. He could get a part-time job at a library, learn to appreciate fine wines, and maybe even tend to a small garden. To think of garnishing his dinner plate with vegetables he'd cultivated would be a complete detachment from whom he'd been for as long as he could remember. It would be a new life and the mere prospect made him smile.

But it was a dream he wasn't sure that he could ever realize. He'd been a principal operator in some of the U.S. military's best kept secrets and had knowledge of things that no one knew, save a handful of high level personnel. And although the emotional burden of his past sometimes screamed for release, his sense of patriotism and duty called to him hungrily, and often.

He had long come to terms that he was usually the most highly trained and capable man for the job, and that task, wherever it called him for the sake of his country, had to be done.

He took another long sip of coffee and turned the pages of the *Washington Post*, scanning every word with honed efficiency. He stretched his legs, eased back in the chair, and silently praised his comfortable attire. He wore old Nike sweatpants and a tattered sweatshirt. Both garments, comfortably faded and nearly worn thin, were a welcome abandonment of the stiff clothes he donned for more than sixty hours per week at CIA headquarters in Langley.

The CIA had many unofficial personnel and he was a perfect example of the term. These contractors were highly specialized and "off the books," hired for narrow duties that usually had no specific timetable. Some could work a few hours per week, while others had a more permanent, albeit unofficial role. Steve was an example of the latter and had been personally recruited by the director a few years prior.

Steve had served in the Army for over thirty years -- many of them entrenched in Special Operations Units -- before retiring as a Sergeant Major. Within hours of becoming a civilian, the director of the CIA had found him. Recruited him.

Steve's war record was perfect and highlighted by unwavering allegiance and understated effectiveness. To his command he was faithful and honest; to his mission relentless and always successful. He was known by his superiors as a man who got things done, by his men as a leader who had both vision and integrity in the field. He fought beside his team in every harrowing situation and always led the way through the madness.

He'd worked in popular campaigns in Vietnam, Grenada, Afghanistan, and Iraq, but the balance of his work was classified and not even recorded. His file, which could only be partially assembled, was the most impressive resume the CIA director had ever seen.

Consequently, and not to his liking, Steve was the only unofficial person to have an office on the coveted seventh floor of CIA Headquarters, which was historically reserved for top officials, including the director, the deputy director, the director of intelligence, the executive director, and their staff. What was more interesting, though, was how quickly he and the director had become such good friends; each other's confidants.

Steve quickly became Director Donald Willard's right hand man and was involved in most of the man's happenings. He also became known at every level as a hands-on operator that everyone wanted to get close to.

At age fifty-six, Steve was very physically fit and ran several miles every other day; the only evidence of aging being the gray that meshed into his thick, dark hair. Standing well over six feet tall, he carried his athletic frame well and commanded a presence that called to people. He was easy to talk to, always honest, direct, and fair; but also tentative, speaking only after thoroughly contemplating every angle. He was determined, deliberate, and calculating, and had all of the qualities the director sought in heading the CIA's anti-terrorism campaign.

As such, Steve led a team of over three hundred and had one of the more visible units inside the CIA. He often cross-referenced data with intelligence agencies and military installations abroad, and worked closely with the NSA, FBI, and the Department of Homeland Security. He arrived at 5:45 a.m. every day and left no sooner than 6 p.m.

He held a thankless position whose successes were rarely acknowledged, but his unit, he knew, was of utmost importance to the American people. And with the intelligence community under increased criticism and scrutiny by the media, the director of the CIA had found no better man for the job than Steve McCallister.

Finishing the *Washington Post*, Steve placed it aside and reached for the *Times*. Laying it out, he sipped more coffee and took a break, thinking of the short vacation he would take at the end of the week. He had a unique friendship with two childhood friends -- Blake and Pete -- and the three were meeting in Lucerne, Switzerland for a quick getaway.

The three had grown up on the same street and had been best friends since pre-school, steadfastly bonding in all of the recreational activities of youth. From pick-up basketball and backyard football games, to cars, girls, and partying, they were always together. In 1970, after graduating from high school, they went their separate ways; Steve and Pete to different units in Vietnam, Blake to Berkeley to study law.

Pete was shot in the leg within days of arriving in Vietnam. After a medical discharge, he settled into the University of Rhode Island in time for the fall semester, concentrated on his studies, and discovered a passion for writing that would greatly change the remainder of his life. He was now married to his best friend Jillian, living in Vermont, and was a very successful and best-selling author of popular suspense fiction.

Blake, who had planned on dodging the draft in Canada, quickly abandoned those plans after learning that his flat feet would keep him on friendly soil. He spent three years in law school and was subsequently hired by the most prestigious law firm in Los Angeles. After becoming a partner, he became extremely wealthy and spent hundreds of thousands of dollars on an extravagant lifestyle normally reserved for movie stars.

It had been fifteen years since Pete had an idea to maintain and even build upon their friendship. Separated by geography, occupation, and lifestyle, it wasn't practical for the three to see each other regularly, so Pete proposed a once per year weekend meeting.

These encounters quickly evolved into more exotic getaways in far-away places, and to make things more interesting, two very important rules were established. First, it was decided that the rendezvous point would be in a different location each year and the destination would be decided, historically by Pete, at the current meeting place. Second, no communication between the three was allowed during the year. At the exact time and designated place, the three friends would meet and engage in conversation, fine dining, and take advantage of whatever activities or sites the location hosted. The second rule was more of a guideline, but each of the friends had respected it, and none of them had tried to contact the others between meetings.

This year they were to meet in Lucerne, Switzerland and it was less than a week away. Steve had mixed emotions about the upcoming trip, though. He was specifically charged with counterterrorism, and a very dangerous faction named al Assad had been monopolizing his time. They were the most venomous terrorist network ever known, and had recently begun to mobilize. Satellite pictures didn't lie. Steve knew he was able to maintain communications and his command off-site, but he felt better being at CIA headquarters.

Al Assad was making the rules, at least for now.

Chapter 4

SIMON STOOD before Almedi Hahn Sahn, the holy leader of al Assad, his head bowed in an attempt to be humble. But Simon was never humble and the pitiful display only infuriated the man further. They were in the basement of a halfway bulldozed and forgotten home near a market place in eastern Afghanistan, and it was time for Simon's report.

Almedi spoke first. "How did he manage to get out of our stronghold, run through the streets of London, and deliver a message to the U.S. embassy?"

"I *did* see the clerk who accepted the envelope inside the building and..."

Almedi cut him off. "I want to know who it was sent to and what it read. You and Falby will get it done. Tomorrow!"

Simon hated working with others. Partners got in the way and slowed him down. Now, however, was hardly the time to offer an opinion. He simply bowed to his master, turned, and looked toward the man known only as Falby.

Falby was a small, compact, and physically fit German mercenary who kept to himself. He looked to be in his mid forties, with short sandy hair, cool gray eyes, and a confident manner that made him look much taller. He was also known as "The Chameleon," a fitting description of his ability to adapt to any situation, both physically and mentally, and always to his advantage. Falby was no one to get close to. Little was known about him and he was as deadly as they came.

Maybe this wouldn't be so bad, Simon thought, as he continued sizing up his new partner. Falby held Simon's stare and spoke directly at him in an even tone.

"If you get in my way or fail me, I will kill you."

Simon laughed, unable to control the outburst. "If you talk to me like that again, *I'll* kill you before you finish the sentence."

Simon was in his early fifties, but was still a brute force of pent up hostility and aggression that few could match, no matter how evil their intentions. He was American-born and stood just over six feet tall with a muscular physique, but most of his strength seemed to come from within. He had a hidden intensity -- a stubborn rage -- that seemed to burn inside him impatiently. And although his volatile mind knew many extremes and often forced uncalculated moves, his enemies had always felt his sting.

He was a master at hand to hand combat and nearly unstoppable with a weapon. He never strayed from a fight, but because his reputation often preceded him, was rarely challenged. His long hair was still black and fine, the bangs falling kindly to frame his strong facial features and bone structure. He was usually dressed in black, emphasizing his pale skin, and his eyes were dark and searching.

Falby remained silent, his jaw tightening. He stood patiently, his stare pointed.

"You know Darwinism," Simon continued. "The weak are always terminated, the strong survive. It's good for the natural order of things."

Falby smiled and shook his head at Simon. "You're right. The weak can *always* be terminated."

"Gentlemen, please!" Almedi intervened. "You are to work together so stop your bickering."

The two men nodded and Falby, who dwarfed Simon by nearly a foot, confidently walked out of the room.

"Let's go. I've got a plan that even you can't mess up," Falby called over his shoulder.

Simon reluctantly followed.

Chapter 5

FALBY ENJOYED going undercover. A passionate and dynamic man, it appealed to his creativity and allowed him to explore the many facets of his inner-self. He was very thorough in his preparation, spending considerable time with different wigs, creams, and facial putties, to sculpt himself into a new person. Black, white, male, female, old, young, skinny, fat, it didn't matter. This was his specialty; an art he enjoyed immensely.

The over weight clerk at London's U.S. embassy felt sorry for Falby the babbling tourist immediately. After all, Falby explained how he'd been robbed of his wallet and beaten by a group of thugs. He needed help with his credit cards, a flight home, and contacting his family. He sat in front of the clerk a defeated man, shaking uncontrollably and asking how someone could have done this to another human being. His mouth was bleeding, his eye blackened, and his glasses, now broken, were hanging from his left ear. Falby seemed one step away from a mental breakdown as his voice strained to tell his sad tale.

The clerk led him to a comfortable room and offered him coffee and a pastry. When the man turned his back, the sad expression left Falby's face and the killer began to spy on his friendly target, who spent most of his time on the phone and directing walk-ins to different departments within the building.

It seemed that the clerk was responsible for a lot of miscellaneous tasks; simple errands like mailing a letter to the CIA. The day before, Simon had seen the man accept the envelope, consider it for a moment, and place it into a mail bin. Falby wanted to take the clerk now, but that would have to wait. He needed more information. Who was it mailed to? More importantly, what did it say about the cause?

Simon waited anxiously in the van down the street, eager to get the job done so he could catch an evening swim at the hotel. He hated his new partner, loathed his arrogance and total disrespect. Who did Falby think he was to speak to him like that?

Without warning, Falby appeared next to the van and tossed a note into the open window. Then he was gone, leaving Simon with many questions and even more contempt for his new partner.

Simon looked for Falby, first turning peripherally to both windows, and then using the side mirrors. Finally, he exited the vehicle and looked up and down the side streets without success. It was as if Falby had disappeared and Simon recalled his partner's nickname. The Chameleon.

The brief note gave a description of the clerk, his name, and the make, color, and location of his car. It also had the time he was expected to get off work. Simon guessed it was up to him to finish the job, but he *had* expected Falby to offer more direction.

After parking the van two spaces from the clerk's car, Simon opened the hood and began inspecting its contents. It wasn't long before a jolly man with a high-pitched voice stood behind Simon to offer assistance.

"Car trouble Mister?"

"Unfortunately," Simon replied, solemnly. "And my wife's gonna kill me if I'm late picking up the kids again."

There was a southern twang in Simon's voice and he turned to face the man, a crooked frown adding to his desperate appearance.

"Are you from the States?" the clerk asked, starting a dialogue.

"Yes sir. Houston, Texas."

"Very good. I've got a pair of cables if you need a jump start," the clerk offered. "I'll get you off and running in no time."

The man quickly moved toward his car trunk and Simon smiled to himself, not believing the naiveté.

"That would be great!" Simon said excitedly, quickly changing his tone and demeanor to one of complete elation. "I *really* do appreciate it. But could we use my cables? They're fifteen feet long and would probably make things easier."

Simon moved behind the clerk in a controlling position and put his hand on the man's shoulder.

"Do you mind getting them from my tool box in the back?"

The clerk was immediately inside the van looking for a toolbox that didn't exist and Simon was right behind him, slamming the rear door shut. The startled man lifted his head, meeting Simon's eyes for the first time. This was no helpless man.

The clerk was easily overcome and wrestled to the van's floor. When subdued and still, Simon spoke calmly in his ear, his hot breath adding to the intensity.

"Shut up. Don't say anything. If you move you're fuckin' dead!"

Within seconds a bandanna covered the man's eyes, another was in his mouth, duct tape holding both firmly in place. His hands were cuffed behind his back and Simon propped him against a large utility box. Simon quickly exited the van to shut the hood and look for witnesses. All was quiet and clear.

The van took a quick left onto Park Lane, eventually easing out of the city via the M-1. Several minutes later, the landscape became much more rural, and Simon took a calculated left and drove a considerable distance into the brush. He saw the blue marker he had left earlier and headed down a bumpy path very slowly, each of the van's tires jumping in turn over deep holes and high ridges. Then he stopped the van and sprang to the rear to speak to his prisoner.

Without any thought or premeditation, Simon took out a long Bowie knife and severed the man's right pinky finger. The man screamed and Simon removed the bandanna to allow the man to see his finger lying beside him, blood gushing from the fresh wound.

"Do I have your attention?" Simon asked, calmly.

The man didn't answer. Instead he looked around the van with a terrified look on his chubby white face, his eyes darting between his hand and detached finger. His screaming ceased, but drool dripped from his chin and his body shook uncontrollably.

"Do I have your attention?" Simon asked again, his tone suggesting boredom.

"Who are you? I don't understand... Please... I beg you," the clerk blurted.

Simon placed a heavy hand on the man's shoulder in an effort to steady him.

"I just need to ask you a few questions," the killer said.

"Don't kill me, please don't kill me. I think you have the wrong person," the man said, shaking.

Simon held up his hand in a quick motion and the man stopped babbling.

"Yesterday, a man gave an envelope to a guard, who walked it up the stairs to you. I need to know what it said, who it was for, and where it was heading. Be as thorough as possible. Your entire future depends on it."

In spite of the circumstances and the dull pulsing pain in his hand, the man regained his composure and spoke calmly. He remembered the envelope instantly.

"I was on the phone when the envelope was given to me. It read 'CIA Headquarters -- Langley.' The name 'Steve McCallister' was written on it. He's a big wig over there."

"Go on," Simon prodded.

"I threw it in the inter-agency mail and resumed my phone call."

Simon was very happy with this. It seemed as though the hole was semi plugged. The fat office worker knew nothing about the contents of the letter and didn't feel it was very important.

This confirmed the story that Yamir had given when Simon cornered him in Hyde Park, and Simon smiled as he remembered the struggle. Yamir had been a skilled and respected opponent, perhaps as deadly as Simon himself, but the fight didn't last long and Simon had quickly finished Yamir.

"Did you talk to anyone about this?"

"No."

The man began to feel better as the intensity of his captor's face turned into an expression of content, a smile eventually cracking at the corners of his mouth.

"Do you have a family?" Simon asked. "Wife, kids, that sort of thing?" "I've been married for twenty two years and have four children." At an attempt to build rapport, he added, "As you can see my wife's a very good cook."

Simon pulled a silver key from his pocket. He held it for a few seconds and then unlocked the man's hands from the handcuffs. The clerk applied pressure to his bleeding hand by pressing it into his ample stomach and curling over to cover it with his large body.

"Okay," Simon began. "You and your finger are free to go. If you tell anyone about this, you and your family are dead."

The man awkwardly scooped up his finger and quickly made his way to the back, using his good hand to open the rear door and still pressing his bloody hand to his stomach. Jumping down, he began to run slowly and clumsily, his gaze frozen on the path ahead, his breathing labored.

The clerk didn't hear the gunshot and was dead before his body thumped against the soft ground. Simon exited the van, locked the door and put the Sig Saur back into his jacket holster. He then slit the man's throat to confirm the kill and stood over the body, reflecting on the recent exchange.

"McCallister," Simon said aloud. He began to think about Vietnam and the Special Forces unit he was a part of. He had known a man named Steve McCallister. He shook his head slowly, remembering the horror his unit had endured. And for what? At least it made him the successful mercenary he was today. He walked back to the van, dismissing the name for coincidence. He focused his attention on the road as he turned right and casually drove back to the hotel. He couldn't wait to sink his teeth into a thick porterhouse and swim a few laps in the heated pool.

Simon reported that the letter was mailed to a man named Mc-Callister at CIA headquarters. He also reported that the clerk knew nothing, and that the letter probably included at least a partial list of their terrorist agenda. He had uncovered that from Yamir after their brief encounter in the park. He had already organized the surveillance and was in the process of planning Steve McCallister's abduction and subsequent elimination.

Chapter 6

AN OCEAN AWAY, two men looked through binoculars from atop a hill. They were about three hundred yards away from the target and hidden just inside the tree line that surrounded a small community playground. It was a dreary morning and the drizzle made light pattering sounds on the backs of their green nylon jackets. They were covered in wet leaves and meshed nicely into the landscape, as they waited for Steve McCallister to emerge from his home.

Just after 4 a.m., Steve walked down his driveway, his confident strides hindered only by the hot coffee he carried in his hand. Although dressed in a black suit, polished shoes, and starched white shirt and non-descript tie, he looked very comfortable, as he scooped up his morning papers with practiced moves and retreated back to the house.

Forty minutes later he eased from his driveway, eventually heading east on Route 193 to CIA Headquarters in Langley. The Ford Minivan was about a mile behind him, just out of sight.

The first words Steve usually spoke each morning were to his three secretaries: Diane, Barbara, and Armor, a portly woman of

Spanish descent. Armor was learning disabled, slightly autistic, and barely passed the required minimum intelligence tests, but Steve respected her dedication to detail. She was open, honest, and direct; unable to commit the selfish acts reserved for higher intellects. She was Steve's favorite, charged with the simple details that kept the office running and was the heart of his administrative staff.

Diane was in charge of day to day internal operations; Barbara was responsible for the external and political side, setting meetings with the president, the different federal agencies, and any rare speaking engagements for the House, Senate, or other government offices. Steve's schedule was usually full from 6:15 a.m. to 6 p.m. Meetings rarely lasted more than thirty minutes and he always had somewhere to be.

He entered his office and walked to the thick U-shaped mahogany desk in the center of the large room. Usually clear of all clutter, he noticed a small piece of paper and reached for it.

He smiled instantly as he read the message. Armor had taken a call the night before and had scribbled the note for Steve's review. He liked the simplicity of the communication. Usually he was paged, emailed, or tracked down by one of the two cell phones he carried. This was a welcome and unexpected change, even primitive, and it reminded him of something he would have received during class in high school when the teacher's back was turned.

Steve was further intrigued by the message itself, from Dana Carpenter, a reporter from *The Washington Times* who had interviewed him the week before. For almost an hour, there were questions about the CIA's counter-terrorism efforts, the ongoing problem of cooperation between the federal agencies, and his opinion of the future of the Middle East and the United States' place in it.

But there were also the delicate glances that lasted a little longer than they should have; the natural smiles that showed her perfect teeth, and of course the suggestive demeanor that both parties were a little more interested in each other than the interview.

The conversation was fluid, each inserting personal pleasantries and playful jokes in between the more rigid, formal questions. But the interview ended abruptly when he was forced to take a phone call and Dana was required to leave.

Steve didn't get to say goodbye and had been wondering about her since. Could the message indicate that she was interested? Or was it a simple follow-up to the piece she was writing? When he thought of it he became confused and he hated feeling the weakness.

He was used to being in complete control; having all available information for any situation he was involved in, but women were different and he hadn't had much experience. Sure he'd had topical conversations, light dates, and occasional flings with the opposite sex, but he was usually naïve to any female advances and had never been in a romantically charged relationship that lasted more than a couple of weeks. He had long convinced himself that because of his occupation it wouldn't work, and he'd followed that line of thinking perhaps too long and to his detriment.

But he wasn't an operator in the Special Forces anymore and therefore not on constant duty in the field. He had much more stability now; a home, an office at the CIA, and even a boring commute in between.

Still, he thought of the hours he was required to keep, the unusual and random travel that could call him away anywhere at any time, and then there were the safety reasons. To think of someone harming anyone he cared for just to get to him was unbearable.

He neatly folded the message and placed it in his pocket, making a mental note to call after lunch. His day would certainly be chaotic until then.

The first meeting every morning was with the director and the department heads. It was a debriefing on the past twenty-four hours. On a global scale, who did what and where? What effect did it have on the security of the United States, its allies, territories, or any of its citizens? Political uprisings, terrorist bombings, and riots were common topics of discussion.

This morning the main subject was the terrorist group al Assad. The faction had been dormant for some time, but now there was a substantial increase in activity. Information came from a variety of sources and had been thoroughly analyzed and cross- referenced.

Steve had reviewed the report from the NSA earlier and it wasn't good news. In the last few weeks, a combination of satellite imaging, human intelligence, interrogations of captured insurgents, and a general rise in chatter in intercepted lines of communications, had yielded an impressive amount of data. The CIA was very concerned that al Assad was mobilizing and perhaps planning a terrorist attack domestically, and Steve was charged with countering their efforts.

After the meeting, Steve and Director Willard met privately for a few minutes to discuss the meeting and catch up on each other's lives.

They walked to the sitting area at the far end of the director's expansive office, and Steve sat on one of the sofas, leaning into it with a hand on his cheek, a statue of staunch pensiveness.

"So what do you think, Steve?" the director asked, still standing.

"They're definitely up to something and MI6 and Interpol have similar concerns. I'll get a summary to the president immediately."

"Are you still going to Switzerland this Friday?"

"Yeah, I'm still going," Steve said. "I know it's not good timing, but I've been meeting my two buddies like this every year for a while now."

"Just keep in touch."

"By the way," Steve began. "I was followed into work this morning by a white minivan. I'm not sure why I'd be of interest."

The director nodded slightly as he processed the information. "It would make me feel better if you accepted the protection you've been refusing. You shouldn't be walking around exposed out there. You have to come to terms with who you are and how valuable the information in your head is."

"I'm always armed, have no family, and very few friends. That's all the edge I need," Steve countered.

"Will you at least start wearing a bullet proof vest for the next few months until we figure this out?"

Steve didn't like the thought of altering his lifestyle, but he recognized that he *could* be in terrible danger. He knew more about al Assad than anyone in the law-abiding world, and had even been solicited for membership in the early 80's. They came to him knowing every detail about him. Almedi Hahn Sahn was their leader then, as he was now.

A very wealthy and dangerous man, Almedi had important and time-tested relationships throughout the legitimate *and* underground Arab world; and he hated the United States with unparalleled passion. No Arab should be told what to do in the sanctity of their divine and holy lands.

"Wear a bullet proof vest?" Steve questioned, sarcastically. "If they want anyone dead, a vest won't stop anything."

"Have it your way, Steve." Changing the subject dramatically, the director added, "So what's this I hear about a certain young and attractive reporter in your life?"

Steve was taken back and his face evidenced it.

"That's okay, Steve, you don't have to talk about it," the director said, enjoying the exchange.

"No, that's fine. I didn't know what little gossipers everyone was. She's the one that interviewed me for *The Washington Times* last week. She's nice."

"She's nice?" the director laughed, finally sitting on the other sofa. "You really expect me to believe that you just think she's nice? My sources say she's hotter than hell."

Steve didn't respond, choosing instead to glance past his boss and into the distance. Sensing his reluctance, the director continued.

"You really are something Steve. You could have your choice of any woman out there and you don't even know it. Look at you, you're blushing."

"I don't know Doc," Steve started, using the nickname he'd called his boss since he first met him. It referred to the director's complete authority and knowledge. Steve was always amazed at how the man seemed to know everything, and could only guess at how many sources fed him intelligence on any number of issues.

"This job doesn't allow room for much else, especially women," Steve added.

"Don't you get lonely, though? I'm not sure what I'd do without Margaret," the older man said, thoughtfully.

Steve turned to the director, changing the subject. A deeply personal man, Steve didn't like sharing his feelings, not even with his closest friends.

"Well, time to go fight the bad guys I guess," Steve said, standing and turning to leave.

"Not so fast, Steve. At least tell me something about this girl."

"She likes RC Cola over Coke and Pepsi," Steve said, as he walked out of the room.

Moments later, Steve entered his office and was immediately met by Armor.

"This came today. It looks much different than the other mail. It came through inter-agency. I thought you might want to open it right away." She stood in front of Steve excitedly, her eyes never leaving his.

She was right. It didn't look like anything that he was used to receiving. The address was hand written sloppily and the envelope was plain. There was not a return address but a stamp showed that it was sent inter-agency from the United States embassy in London.

"Has it been cleaned?" he asked, referring to the X-ray and 'Hazmat' screening that was done to anything mailed to the CIA.

"Of course."

"Thank you, Armor. You're the best," he smiled, waiting for her to exit before opening the envelope.

Inside was a one-page letter that had obviously been written in a rush, and as he scanned it, his demeanor suddenly changed. It detailed a potential terrorist action, including a location, date, time, and method. Whoever sent it was either the author of an elaborate hoax, or someone inside al Assad.

Steve sat at his desk and read the letter once more. He was relieved to have the information, but concerned that the CIA or any other allied intelligence had not picked it up earlier. Then his mind wandered to whoever sent the short note and where it originated.

After making several well-placed calls to hopefully confirm or deny the alleged attack, he read the letter a third time; studying everything from the hurried style of the words, the slight downward slant of each sentence, and the spacing. Then, using tweezers, he placed the paper directly in front of him and used a magnifying glass to examine the paper itself. Something was on his mind and it didn't leave him all day.

In the late afternoon Steve learned of the murder of an embassy employee in London, and the killing of another man in Hyde Park. The latter appeared to be a vagrant without any identification, but when the photo of the man came across the wire, it answered the one question that had been biting at Steve all day.

Chapter 7

THE CLERK'S DEATH made the London headlines. Simon enjoyed reading about his work in the paper, learning about who he killed, how they lived, and so on. He would sometimes go to their funerals to learn more. He wasn't above putting a rose on his late victim's casket as it was lowered to its final resting place, a somber look on his face. He never regretted it. It was his specialty.

Wayne Earshing had been employed at the U.S. embassy in London as the front desk clerk for eighteen years. He was loved very much by friends, family, and coworkers, judging from the number of people who gathered outside for the service. It was the largest and longest funeral Simon had ever attended, with speeches, stories, and prayers as the group remembered Wayne, the most innocent and decent person that had ever graced the earth.

"He was an angel," one man had said between sobs. "God needed him back."

Simon saw his victim's wife immediately and remembered what a good cook she was. *And those must be his four children beside her,* he thought. The youngest was wearing a pink bonnet, looking around innocently, oblivious to the situation surrounding her. She was told that today she would say her final good bye to daddy, but she hadn't seen him yet. She wondered where he was.

The oldest child cried uncontrollably and was being consoled by an older man. Simon could not hear what he was saying, but as he talked the sobs got louder and then eventually stopped as her pink face affixed in a permanent frown. The middle two children were playing a game of tag, and Simon wondered why they weren't in mourning over the tragic death of their father. They would never see him again.

Simon sat in a chair in the last row with a folded newspaper; his head bowed low as he read the much smaller story of the other man he'd killed. According to the local police he was a vagrant with no identification, possibly killed by the other homeless in the area.

Simon smiled. *That was the real story.*

Chapter 8

THE OPUS BAR AND RESTAURANT is located in the Neustadt District of Lucerne, Switzerland and is one of the better known café's near the water; popular for its outdoor seating, good food and drink, and proximity to Old Town.

The rendezvous, per the plan a year earlier, was to take place at 2 p.m. It was a cool day, with a high blue sky and magnificent bright sun. The tourists sipped their coffees, teas and wine, ignoring any sense of time, and taking advantage of the beautiful afternoon. Steve and Pete were among them.

The pair hadn't seen or spoken to each other in over a year, and neither had spoken to their third friend, Blake. This was one of the rules they had agreed to since the excursions began, and it had been an essential part of maintaining the intrigue they sought.

Pete had always planned the meeting itinerary and destination. He disclosed the next rendezvous point at the current meeting place, and always took pride in accounting for every detail.

Lucerne, Switzerland was to be the fifteenth rendezvous the three friends had enjoyed, and it had been revealed while the three were visiting Egypt the year before.

"Great job Pete," Steve said, raising his glass of merlot and studying his long-time friend.

Pete was the same age as Steve, but always managed to look much younger. He was of average build, with a full head of blondish red hair that had been parted the same way since elementary school. He was a very deliberate man, even meek; his only rebellions being his daily cigarette and two beers.

"Thanks buddy. It's always my pleasure," Pete replied, taking a pull from his Heineken.

"So where's Blake?" Steve asked, looking expectantly at the people walking on Bahnhofstrasse Street.

"I don't know, probably got hung up with some blonde or at a bar."

"Or both," Steve cut in and the two laughed.

Blake had always been the most dynamic of the three. His personality knew many extremes and often tested immaturity and genius in the same breath. Many people found him abrasive and overbearing, while others saw a certain charm and spirit that most people lacked. As a trial lawyer, he worked magic for his clients and was easily the most visible partner at his law firm. Success came easy and so did the money.

Blake stood six feet tall, but seemed to be shrinking over the years as his waist line expanded. Once athletic and active in all kinds of sports, he now confined himself to his office for more than sixty hours a week. He drank coffee by the pot, whisky by the fifth, and exploited every excess. His thick, graying hair had steadily receded with age and his broad face was now a permanent shade of pink.

Pete especially liked Blake because of the stories the man could tell; Steve found him entertaining more than anything. Still, both men agreed that he added buoyancy to their special bond and they wouldn't want it any other way.

"So how's Jillian?" Steve asked.

"She's wonderful. Every day keeps getting better. I know it's a guy's weekend and I'd never mention this to Blake, but I really wish she was here."

"Yeah, I know and maybe some day it'll happen. But for a few days a year, you have to look at us instead."

Suddenly, a man rushed the table with a large yell, taking both men by surprise and disrupting the immediate area. Steve moved quickly with practiced moves, instinctively tackling the man and immobilizing him in a strong headlock.

The cafe patrons stared at the two men wrestling on the patio floor; some gasped while others stood. Then the mood lightened as recognition set in and Steve released his grip on Blake. Late again and making a grand entrance.

"Very funny," Pete said. "Now that you've made asses of us all, can we please sit and enjoy ourselves?"

"I don't want to enjoy myself in front of all these nice people," Blake said, making a jerking motion with his right hand.

The three laughed and a waiter appeared to take Blake's drink order, the usual triple Tullamore Dew with one ice cube. Several people looked over in disgust, not believing the loud and obnoxious behavior of the three Americans.

"Anyway," Blake continued, settling into a chair. "We can't get kicked out of Switzerland, can we?"

"I think we're safe with Steve here," Pete started. "But didn't Germany get kicked out in World War II?"

It was a rhetorical question, and Pete and Steve took a moment to drink. An old Swiss man, however, glanced over and spoke in a slow, raspy voice.

"Germany never occupied us!" he scowled. "And if they tried we would've defended ourselves to the end!"

Pete and Steve nodded to the man assuredly, hoping they wouldn't be dragged into a long discussion. They glanced at each other in silence and smiled, eventually looking to Blake. They knew what was likely to happen, and couldn't help but look forward to the entertainment that was sure to follow. Blake seemed to know something about everything, and had no problem arguing any subject, even a Swiss citizen in his own country.

Blake had interesting social skills and nothing proved it better than his college and law school years, which were the perfect incubators. He craved knowledge and sailed through every class with A's, all information easily understood, analyzed, and absorbed. But there was always a party to go to and Blake was usually the last man standing.

"Actually, Germany *did* have a plan of attack in 1940," Blake said, turning to the old man.

"Really? Why don't you tell me about this attack that never happened," the old man laughed sarcastically.

"Die Schweiz muß noch geschluckt werden," Blake smiled, speaking in perfect German. "It translates to 'Switzerland must still be swallowed.' Germany could have overrun the Swiss people but there wasn't a geographical or strategic advantage to your landscape. Especially after they took France."

The old man blinked a few times, nodding. "Go on."

"And why would Germany want Switzerland? Swiss banks laundered the gold that Germany took from their neighboring countries, and Switzerland needed coal from Germany after France was defeated. All in all, Germany and Switzerland had a subtle understanding that allowed both sides to benefit. And although Switzerland helped both the Axis and Allied forces, the history books still remember her as neutral."

"We still would have defeated them," the old man said.

"You may be partly accurate, because Germany didn't have a point of attack. Switzerland didn't -- and still doesn't -- have a centralized government. The twenty-six cantons have the authority, and with no way for Switzerland to officially surrender in whole, the Nazi's would've had to fight an entire people, not a country."

"So I'm right. We would have never allowed them in."

Blake's whisky arrived and he was easily distracted.

"Gentlemen," Blake said, returning his attention to his friends. "Here we are together again. We've come a long way together. Here's to us."

It was the same toast Blake gave every year and the whisky, beer, and wine came together above the table. The three men enjoyed the moment, regarding each other; each absorbed in self-thought and reflection. Pete was the first to speak.

"So how were your flights?"

"I wrote three motions and drank several martinis with a Spanish chick," Blake said. "We kissed good-bye at the airport. I would've scored if she wasn't married."

Pete shook his head, smiling at the thought. He wanted to inquire further, but he knew that it was probably true. Blake rarely lied; he had no reason to.

He turned to Steve, smiling. "How was your flight? Any martinis?"

"I hitched a ride to Germany on Airforce One with the president. He has meetings all this week. Then I took a prop plane to Zurich & rented a convertible for the short drive here."

"Well excuse us, Mr. Big Shot," Pete joked. "How is the president anyway?"

"I don't know. It was so last minute he didn't even know I was on board. He's an asshole anyway."

"Well enough about the boring shit," Blake said, turning to Pete. "What's up for the rendezvous next year? Where are we going?"

"I was hoping you'd ask," Pete said confidently, pausing to finish his Heineken to prolong the moment. After so much planning, Pete loved to unveil the rendezvous destinations and itinerary.

"We are headed for a ten-day journey into the Australian Outback, after diving at the Great Barrier Reef. I've got the tickets, rooms, schedule, and all of the details in these envelopes. Everything's paid for and confirmed, a year in advance."

Pete smiled as he placed two envelopes on the table.

"I'm sorry Pete," Steve said, painfully. "But I'm planning the next rendezvous."

"What're you talking about?" Blake practically yelled. "Petey-boy's been doing this for years, you can't just nix all of his work. Besides, he's the creative author guy and probably plans a better trip than you could ever dream of."

"Like I said guys, I'm sorry. But Australia isn't gonna happen. I'll reimburse you for the cost, but it's impossible."

"Why is it impossible?" Blake challenged. "You don't even know *when* it is."

Blake eased back into the chair, his hands clasped in front of him. It wasn't that he wanted to go to Australia as much as he enjoyed a good debate.

"It's just impossible," Steve said, leaning closer to his friends and speaking in a whisper. "We're going to southern Chile, the Hotel

Miramar. 7 p.m. on June 4. It's located in a very small town called Copas, just north of Puerto Natales. I'll be on the third floor awaiting your arrival."

The others were taken back to hear of Steve's proposal. The way he spoke with such confidence and precision about the supposed meeting. Empty moments passed with Blake and Pete sitting in silence, digesting the quick turn in conversation. Steve casually sipped his wine.

The waiter came over and snapped the trio back to reality, inquiring about any food orders. Blake ordered another round for the table and then looked at Steve with a piercing glare.

"Fuck you, man. I'm going to Australia."

"Blake, it's out of the question. It's just not going to happen. I'm sorry."

"Maybe if we knew why it was out of the question, we could better deal with it," Pete reasoned.

Pete was usually the intermediary between Blake and Steve, anchoring their friendship with a fatherly influence. He rarely jumped to conclusions and always made principle-based decisions using the information available.

Steve turned to Pete and smiled, appreciative of the thought. "I'm sorry but I can't, and you must *memorize* the rendezvous point and not disclose it to anyone. Not the cleaning lady at your law firm, or the chick that you're sleeping with Blake. No one, and that means Jillian too, Pete. Also, don't *ever* repeat this conversation, not even to each other or to me. This discussion *never* happened. Memorize it and forget about it until June 4. *Please* trust me."

Pete and Blake fell silent as they stared at Steve. In a hushed whisper, the CIA man repeated the destination information to his friends, who listened in stunned silence. When finished, Blake looked up in disbelief, still not fully understanding Steve's reasoning.

"Steve, with all due respect, this is outrageous. We..."

Steve's closed fist hit the table with such force that many of the neighboring tables looked over in surprise. Steve's wine spilled and the liquid raced toward his white sleeved shirt. He made no attempt to move his arm, however, and it instantly stained his sleeve. He looked at his two friends and repeated his request in a forced whisper.

"I should not have to beg for this guys. This is *very* important. You must meet me there no matter *what* happens."

Finally sensing the stares from the other patrons, Steve wiped up the spilled wine. He leaned closer, his hands tight on the edges of the table, as he looked back and forth between Pete and Blake. In a very low and measured voice, he spoke once more.

"Let me qualify this to make sure there are no illusions. No matter *what* happens, I *will* be there."

Steve said this with such emotion that it was finally clear that Chile was indeed the next meeting point. No further discussion was necessary.

Blake drained the rest of his whisky as he eyed his friend. He couldn't help but wonder why Steve was so determined about the new plan, but conceded defeat after Steve's emotional plea.

"By the way Blake," Steve said. "How do you know so much about World War II and Switzerland?"

"And how do you speak German all of a sudden?" Pete jumped in.

"Last year I was banging a German chick all summer long."

"How did *she* know about it?" Pete asked, still flabbergasted.

"She was married to a history professor."

They erupted in laughter and emotions eventually returned to normal. Steve later quizzed his friends about next year's plans and the drinks kept coming. Blake bragged about his partnership promotion; Pete wanted feedback on his latest novel idea. Steve, the most reserved of the three, continued to sip wine, wondering if he'd come across too strong.

The rendezvous couldn't have come at a worse time and Steve knew people could be watching and listening. He just hoped that if al Assad *was* here, that they regarded this as an innocent gathering among friends, separate from anything he was involved in.

From across the street, on a jagged rooftop, two men witnessed the reunion. Their listening devices had picked up most of the conversation and they'd seen the meeting through binoculars. They retreated to the rear in silence, as one of them reached for a cell phone.

Chapter 9

FOR THREE DAYS, the friends ate hearty meals, smoked expensive cigars, and enjoyed happy hours at the quaint pubs that hugged the cobblestone and vehicle-free streets of Old Town. They caught up on every detail of each other's lives since Egypt, and because of Blake, saw everything that the university town had to offer.

They walked the Squares of Old Town and paused for photographs at the Lion Monument, visited both of the famous covered bridges, and walked the Glacier Garden. On the last day they opted for some exercise and climbed Mount Pilatus, admiring the picturesque views of the Alps and Lake Lucerne, or the "Vierwaldstattersee," as Blake pointed out.

Steve, who had always been an introvert, was even quieter than usual. Pete didn't mention it, but couldn't help wondering what was troubling his friend. That evening, Steve drove Pete and Blake to Zurich International airport, where they parted and would eventually regroup the following summer in Chile.

Blake wasn't accustomed to the physical demands of the day's long hike and was sleeping in the back seat, while Pete regarded the beautiful landscape as it flew by. Steve negotiated the highways with ease as he carefully monitored the rear view mirror for any sign of a tail, especially as they drove through Sihlbrugg and Thalwil. He didn't like being so vulnerable. The route was unsecured and they were an open target, especially for an invisible enemy who could do as they pleased.

Arriving at the airport did little to relieve Steve's uneasiness. It was very open and because of the hour, hosted few customers and even fewer employees. He pulled to the curb, immediately waving off two boys who offered to handle the bags. Standing up and stretching, Steve looked at his two friends and smiled.

"Well Pete. It was fun. Like always you did a bang up job in planning."

Turning his attention to Blake, Steve held out his hand. "I'll see you next year. Good luck with your practice and I'm sorry about Australia."

Blake looked at his hand and instead of accepting it suddenly embraced Steve, rocking him back and forth in a joking manner. "No problem man, you know I love you."

Pete watched the scene, smiling. "You're not even drunk yet and you're hugging guys?" he said.

"Oh yeah," Blake said, feigning confusion as he reached around and squeezed Steve's rear end.

Steve jumped back and Blake hurried toward the door with Pete laughing in tow. Soon they both disappeared inside the airport. They would fly to New York and Boston, respectively, and then back to their individual lives.

Starting the engine and pulling away from the curb, Steve turned on to the N3. After about ten miles, when convinced he wasn't being followed, he pulled off and parked behind a row of trees. He took a brief case from the trunk and placed it on the hood. Then he took out his Sig Saur 9 millimeter and rested it at the base of the windshield.

He dialed the CIA director's direct line. Like the phone he was using, it was secure and the number frequently changed.

"Hiding behind a row of trees isn't going to fool anyone, Steve." the director said, picking up within one ring.

Steve looked to the blackening sky and thought of the techies at the NSA that kept an invisible and constant eye on anything they chose to.

"You never fail to impress, Donald. Don't you ever sleep?"

The director was suddenly grim. "Our intel confirms that the letter you received is valid, but there's little else to fill in the gaps, except for a dead body that was found in London the other day."

"Go on," Steve said.

"We asked London police to give us information on every murder that had occurred within a week of the letter. It seems that there was a man found in Hyde Park. He didn't have any identification and there are no leads or witnesses, but his fingerprints match those found on the letter, and it looks as if he was severely beaten and tortured."

"Anything else?"

"Yeah two things," the director said, carefully. "He had a Special Forces tattoo and the pinky finger on this right hand was cut off."

Chapter 10

THE SIGHT OF POLICE had always made her nervous. She'd been in and out of police stations all her life, sometimes as a complainant, sometimes as a suspect. Petty theft and drugs; then domestic violence, aggravated assault, and three prostitution busts by the time she was nineteen. Growing up was hard for Peggy Reynolds. Until she met Blake Edwards.

They met at a strip club in Los Angeles. Not the gentleman clubs of late with their cigar bars and well-dressed security personnel. She worked at Mo's just off Sunset Boulevard in Hollywood.

It was small, dark, and dirty; and fronted for a variety of illegal happenings. She would dance during the day and work the streets at night. Blake would come in almost every day to see her. He'd always dress down for the occasion, wearing blue jeans, boots, a faded t-shirt, and a baseball cap. Attorneys were hardly accepted in the district, and advertising success was not the most appropriate way to make a friend or even stay alive.

At first he was attracted to her legs. They were long and perfect, ending with two gold anklets that rested atop fire engine red, high heel stilettos. She would shift her weight perfectly, watching Blake with an electric gaze. As with all big tippers, she would visit with him afterwards.

They'd talk and laugh, drinking cheap canned beer and smoking Marlboros until after close. She was like no other woman he had ever met. To him, dating was a ritual that included dinner, maybe the theatre, and ultimately sex. This girl was the only woman who ever laughed with him. She wasn't from money and didn't place much importance on materialism. They would talk for hours, sometimes at Mo's or at the twenty-four hour coffee shop down the street.

He told her about his partnership, his cars and expansive home; his vast knowledge of tax law, all of the clients who loved him, and the paralegals who emulated him. She wasn't overly impressed with his stories, she just liked the way his face lit up as he told them. Inside he was a child who still needed confirmation and attention. He was trapped in a fast lifestyle centered on money and image; she was trapped inside a world of loneliness, desperation, and addiction. Together they were happy, simply enjoying each other's company, and for the first time Blake tried to help someone other than himself.

He arranged for a furnished apartment in Venice Beach and a secretarial job with his firm. He bought her a new wardrobe and promised her the stability she always longed for. Finally, Peggy caught a break.

But now the police were studying her. In the conference room of Blackberry, Schmitz, and Warwink, the questioning began, and although she was not the topic of discussion, her uneasiness was apparent.

The uniformed cop spoke first. "Peggy. Please explain to the detective exactly what you saw."

Detective Ray Monroe was a thirty year veteran of Homicide. He was a black man in his mid-fifties and hid his age very well, in spite of his graying hair and peppered beard. His pale green eyes looked down at Peggy Reynolds, the only eyewitness to the abduction of Blake Edwards.

He rarely worked kidnappings; it wasn't his area of expertise. But when a partner from the most prestigious law firm in Los Angeles gets violently taken in plain view, exceptions were made.

"Well," Peggy began, "I just started working here three weeks ago as one of Blake's secretaries. I was filing a brief when I looked out the fourth floor window and saw Blake in his BMW stopped at the light at the corner. All of a sudden, two guys, both wearing masks and waiving guns, broke his passenger and driver's window, got in the car and peeled off."

She put her head into her hands and began crying softly, finally looking up as the next question was asked.

"Was there any suspicious activity prior to the abduction? Was Blake involved in anything unusual?"

Peggy's facial expressions made her more and more transparent to the seasoned detectives, who immediately knew she was hiding something. Her intentions were harmless enough and hardly material to Blake's kidnapping, though. She simply didn't want to advertise her past life. She had finally made friends and people had accepted her as a hard-working person. She also didn't want to embarrass the only man who had ever been kind to her. She bit her lower lip and stared blankly at the two officers who moved closer.

After a few seconds, she said, "Look. I'm only his secretary. It's not like I know him intimately or anything. I just saw what I saw."

The questioning lasted several more minutes, the two officers not learning much of consequence. Finally, Detective Monroe rose from his seat. He extended a hand through his cheap brown sports jacket and gave Peggy his business card.

"If you think of anything else, please don't hesitate to call."

The men turned and walked out of the reception area and into the elevator. When the door shut, Peggy's pulse returned to normal and she let out a large sigh of relief. *I hope Blake's okay*, she thought to herself as she crossed her legs and tried to concentrate on the file in front of her.

Chapter 11

AS A SOPHMORE in high school, Senator Joyce Monahan had been captain of the varsity cheerleading squad. In college, she was president of her college sorority. She was the first female senator in the state of Missouri and definitely the most vocal. The walls of both of her offices were covered with honors, awards, and acts of achievements, yet no one liked her. Not her staff, her husband, or the politicians who worked with her.

She would speak on any topic that would result in media attention. Face time was free advertising, and more advertising meant more potential votes. More votes meant more power.

All her life, it seemed that Senator Joyce Monahan was unstoppable. Everything went her way. But that changed when she spoke out against a specific terrorist faction and spearheaded a federal committee against terrorism. She gave endless criticism to the most dangerous terrorist groups in the world, pointing out specific attacks and making up others. She attacked the CIA, the president, and the Department of Homeland Defense. Everyone was incompetent and she promised change for the future.

She was joined by Senator Jack Keeler from Michigan. A long-time Democrat, he had served for four terms and felt a need to start justifying his position. Riding the coattails of Senator Monahan's ambitious campaign, he thought, could only help. It was a popular topic and Senator Monahan was very visual, speaking at every venue that would have her. Together, they thought they could conquer the world. But they were wrong.

Al Assad was on Senator Monahan's list. Because of their secrecy and commitment to perfection, little was known about their terrorist attacks. They weren't at the top of her list, nor were any specific actions mentioned, but al Assad was on the list.

And now she and Keeler were on theirs.

Simon enjoyed these kills. High profile and very detailed, they would be simultaneous. There were three months of data available on the daily activities of both politicians. Simon knew their eating habits, driving routes, and sleeping patterns. He also had their social and political calendars. Simon was to eliminate Monahan, Falby was assigned to Keeler.

In two separate cities, the two assassins waited patiently for the final order.

Chapter 12

THE STENCH WAS HORRIBLE, the sight was even worse. In his entire career in homicide, Detective Monroe had seen a lot, but he was still taken back by the scene in front of him.

It was clearly the remains of a black BMW. The fire was contained, somehow to the front half of the vehicle, leaving the rear in perfect condition. Not a scratch. Identifying the owner wouldn't be a problem. Identifying the headless, charred body in the passenger seat, however, presented trouble. Initial attempts to move the body resulted in limbs falling off the torso, some of it instantly turning to black dust at the coroner's feet.

Detective Monroe was going to work late. He had a hunch that the remains probably belonged to Blake Edwards of Blackberry, Schmitz, and Warwink. They would perform an autopsy, look for leads, and take the investigation from there.

———————

Simon the jogging assassin ran along Barnes Road, in the prestigious community of Ladue in St. Louis County. He wore Nike running shoes, black sweat pants, a forest green hooded sweatshirt, and a waist pack that fit nicely across his mid-section.

The night sky was clear and the stars were out accordingly, creating more light than Simon would have liked. The fall air carried a chill and he welcomed the breeze on his sweaty face. Halfway down the street, the killer deviated from the sidewalk and made his way into the adjoining forest that lined the St. Louis Country Club grounds.

Hidden from the road by trees, he removed his sweatshirt and turned it inside out. Outfitted in black, he maneuvered through the woods and to the southern perimeter of Senator Joyce Monahan's primary residence. His night vision equipment worked extremely well. It was daylight at 3:43 a.m.

At the base of the outer fence, Simon dropped to his knees and powered up the radio frequency jamming transmitter he'd manufactured earlier in the week. He knew the estate was protected with wireless sensors and his unit easily flooded the signal, disabling it even though the master alarm showed otherwise. Moments later, Simon jumped the fence and quickly made his way to the rear of the home. He stopped and listened again. Nothing.

He eased up the rear staircase that led to the second floor patio and came to the back door, entering easily and without hesitation. Having memorized the layout of the house, he moved in the dark with amazing precision. A table here, a piece of furniture there. It wasn't long before he found himself outside the closed bedroom door of his victim, listening intently.

He slowly turned the doorknob and entered, closing the door behind him. He saw two sleeping bodies beneath the covers, one snoring loudly, the other in complete silence. There was about two feet of space between the two and both were partially covered with blankets. Simon removed his pistol, attached the silencer, and walked toward the sleeping body on the right, eyeing it closely. *So this was the bitch on a mission*, he thought. *Hello senator.*

He pointed the gun at her and aimed, moving back slightly before firing a slug into her forehead. She never felt a thing, although the impact made her body shake, instantly waking her husband. Simon punched him several times, breaking his nose and immediately sending him back to sleep. He needed to live.

Then Simon opened a small bag and sprinkled several newspaper clippings on the floor.

In Ann Arbor, Michigan, in the plush accommodations of Senator Jack Keeler, Falby had a very similar experience.

Chapter 13

IT WAS THE OFFICIAL FINDING that the charred body was Blake Edwards, a partner in the law firm of Blackberry, Schmitz, and Warwink. The report concluded that he was a murder victim in a carjacking that had gone terribly wrong. Fearing forensic evidence, the perpetrators had burned the car and the body, making it almost impossible to identify. There were no suspects and very little evidence.

The funeral took place on a beautiful day in L.A., with modest cloud coverage and a steady breeze that made the bright sun tolerable. One of al Assad's finest killers -- a man known as Hortence -- was tasked to gather data on the attendees and to make a quick retreat to report what he had learned.

Hortence was in his early fifties and stood just under six feet tall with a modest build. He was Hispanic by birth, wore his dark hair very close, and had no outstanding features. His general look was non-descript, and he took pride in being able to modify his accent, dress, and overall demeanor to melt into any situation he wished. His look was common; the average person probably forgot him the moment he was out of sight.

He patiently watched from the sixth floor of a building window, just across from the cemetery.

The evening before, the Wake had lasted three hours. It was closed-casket, obviously, which made it more tolerable to carry on normal conversations in the parlor. Those present included clients, co-workers, most of the thirty-one partners of the firm, and friends, including Peggy Reynolds. Detective Monroe stood in the back throughout the service, taking mental notes. Everyone seemed unusually upbeat and seemingly emotionally detached from the deceased, as they discussed the work week, recent vacations, and general business.

The mood changed when Pete arrived. He approached the casket, knelt, and began sobbing softly. Those nearby moved away, resuming their conversations in the rear of the room. Pete and Blake had been friends since childhood. They were together the week before in Switzerland. *How could this have happened?* he thought to himself, sadly.

Hortence saw the helicopter get closer and closer. It was flying very low and coming directly at him. He moved further inside the room, turning off the light and checking to make sure the door was locked. Looking out the window, he was relieved to see that the helicopter had changed direction and was landing in a clear grassy area, just a few hundred feet from the small group of mourners who were leaving the funeral service. They all looked over, wondering why a helicopter would land in a cemetery.

Immediately upon touchdown, two large men, one black, one white, but looking very similar, jumped out and evaluated the scene. Following them was Steve McCallister, just in from Andrews Air Force Base and thirty minutes late to the service. The helicopter blades became still as he briskly walked toward the small dispersing group. Pete furiously moved toward the helicopter and met Steve half way.

"What the hell are you doing?" Pete exclaimed. "This is a cemetery!"

Steve kept walking past his friend. "I know. Do you think I wanted to do it this way?"

Pete turned to follow and the two stopped near the coffin. All of the attendees had cleared the area, and most were either beyond earshot or already in their cars. Steve placed both of his hands on

Blake's smooth wooden casket as he studied the ground. His look was one of concentration and he appeared to be in pain as he took a moment to gather his thoughts. Pete remained unmoved, eyeing Steve with contempt.

"I'm not through with you," Pete said.

Steve remained steadfast, his eyes now closed, his lips moving slightly as he silently prayed. Pete softened and put his arm on his friend's shoulder.

"Is there something you want to talk about?" Pete started. "You were acting strange last week. Talk to me."

"I don't know what you mean," Steve said, squaring himself against Pete. "This is a tragedy and it's unrelated to anything I'm involved in." Steve's tone seemed scriptish to Pete, even rehearsed.

"Then why the protection? Why the helicopter? Why the suspicious behavior? This isn't you. Does this have anything to do with Chile?"

"*Don't* say another word!" Steve yelled, his face red. "Don't you *ever* talk to me about that. I'm sorry this happened but there was nothing I could've done!"

Steve left Pete and walked to the helicopter. With a hand motion to the pilot, the huge propellers were in motion and soon Pete was alone in the cemetery.

Hortence documented the entire exchange.

Chapter 14

MOHAMMED WAS SELECTED for his energy alone. Straying from traditional assignment procedure, Almedi Hahn Sahn had charged a fifteen-year old boy to carry out an attack in the heartland of the United States. The American Mid-West.

What the boy lacked in training, he made up for in enthusiasm. Shadowing Almedi everywhere he could, Mohammed would do odd, random tasks for his master, methodically carrying out each assignment, usually in less time than allowed and always to perfection. He had begged for an opportunity to attack the infidels and Almedi had granted it.

Inexperience didn't seem to be a factor, though. The young boy had made all of the planned connections and had met his contact in Toronto without incident. From there, the pair easily entered the United States near Niagara Falls, with Mohammed looking like the bored teenage son of a tourist. They continued into eastern Cleveland, where the boy was checked into a cheap motel directly off I-90 and given two large boxes.

When alone, Mohammed quickly inventoried and separated his supplies. He carefully removed a map of downtown Cleveland, detailing the area known as The Flats. Attached there were several photographs of the designated area where Mohammed was to stand and open fire into humanity at exactly 12:30 p.m. the following day.

In an envelope there was $400 in small bills, a Koran, and detailed instructions on his mission. The note was written by Almedi himself and detailed exactly what Mohammed was to do. The boy read the note quickly and then reread it, fully intending to follow the instructions to perfection.

Next, Mohammed separated the weaponry from the many boxes of ammunition rounds that were carefully stacked. He smiled as he held the HK MP5 submachine gun, noticing how similar it was to the older HK54's he'd practiced on in Pakistan. The HK MP5 was brand new and he grinned at the revelation.

The German-made HK MP5 is easily one of the best sub machineguns available, and had been deemed perfect for the attack. Extremely compact at just over 19 inches in length and weighing about seven and a half pounds fully loaded, it can shoot several hundred rounds per minute and can carry a thirty round magazine clip.

But Mohammed was to switch the selector to a three-round burst to maximize lethality and accuracy. With a machine gun in his right hand and a duffel bag of magazine clips on his left shoulder, he was to spray fire at everyone in sight, changing clips about every ten seconds until all twenty were gone. He'd practiced the physical motions for days, having prepared mentally for even longer.

Mohammed methodically disassembled the gun into its six parts, intently studying the roller-locked bolt system, retractable butt stock, and free floating cold hammer-forged barrel. He then reassembled the gun and turned his attention to the twenty clips and the thirty 9 x 19 millimeter Lugers they each held, making sure that all of his messengers of death were neatly aligned.

Tomorrow Mohamed would walk into immortality. He would fulfill his last task for the cause. To perfection.

Chapter 15

A BLARING HORN awoke the boy, nearly sending him flying off the small bed. Disoriented at first, he quickly regained composure and became excited at the day's events.

It was mid morning and the sun had already burned off the morning haze. Weather reports promised a clear, autumn day in the mid-sixties; perfect for the task at hand.

Mohammed slowly stood and leaned against the only window, studying the constant flow of traffic mere yards away. The cars and trucks went by so fast, the different noises of tires, engines and mufflers blending into a dull monotone that rose and fell at random.

After relieving himself in the bathroom, he moved to the floor and prostrated himself facing east on his sajjafiamda in deep prayer for nearly two hours.

Then, as if an alarm had sounded, the boy rose with robotic confidence. He gathered the two duffel bags and walked out of the room and to the corner where several taxis were promised to be.

Mohammed produced a note that read "Cleveland Flats," and looked to the cabbies waiting on the corner. A large, muscular man waved him over and soon they were on I-90 and Mohammed was thinking about his mission.

Almedi Hahn Sahn was very specific about the time and place of the attack. *12:30 p.m. at The Flats. Just as the Americans flocked for a favorable lunch table, begin shooting. Shoot all twenty clips. Don't stop. Rapid fire in every direction. Do it for the cause. Do it to perfection. This is your jihad.*

Several minutes later, the taxi stopped and the driver looked to Mohammed expectantly.

"Alright kid," he said, his large hand on the passenger headrest. "This is it."

The boy looked up, unsure of what to do, but instinctively grabbed a fifty-dollar bill with a note scribbled in his native tongue that read "transport."

He gave it to the cabby and quickly moved to the door, swinging his legs to the pavement.

"Hey kid," the cabby yelled, and Mohammed almost reached for the gun to affect a quick escape. "Thanks for the tip."

The boy, clearly not understanding, turned and began walking per the instructions in his right hand.

Mohammed stumbled along; looking at the many people that hurried past him and the mammoth buildings in the immediate distance. He tried to move with the busy crowd, not attuned to the different flashing lights and foreign signs all around him.

Finally, he looked past an intersection and into a large clearing, with cobblestone flooring and an old brick wall on the far side. There were many bistros and outdoor cafes; street performers and artists were setting up, and people swarmed the area in search of tables with large umbrellas. Pigeons stirred to the left, and Mohammed turned to see an old bum yelling at the in-flight birds.

Without anyone at his side, the boy began a brisk walk toward the area he had memorized from the pictures the night before. He sat on the edge of a park bench, waiting for the designated time. The killing time. At his destination, he awarded himself a moment of repose and took in the warm sun on his face, enjoying the pleasant breeze that was fragranced by the scents of the area.

He thought of Almedi Hahn Sahn and the cause. *These people don't care about us or our ways. They fight from across the sea, judging us without understanding. Send the message, Mohammed.*

55

The boy glanced at his watch and noticed the time. One minute. He arose to tingling legs and a strange uneasiness. His throat dried and the sun seemed to grow hotter. His clothing felt heavier and more constricting. With heightened senses, Mohammed became aware of every noise, of every person. This was it!

He quickly opened both duffel bags and as practiced many times before, stuffed a clip in the MP5, allowing the empty bag to fall to the ground. Then he unzipped the other bag containing the clips and within moments was poised for action and in position, mere yards from a crowd of hundreds.

In his tongue, he shouted a short statement of freedom and moved the weaponry to his side. Just before he was able to shoot, though, several bullets ripped into his small body. Stunned, his brown eyes grew wide, the gun fell, and he dropped to the ground, fighting desperately for air and curling into a fetal position.

Several armed men appeared and surrounded the fallen boy. People screamed and ran. Others, just arriving, stood motionless and asked each other for details that nobody knew. All of the shots were from silencers and nobody heard a thing. A wall of men hid the boy from view, while other federal agents aggressively moved spectators from the quickly expanding perimeter.

Important looking men guided a waiting ambulance to the scene and an EMT stooped to the would-be assailant's side, checking his pulse and looking into questioning eyes.

"Get him in. We've gotta go now!" he yelled.

Within moments, the ambulance, followed by several blue sedans raced away, not to the hospital, but onto the interstate and to a park in Bay Village. When the cars came to a stop, a well-dressed man approached the boy, leaning between two EMT's that were busy working on him.

"Can you hear me, son?"

Nothing but a few blinks.

"Can you hear me?" he repeated, this time brushing the boy's hair with a gentle hand.

The boy, wide-eyed, began murmuring a prayer and looked into the distance. The man leaned back to offer the boy some breathing room. He needed him to live, information was crucial. What did the boy know about al Assad's next target? Lives depended on it.

With a sudden jerk that seemed impossible for his condition, Mohammed reached into a loose pocket, took out a small capsule and moved it between his lips. The agent moved to open the boy's mouth, finding no resistance, but unable to retrieve the pill.

"What the hell was that?" he blurted, looking from right to left. "Did *anyone* see that?"

Others came to his side, and Steve McCallister looked into the young boy's eyes as they became dilated, shuttered, and eventually halfway closed. A couple of involuntary jerks of his body followed, and a frothy white substance accumulated on the boy's lips. Death was ushered in quickly and the eyes were soon glazed over.

"It was cyanide, dammit!"

Chapter 16

PETE SAT ON HIS DECK in Hall Mount, Vermont, drinking a Broken Hill Lager, his favorite Australian beer. Last week's frost had been cruel to the trees. Many of the beautifully colored leaves that brought tourists to the area were now scattered on the ground, tattered and dirty. Those that resisted nature hung on the trees limply, dangling in the slight breeze.

It seemed that the world had changed. In writing his novels, he was intimate with mass murderers, criminals, and general human slime. He invented them for a living. But coming face to face with the horror of his friend's tragic death consumed him and he suddenly felt aged and detached. Still, the scenery offered a complacency that was unchecked by the horrors of recent events. He took a drag of his cigarette and looked to the fading horizon.

Two beers later, Pete found Jillian in the kitchen.

"Hey honey," she offered, warmly. "You seem so distant. Wanna talk?"

"I'm okay babe," Pete lied.

But then his eyes began to water and he cupped his face with his hands. Jillian moved to him and held him tightly, waiting for him to speak.

"I just need some time. I met Blake in preschool and now he's gone. It's just hard to believe."

"I know," Jillian said, and she nestled her head into his chest.

Pete was suddenly caught in the moment and again reminded of how much he loved his wife, his best friend and partner. He smelled her perfume and took in her essence, as her long dark hair hung down to his forearm.

"We'll get through this together," she added.

Tears rolled down his face as she hugged him tighter. He bowed his head and looked at the tiled floor.

"And Steve's been acting so strange," he said, collecting himself. "He shows up to his best friend's funeral in a helicopter? That's just not like him."

"Why don't you give him a call, honey?"

"I can't."

"Oh forget your stupid rules Pete."

Jillian, becoming frustrated, let go of her husband and moved around to face him. She took his hands in hers.

"It's over Pete," she started, her head shaking slowly. "Blake's dead and he's *not* coming back. Forget your rules about not contacting each other between meetings. He's dead and you have serious questions about it. Call Steve. He may know something."

"Maybe in a couple of weeks."

Jillian sighed and pulled away. She put her hands in her jean pockets, shrugged her small shoulders, and looked at her husband with soft brown eyes.

"Is there anything I can do?"

"Come here babe, I'm sorry," he motioned.

She walked over and they fell into each other's arms once more.

"I love you more than anything," he said, stroking her hair.

"I know honey. I love you too."

The leaves offered perfect camouflage to the man on the forest floor. He captured Pete's time on the deck and the brief conversation inside the home on both tape and film. He waited for several more hours with very little to document, and then disappeared into the darkness.

Chapter 17

THE INSIDE of the dilapidated building contrasted the outside with such dichotomy that it never ceased to amaze Falby. Located in western Pakistan, the leaning structure had been bombed several times and had undergone many facelifts, yet it currently housed the leader of al Assad.

In the foyer, trash was scattered about, walls were missing, and rodents scampered in and out of random holes in the concrete. On the second and third floors, however, there were magnificent rugs, flowing curtains, and expensive furniture. There was a marble staircase, fine art, and a large conference table; at the head of which sat Almedi Hahn Sahn, the holy leader of al Assad. Falby stood in front of him.

"Good job in silencing the two politicians. You have done your cause a great service."

"Thank you," Falby responded, humbly.

"How are your comrades doing with the rest of our agenda?"

Falby nodded. "I have heard nothing of Mohammed and his task in Cleveland."

"Neither have I and that concerns me. What about the others?"

Everything is on schedule. Our people are in place in the American cities you requested."

"Excellent!"

"Sir," Falby started, cautiously. "We need to know the details of your plan. I need more information."

Upon saying this, two of Almedi's bodyguards looked over. Nobody questioned Almedi Hahn Sahn. Falby regarded them both with a pointed glare that forced them to look away. Then he returned his attention to Almedi.

"How are Steve McCallister and the CIA?" Almedi asked.

"They are in receipt of the letter. It arrived a week ago Monday. They're shocked at the assassinations of the two senators and believe it to be us. Steve was personally distraught by the death of his friend, Blake Edwards. As you know, Hortence was monitoring the funeral."

Falby rested a large envelope of pictures in front of Almedi, documenting the actions of Steve, Blake, and Pete over the past two weeks. Accompanying each photo was a one-page explanation. In deep thought, Almedi Hahn Sahn looked over each picture carefully.

"Order your people to interrogate and kill his other friend Pete. If he knows nothing, the hole is semi-sealed and we can move on to McCallister. We need to know what Yamir's letter said about our future actions."

"What good would taking out McCallister do? He's in the CIA; the wheels would continue to function with or without him. It's a dangerous move."

"Leave me, Falby." Almedi Hahn Sahn said with a hand motion, as if waving off an insect.

Falby stood for a few moments indifferently, but then took a few steps back, turned and left the man alone. Almedi Hahn Sahn looked up in prayer and smiled. *It's almost time.*

Chapter 18

JILLIAN SLEPT SOUNDLY, a good idea considering the weather. Fall was beautiful in Vermont, but it brought brisk winds, low temperatures, and sometimes icy rain. Warm flannel sheets on a damp Saturday morning was better than venturing outdoors.

But Pete had been gone a lot lately, and there were mandatory house projects that couldn't wait another minute. Home Depot was about fifteen miles away in Chittenden County. He hadn't driven their new Jeep Grand Cherokee in a couple of weeks and didn't mind the drive.

About a mile behind Pete, driving a white, unmarked utility van was a very dangerous man. He wasn't thinking of weather conditions or sleeping in. His only focus was extracting information from Pete and then killing him. He was holding at thirty-five miles per hour as Pete's vehicle came into sight. A motorcyclist was also trailing about a half mile behind.

Inside the Jeep, Pete was whistling a Simon & Garfunkle tune, oblivious to the danger behind him. In the van, the man was going over the plan that had been rehearsed a hundred times. They were both approaching an intersection on the windy road into Winooski. It was a four-way stop, rarely traveled at early hours on cold and wet Saturday mornings.

Three hundred feet before the stop sign, Pete began to slow the Cherokee. Behind him, now at two hundred feet and closing, was the accelerating van.

After Pete came to a stop and started through the intersection, he glanced in his rear view mirror, seeing an out of control van, its driver frantically applying its brakes. In a matter of seconds, the two automobiles met. The impact was lessened as the braking van met the accelerating Jeep, and the two vehicles moved to the side of the road to assess the damage.

Pete took a few moments to leave the Jeep, removing his cell phone which was charging in the cigarette lighter. The other driver was already bent over, looking at both bumpers. With pen and paper, Pete approached the man, who stood with his arms at his sides, an apologetic smile across his face.

"I'm really sorry about this. I was speeding and didn't realize there was a stop sign until I was on top of you," the man said.

Pete was forgiving and cordial. "That's okay. It happens to the best of us."

Pete crouched to look at the bumpers, the van more damaged than the Jeep.

"At least I got the worst of it," the killer said. "Come over to my van and I'll give you my insurance info. I think I even have an umbrella for you."

"Sounds good to me," Pete said, as he followed the man to the rear of the van. He stood in the pouring rain as the man disappeared inside and produced an umbrella.

The van was a newer model, but the inside looked aged and worn. The seats had been removed and oversized toolboxes lined the sides. The killer sat on a large black box, staying out of the rain. Pete figured this to be a good idea and jumped into the van to join him.

"Mind if I jump in?" he inquired.

"Not at all. Have a seat," the man replied, motioning to the large black box across from him.

As Pete sat down, the man took a 9 millimeter Beretta pistol and smiled confidently.

"Don't say a word," the man said. "I have a few questions for you. The better you answer them the quicker you can get to Home Depot, and back to fixing the downstairs bathroom."

Pete was in shock, his face showing complete astonishment. Then his eyes lowered to the gun and he became numb with fear. Everything seemed to move in slow motion. He heard the man speak and understood the words, but he didn't know how to respond. He trembled, partly due to the cold rain that had soaked his clothing, but mostly because of the intensity of the man's face and the gun that was leveled at him.

"What's going on?" Pete managed.

"Just be completely honest and open, and everything'll be okay. Tell me what you know about a terrorist group called al Assad."

"They've been on the news and in the papers..."

The killer quickly interrupted. "Tell me about your relationship with the CIA?"

"I have a friend that works there, I guess, but I wouldn't call what I have with the CIA a relationship."

"Talk to me about the conversations you've recently had with Steve McCallister."

The first two questions were almost rhetorical, but the man had asked this one differently and leaned closer to his captive to be sure of the response.

"My friend Steve? What's he have to do with anything? We're friends, good friends. I hung out with him in Switzerland last week and saw him briefly in L.A. a couple of days ago. We talked about a lot of things."

"Did he tell you anything about recent activity in a terrorist group? Anything about his current work?"

"Steve wouldn't do that," Pete countered. "He's been very secretive all his life. He doesn't talk much, especially about his job. He's the typical alpha male."

There was a very certain tone in Pete's voice and the trained killer knew he was telling the truth. Hunching over and walking backwards, the man made his way to the rear of the van and stepped out. The whole time, he pointed the gun at Pete. Sensing the worst, Pete panicked and froze. He closed his eyes, unsure of what to do.

A distant gunshot startled him, snapping him back into reality. He looked at the man, only to see him slumped over sideways, blood gushing from a large hole in his neck. Not thinking, Pete jumped over the dead body and onto the road. He heard voices in the distance and saw men running toward him.

Pete quickly entered his Jeep, started the engine and sped away. He looked in his rear view mirror and saw a group of men surrounding the van with guns drawn. A couple of them excitedly waved Pete to stop, but he only accelerated faster.

Trembling and out of breath, he opened his cell phone and called Jillian. She always knew what to do. She answered after several rings.

"Hello?"

"Hey it's me! Get dressed and get the hell out of there! Listen, I..."

"Pete, what's the matter?" she interrupted. "Slow down."

"There's no time for that. Get the hell out! They're after me!"

The motorcycle appeared out of no where. The cyclist was riding parallel to Pete and reaching into a knap sack on his lap. Suddenly the window shattered as a deafening gunshot rang out. The cell phone flew out the window as Pete instinctively swerved into the cyclist, sending him skidding into the nearby woods. The Jeep couldn't recover from such an abrupt maneuver and crashed into a grouping of trees at about forty miles per hour.

The collision sent Pete into shock as he stumbled from the car and fell to his knees on the grassy roadside. His jeans quickly turned dark blue as the cold wetness was absorbed. Everything seemed to be in slow motion yet he had all his senses about him. He could hear the birds, feel the rain, and could smell the damp grass, but he couldn't think clearly. Finally, he got up and slowly walked back to the Jeep, which was banged up and bellowing white smoke from the closed hood. He sat inside with his legs out of the vehicle.

Who was that guy? How did he know about my home improvements? What did this have to do with Steve and the CIA?

Suddenly it hit him. Steve's strange behavior, Blake's death, the last half hour. Everything had to be related. Remembering the motorcyclist, he began jogging down the road. The motorcycle was easily visible, smashed into a few different pieces and lying in the middle of the road. Green fluid gushed from its battered side. The cyclist was not very far, lying on his stomach near the shoulder, a gun a few feet away from his unmoving, outstretched hand.

Pete picked up the gun and stood over the motionless cyclist, not knowing whether he was living or dead. He inspected him from a few feet away. Lying on his stomach, there was no visible sign of injury. Pointing the gun at the body, Pete lightly touched his side with his foot. Still no movement. Pete backed up and watched the body for several seconds, looking for any breathing. Sensing no danger, Pete dropped to his knees and turned the man over. He instantly felt the limpness and several broken bones. Looking at his chest and stomach, he noticed blood and gaping holes, revealing massive internal injury. He was dead, or soon would be.

"Better you than me pal," Pete said, aloud.

He stood and studied the gun; a Sig Saur 9 millimeter semi-automatic with a rare fifteen-round clip. He hadn't handled a gun since Vietnam, but didn't feel uncomfortable ejecting the round from the chamber and sliding the clip into his left hand. If his suspicions were correct, he would have to get a lot more aquatinted with guns.

He looked up the road and saw his Jeep, still smoking. Looking down the road, there was nothing. Down the hill and into the forest was decidedly the best route.

In a morning that was full of craziness, taking a trip through the woods seemed to be an okay move. Running down the landscape, he could see his breath in the crisp morning air, but still he perspired. His adrenaline was at top speed as he dodged trees and jumped small brush. He had to contact his wife again. Surely, she would know what to do.

Hortence couldn't believe his luck as he happened to see Pete appear from the dense tree line behind a convenience store. He knew that things had gone terribly wrong a couple of miles north, and was glad his general sweep of the outlying areas bore fruit.

The abduction would happen, it just wouldn't be easy. Being a Saturday morning, the traffic was constant and potential witnesses were everywhere.

The seasoned killer continued his slow drive and eventually parked in an adjacent parking lot. Then he took out a cell phone and made a call.

Chapter 19

JILLIAN SAT AT THE CORNER BOOTH, nervously sipping her coffee. Her eyes darted from person to person, looking for the slightest hint of abnormality. She was wearing a heavy black overcoat, and although the restaurant was a comfortable temperature, she felt a chill. She cupped her hands around her second cup of coffee and slumped over so that her head was low to the table. She would seem less conspicuous that way, she decided.

It was mid-morning and she was at the Denny's in Ferrisburg, just as her husband had instructed. She'd hastily packed a week's worth of clothing and taken the $15,000 in cash from the house safe, just as he'd told her. Then she'd made several unnecessary turns to make sure she wasn't followed. Now she sipped her coffee, trying to fit in with the other customers, most of whom were in deep conversations with friends or family.

There was a lot of commotion when Pete called from his cell phone almost two hours earlier. Then silence. She was immediately awake and dressed, awaiting another call. It came several minutes later from a pay phone at a 7 Eleven. Fearing that someone could be listening, they kept the conversation short. She was very inquisitive, but he had assured her that all was well for now, and to follow directions and move quickly. He had told her to go to the place "where the bald man slept," an inside joke from several years earlier when at 3 a.m., after a long date, they visited the Denny's for a late night milkshake. An old, bald man in the next booth had fallen asleep in his eggs.

Pete was confident that the terrorists couldn't interpret the message, and he prayed that no one had shadowed Jillian, as they did him. He had told her he would meet her at 10:30 a.m. So she waited.

She was about to order a pastry when her cell phone rang and she reached for it excitedly.

"Hello?"

"Babe, it's me."

"Where are you? Are you alright?" She pressed the phone to her ear, hoping it would bring him closer.

Pete calmly explained the morning's events in great detail, and reiterated his concerns about Steve's suspicious behavior in both Switzerland and Los Angeles. Still, he didn't tell her about the rendezvous point for the next year, or how adamant Steve had been about its importance. He didn't talk about how Blake's death could be related, or that Steve was probably connected to the morning's events. He wanted to isolate her from the madness.

"I'm not going to meet you there like I said," Pete said. "I need you to leave town and drive all day and into the night. Get as far as you can from there. Pay cash for a room and decide where to go from there. I don't want to know where you're going. I just want you safe."

Jillian slumped into the cushy booth.

"Why can't we leave together?" she challenged. "We'll be safer that way."

"No. I think we're both lucky to be alive as it is, and hopefully neither of us has been followed. I don't want to risk you staying there any longer."

Jillian was silent as she thought about the sudden turn in events.

"Jillian?"

"I'm here," she managed, and Pete could tell that she was close to breaking down.

"I need to think things through. The only way I can concentrate is to know you're safe. I know it's hard but you need to do this."

"When will you call me?" Jillian asked.

Outside the convenience store it began to mist. He looked to the low gray sky and took a moment to allow the falling spray to refresh his sweaty face. For a moment he forgot the current crisis.

"I'll call when I know more."

His words became soft as tears welled in his eyes. His throat seemed to narrow and his mouth dried. He wanted to console his wife; wanted to leave town with her and hold her all night.

She wanted to reach through the phone and hug him. Everything was fine when they were together, and now he'd made a decision to separate for who knew how long? For two people who never needed each other more, both fell silent for a long moment.

"Are we gonna be okay?" Jillian asked, defeatedly.

"Of course," Pete responded, quickly. He surprised himself with this unexpected air of confidence, but decided that it would help Jillian's mindset, so he continued.

"I just need to know you're safe. We'll be together soon."

They both believed the lie for the moment. It was refreshing to hear about everything returning to normal, but soon they were gripped by reality and more tears followed. Eventually, the conversation ended, each having a separate and undefined agenda.

Pete hung up the phone, regarded the immediate area, and walked across the street to a truck stop. He spotted a large rig filling up on diesel, the driver emptying trash from the cab.

The trucker wore a dirty red baseball hat with cheap mesh backing and a stained bill. His designer jeans seemed too blue, and the pants gave way to imitation snake skin boots. He wore a gray sweatshirt with a jacket vest and an unlit cigarette dangled from his mouth.

"How ya' doin' buddy?" Pete started.

The trucker continued to empty his cab of fast food bags, styrofoam coffee cups, crumpled cigarette packs, and candy wrappers.

"Just fine."

"I'm actually in a bit of a bind," Pete said. "I saw you pull in from the north, which makes me believe your headin' south?"

"Yeah?" the trucker replied, realizing he was being hit up for a ride.

Pete sensed the man's hesitancy and moved around to face him.

"I don't mean to bother you, but I could drive if you'd let me. It can get lonely on the road, and I'm always good for a few jokes. You could even get some rest."

The trucker finally stopped and took a hard look at Pete, who stood with his arms outstretched, a look of uncertainty on his face. The man was taken back by Pete's honesty. He quickly surmised that he wasn't a freeloader or runaway, rather an educated, well-mannered guy that was down on his luck. Sensing no danger, the trucker decided to help him.

"What's your name, buddy?" the man asked, extending his right hand.

"Sam... Sam Gunther," Pete replied, remembering his favorite teacher in high school. He didn't like lying about his name, but his guilt quickly dissipated as he reflected on his present situation.

"I'm Phil."

They shook hands and exchanged brief smiles. "I'm headed to Atlanta, transportin' pipe valves and shit. You're welcome to come along for as long as you like."

"Thanks Phil," Pete said with a smile. "I'll get some food and coffee from the shop here. Do you need anything?"

"I'm fine," the trucker said, already resuming his cleaning efforts in the cab.

Pete began walking to the gas station store. He put his hands in his pockets and walked like a man without a care in the world. Still, he was very realistic. Getting a ride south was a huge win, but he still had a lot on his mind and he was sure that bigger problems awaited him in the near future.

Chapter 20

STEVE'S FACE TIGHTENED as he listened intently to Special Agent Holbrook's report of the incident. Two terrorists were dead, Pete's jeep was crashed into a tree, and both Pete and his wife were missing.

"Let me begin by asking a question," Steve said, slowly.

"How many *fucking* agents do we have on this?"

"Twelve Sir, just as you requested."

"How many were watching the house? How many were watching the assassin? And why didn't we know about this other prick on the motorcycle? Where did *he* come from?"

These were rhetorical questions, the agent decided, and any attempt to answer them would prove futile. The whole thing went down sloppy, and as agent in charge, Holbrook simply lowered his head, spoke into the receiver and apologized.

"I want a full report immediately." Steve commanded. "I want these two dead assholes identified, and I want Pete and his wife found!"

"Yes sir," the agent managed to say.

"I'm sending you fifteen more men, Holbrook. I want everything in a forty mile radius turned over. By now al Assad probably knows that two of their soldiers are down and they'll be after Pete, and possibly Jillian, with a vengeance. I want updates every hour."

The call over, Steve fell into his chair and lightly tapped the receiver against his head. The small rhythmic gesture of cause and effect steadied him. He looked at his wall of honors and medals and placed his feet on his desk. *You have no idea what you're up against Pete,* he thought to himself sadly.

He allowed a small moment of relaxation and then heard a knock on the door. Keeping his feet up, he yelled, "Come in."

Director Willard appeared and plopped into an oversized chair. "In on a Saturday, huh?"

"There's no such thing as a weekend with this job, Doc."

"Still you should get some sleep, Steve. You look like shit."

"Thanks."

"You've worked in L.A., Cleveland, and D.C. within three days. Why don't you get outta here?"

Steve smiled, rubbing his temples.

"Tough break about the kid dying before you could question him."

Steve was unresponsive, so the director pursued the issue further.

"Does al Assad know?"

"I doubt it," Steve said. "We covered our tracks extremely well. Even the people in the immediate area don't know what happened and the media hasn't been a factor. We were out in less than two minutes."

"I feel very good about the job you're doing, Steve," the director said.

Frowning, Steve clearly didn't agree and he waved off the compliment.

"We got lucky Doc, clear and simple. We didn't know *who* we were looking for. One of our spotters saw the large, awkward bags the kid was lugging and followed him through a scope. When he made his move, he was taken down. We were seconds away from a massacre and that's hardly grounds for celebration."

"At least you killed the son of a bitch."

Steve sighed. "We killed a kid, Donald. Yes he was al Assad and I'd order that shot all day long, but he was still just a kid."

The director nodded and fell silent, and Steve suddenly felt uncomfortable with his presence.

"Look, I have a call to make. I'll see you later, huh?"

Steve picked up the phone and dialed Dana Carpenter's number. He'd been thinking of her since their interview and needed to speak with someone who wasn't in law enforcement. His mind had been reeling for several days and he needed a break from the madness. The director lifted his large body from the chair and left the office with several short strides.

"We'll talk later, Steve," he called over his shoulder.

Dana answered almost immediately, leaving Steve little time to transition.

"Hi, it's me. I mean, Steve from the CIA. Steve McCallister. Sorry to bug you on a Saturday."

"Hi Steven," she sang. "Thanks for returning my call."

He was taken back by hearing her use his proper name and he liked it. No one called him 'Steven.' He smiled, then became slightly flustered and sought refuge in conversation.

"I apologize for last week. I was going to walk you down, but I..."

"I understand. I just wanted to follow up on a few points with you. Could we meet for lunch or something?"

On each end they were smiling silently, both in hopeful anticipation of the other's words. Steve became more confident and started thinking of an appropriate place.

"This may sound crazy," Steve started, "but how'd you like to take a long walk near the monuments, maybe catch a quick bite in Georgetown?"

"That sounds nice. I live right in Adams Morgan. Where do you want to meet?"

"How about the Lincoln Monument at 11 a.m. tomorrow?"

"I'll see you then."

Chapter 21

PETE'S FOREFINGER slid easily over the smooth window glass as he drifted into thought. The trucker had thankfully been respectful of Pete's privacy.

After an hour of small talk and surface conversation, very few words were spoken. Pete stuck mainly to cosmetic, generic information, and although he did a good job of disguising his true motives, he was sure the trucker saw through the facade. Pete was hoping the man's patience would last until Washington D.C.; another six or seven hours.

He thought of Jillian non-stop, praying she was okay wherever she was. How he hoped she was hundreds of miles away, getting some rest and not worrying about him. She was so fragile and he hated thinking of her in any pain or discomfort. Surely Steve would offer insight into the living nightmare they'd been forced into. He just had to get to him.

The whole thing had to do with Steve, Pete knew. In Switzerland, his friend hadn't been himself. Pete had always known Steve to be in complete control ever since they were children. Nothing worried him and he always came out on top. Whoever these people were had rattled him.

And then Blake was killed. Although people are carjacked everyday, how many are murdered so grotesquely? And burned? At the funeral, Steve was elusive, strange, and distant, leaving even more questions.

Earlier, Pete's would-be killer had asked about Steve, and although the horrific scene unfolded quickly, Pete now realized that the shot that killed the man hadn't come from the enemy. It was probably from the FBI or CIA, which meant that he'd run from the very people that were trying to protect him.

Pete was torn. Should he contact Steve and the authorities now, or bide his time making slow progress south? He feared that calling anyone could compromise his ride in the truck, and he *was* thankful for the time to think. But maybe everyone would be safer if he sought protection now. He decided to wait and anonymously slip into D.C., making contact with Steve then.

Pete slept lightly for a couple hours before being awakened by a yell from his trucker friend.

"What the hell are you doing!?" the man yelled at an old Buick that was driving erratically.

It had been tailgating the truck for some time, and after moving beside them, sped in front of the truck and swerved back and forth, slowing down and speeding up. The windows were tinted black and the driver handled the car like a professional. Then it sped off, its red taillights becoming smaller and smaller until they disappeared into the winding asphalt horizon.

Flustered at the short incident, the trucker exited into the next truck stop to take a break from the road. The tank was almost empty and he decided to refuel, get some cigarettes, and have a talk with his passenger.

Sensing the man's suspicions, Pete's mind sprang to attention. He thought about what he'd told the man thus far and how he could prolong his stay in the truck. He had a good thing going and didn't want to be stranded at a truck stop in New Jersey.

The trucker parked the rig and climbed out to start the fuel pump before heading to the convenience center. Moments later, the trucker climbed in the cab with two cups of coffee, handing Pete one of them.

"Okay, buddy," he began. "I'm not stupid. What's goin' on?"

Pete took a sip of his coffee, using both hands to raise the cup to his lips. Even after he drank, he kept the cup close to his mouth, the steam warming his face. He was unsure how to proceed. If he told the trucker too much, maybe the trucker's life could be in danger. If his response was too generic or unbelievable, he'd be without a ride.

"You've been very good to me Phil," Pete began. "You selflessly gave me a ride and I'm greatly appreciative. But for your own good I can't tell you anything. I need to get to D.C., preferably without being seen. It sounds strange I know, but people's lives are in danger and I'm one of the good guys. All I can tell you is that you are doing me a tremendous favor and I will never forget it. If at all possible, I'd like to continue on with you, but I will respect your wishes if you don't want me to."

"Is what you're involved in illegal?"

"Absolutely not. I just don't know who to trust and involving the authorities at this point could prove detrimental."

"What was all that shit with the Buick?"

"I have no idea, but I really doubt it has anything to do with me."

Pete took another sip of his coffee and looked straight ahead. True, he didn't think the car had anything to do with him, but he couldn't be entirely sure. He just needed a ride and wanted to get out of the conversation and on the road as soon as possible.

"How about I drive for the next few hours while you get some rest in the back?" Pete asked hopefully. "I used to drive rigs like this in Vietnam. You can make Atlanta well ahead of schedule."

The fuel line stopped pumping and made a distinct sound. It broke the tension in the cab and Phil smiled at Pete.

"Alright, maybe I'm just exaggerating. But let me know if that asshole comes back."

"Will do boss," Pete replied with a quick salute.

Pete jumped from the cab, replaced the fuel handle and turned the gas cap. Phil schooled Pete on the basics of the truck's transmission, and Pete worked the clutch while Phil changed gears. Soon they were back on the New Jersey Turnpike and moving steadily at 65 mph.

The late afternoon sun was beginning to wane, casting a soothing orange glow, and Pete felt good about buying more time. If he could keep up good relations with the trucker, he could hopefully be in D.C. within the next several hours.

Then he noticed the Buick a half mile behind him. The driver wasn't moving erratically or attempting to pass the truck. Whoever it was seemed to be lying in wait and doing it very patiently.

Pete's eyes darted from the side mirrors, his resting passenger, and to the road in front of him. His throat went dry, his heart began pounding, and he felt hot all over.

Phil slept soundly, unaware of the danger that lurked in their immediate future.

Jillian decided to travel west, first taking the ferry into Port Kent and then Interstate 87 to 90 West, stopping only for gas and quick rest room visits. Too upset for food and too scared to rest, she kept a steady pace and drove well into the evening. But the drive did little to ease her mind. She could only think of her husband and having him safely by her side again.

She rethought the day's events until she was mentally exhausted. Paranoia fueled her imagination and she became suspiciously aware of everything around her. Who was after her husband? Were they following her as well? Every car was a possible threat and anything could happen. It already had. So she drove.

Near Erie, Pennsylvania, she decided to start south on I-79, where she could eventually lose herself in the landscape of West Virginia. More importantly though, she would only be a few hours drive to D.C. and to where her husband would hopefully be by day's end.

After driving through Bridgeport in West Virginia, she turned onto Route 20 in search of a room. Just after 8 p.m., she saw the faded sign of a small roadside motel, and turned off the dark road to park in its unpaved lot.

She opened the car door and looked around cautiously. She was standing in an ocean of bright white stones, which reflected the light from the two large buzzing lights overhead. The black sky was a magnificent backdrop to the large ivory moon that seemed to shine brighter than she could ever remember. She wondered how such chaos could reign in a world that was so beautiful, so peaceful. An unexpected breeze caught her off guard and she briskly walked to the front office. The stones crunched under her black leather boots and the sound was magnified in the cool, crisp air.

The office was dark, and if it weren't for the orange neon sign advertising a vacancy, it could pass for an abandoned building. Jillian rapped on the window until a light came on inside. She was greeted by an old man in a dark robe. He waddled to the window and turned on a small desk lamp that brightened the office and showed his harsh features. His body leaned as he stood, and his head seemed to be permanently stuck to the right, as if he'd survived a recent stroke.

"How are ya?" he grunted in a hoarse voice. "Ya' need a room?"

"Yes sir. Do you have any king size beds?"

The man smiled at the ridiculous request.

"This aint the Marriott Miss. Some of the rooms aint even been used in quite some time. I can give you a single bed for $38. Is that okay?"

Jillian quickly produced two twenty's and placed them on the desk. The man took the money without providing change, quickly forcing the bills into his side robe pocket. Then he eyed her wearily.

"You okay, Miss?"

"I'm really tired," Jillian said, quickly. "What number is it?"

Jillian wanted to get into a room and get some sleep. She hoped that the uneasiness in her stomach could subside long enough to get some rest; maybe her dreams would be more pleasant than the situation she found herself in.

The old man threw a key on the counter on his way back to bed.

"Number 34," he called over his shoulder, as he waddled away and turned off the light.

Upon entering, she immediately fell into the small bed that consumed most of the room. It wasn't what she had in mind, but she hadn't passed a nice hotel for quite some time.

A half mile up the road, a cell phone came to life.

"I got her," the voice said. "What do you want me to do?"

"Where is she?"

"A small motel near Peeltree, West Virginia."

"Let her get some rest. I'll be in contact."

The conversation over, the man moved the blue sedan into a dark lot and waited. He eased into the leather car seat to wait out the night, turning on the radio in an optimistic search for an oldies station.

Chapter 22

WHEN THE TRUCK SLOWED, the Buick reduced its speed and kept a steady distance. Inside, Hortence reached for his cell phone and called his superior.

"I'm on the New Jersey Turnpike about a half mile behind him. Positive identification."

"We need him alive," the voice was quick to respond.

"What about the trucker he's befriended? Should I eliminate him?"

"Absolutely not. It would cause more trouble than it's worth. I doubt that he'd share anything with a complete stranger. I need this done within the hour."

"No problem," Hortence responded confidently. "Within the hour."

He placed the phone in his pocket and returned his attention to the truck. He had memorized the map and the approaching exits. He was going to acquire Pete for interrogation, but it was up to Pete as to how. Quietly or violently, Hortence didn't care.

If Pete pulled over or used the radio to signal for help, he'd have to take him immediately. If he motioned to a police car and the two pulled over, he would have to deal with the officer. If he pulled into a truck stop among other people, he would still abduct him, but not think twice of immobilizing any heroes that might mistake him for a petty carjacker. Hortence waited patiently and monitored all frequencies.

The one element that Hortence couldn't account for was if Pete was aware of the New Jersey State Police Station in Hightstown, which was only about ten miles away and just off the turnpike. He doubted Pete knew of this potential safe place, but Hortence never underestimated his adversary.

He knew the truck would need to refuel within the next few hours, and that only helped the situation. He also knew that Pete saw him in the side mirrors. When the victim was scared, the abduction and subsequent interrogation was always easier. In his experience, people reacted to stress with confidence or fear. With Pete, Hortence suspected the latter, and fearful people made foolish mistakes.

Hortence had planned the abduction very carefully. Pete just had to make a move.

Inside the truck, Pete's hands were shaking as he unknowingly drove ten miles under the speed limit. A dull feeling throbbed in his stomach and an acidic taste had formed in his mouth. The whole day had been a blur. He knew that the terrorists had killed Blake, most likely because of Steve and what had happened in Switzerland. But nothing *had* happened in Switzerland. Then it hit him.

Steve had key information about terrorist activity, and they probably thought that Steve had told Pete in Switzerland. That being the case, he was being hunted for no reason at all, and the CIA or FBI was looking for him and Jillian to *protect* them. He wished he would've gone to the authorities in the first place. At least then, Jillian would be safe and Pete wouldn't be on the run.

But he hadn't done that and he had to deal with the present. An assailant was behind him, probably armed to the hilt and ready to risk anything to guarantee Pete's capture.

Pete looked at the snoring trucker in the backseat, hoping they knew he was oblivious to everything. Then again Pete didn't know anything either. He decided that his best route was to pull into a truck stop, hopefully among people, and ease into the public place. Pete still had the handgun from the crash scene earlier and could feel the heavy bulkiness in his jacket pocket. But a counterattack was something he didn't know if he was capable of.

He passed a sign advertising a rest stop and had noticed there was a McDonald's and Cracker Barrel restaurant at the plaza. He only hoped that it would be busy.

An occasional car passed the truck and Pete was amazed at how everything felt normal. He could think of trivial things like the dentist appointment he scheduled in the upcoming week, and hoping that they wouldn't be upset with him for not showing. It was like living in a dangerous dream, yet still having all your faculties about you.

Pete exited the ramp and approached the large service area, immediately surveying the area for people and safe refuge. The Buick pulled in right behind him, mimicking the truck's speed. Pete looked to the left and saw several trucks sleeping silently at the far end of the lot. His main focus, though, was on the diesel fueling station straight ahead. It was large and open, with tall overhead ceilings, and it was vacant.

As the truck slowed near the pumps, Pete unfastened his seat belt, unlocked the door, and got ready to run. As the truck rolled to a stop, Pete looked back, whispered a thank you to Phil, locked the doors, and ran to the restaurant. He hoped that Phil being asleep would offer his new friend protection.

Looking back, the Buick was parked, but the driver didn't seem in a hurry to follow. Seeing this, Pete slowed to a walk as he approached and entered through the twin glass doors of the Cracker Barrel.

Pete was instantly consoled by the familiar smell of the kitchen's busy grill. He realized he hadn't really eaten all day, but decided not to give into hunger just yet. He stood for a moment to regain a hint of composure.

He walked through the dining area and into a hallway with convenience stores at either end, rest rooms beyond that. Even though he had to use the bathroom, he hesitated at being confined to such a small area. Walking further, he noticed a wall of pay phones and ran toward them.

He dialed 911 and excitedly explained to the operator that he needed the police as soon as possible. Hanging up, he leaned against the wall sweating. Then he remembered Phil and hoped that he was okay. There seemed to be more people in the restaurant now and he felt safe spying on the truck from afar. It was unmoved and the Buick was gone. He turned to one of the convenience stores and bought a pack of Marlboros. He hadn't had a smoke all day, and this one would be especially relaxing.

He walked out a side exit and leaned against a brick wall exhaling the first puff of smoke. Then a man in a police uniform exited the door and stood between Pete and the building.

"Sir, did you call for help?"

"Yes I did!" Pete said, excitedly. "Man you guys are fast!"

The officer began walking away from the building and Pete instinctively followed, feeling completely at ease. When they turned the corner the Buick was only a few feet away, its doors swung open. Hortence, the fake officer, grabbed Pete's arm and shuffled him toward the car.

"Get in Pete. It'll be better for you this way."

Pete didn't fight the losing battle. He moved to the car and was helped into the back seat as Hortence cuffed his hands and legs. Inside, the windows were dark and when the door shut with a terrible thud, it felt as if he was sealed in a cocoon.

Pete looked to his side and realized there was another man in the back seat. He had long black hair pulled tightly into a ponytail, and his dark eyes seemed to peer into Pete's soul. He had a very distinct and piercing look and Pete shivered at the sight.

"Hello Pete," the man said, softly. "My name is Simon."

Chapter 23

FALBY HUNG from the north end of the Golden Gate Bridge in San Francisco -- just as he'd done several times before -- praising the weather. It was a foggy night and he couldn't have asked for better conditions, especially for the task at hand.

He was wearing stained blue jeans, brown work boots, and a warm flannel shirt. He carried a large backpack, which although bulky, was very lightweight and moved with him easily. He scaled the large iron leg of the bridge with utmost efficiency, caring little about the occasional traffic above or the freezing water over two-hundred feet below. His night vision did wonders as he patiently analyzed the composition of the structure's legs, speaking the details slowly into a compact, hand-held recorder.

He needed one last look at the construction, weight, length, width, and density of the bridge's legs in order to make any final adjustments. He had read about their composition from a variety of sources, and even looked at the original blueprints at the city's bureau of public records. But this information, although valuable, would merely confirm what he would determine for himself. He was extremely thorough and required the most current and reliable information available. It would make it easier to construct and apply the necessary explosives to bring the bridge down.

He finished his study in less than an hour and just before 5 a.m., after throwing his equipment and clothing into the bay; he changed into running shoes, sweats, and tied the flannel around his waist. He neatly tucked his recorder into an inside pocket and began to jog toward his car, located at San Verdir Park just a few miles away.

The sun rose slowly on the horizon, peeking through the morning fog and warming Falby's face. He noticed a jogging party just ahead and increased his stride and pace to join them. It was rare that he talked to anyone in his line of work and he enjoyed random camaraderie from time to time. After a few introductions and pleasantries, he meshed into the group and Falby the friendly terrorist was enjoying his morning jog.

———————

Just within the city limits of Philadelphia, in a secure location, Pete had just survived the second round of interrogations. He was beaten, drugged, and bound, drifting in and out of consciousness and hoping for a quick death. His pinky finger lay on the concrete floor, abandoned like the soda bottle next to it. Chills ran through his body at random and a thick sweat covered his entire being.

At dawn, his captors deemed him useless to question, at least for the next few hours, and left him to check on other endeavors.

He was barely alive.

Chapter 24

BY MID-MORNING it began to rain lightly. Several men were scattered about the small motel parking lot, two more were on either side of the door. All were waiting for the call to take her.

When it came, she was in the shower. She heard the raps on the door and was immediately scared. Thoughts ran through her head like lightening. Who could possibly know she was here? What did they want?

When the knocking persisted, she turned off the water and hastily wrapped a towel around her body. She ran from the bathroom, looking for a phone to call for help, but there wasn't one.

The knocks kept coming and became louder, as she was now much closer. They sounded like fists pounding on the cheap wooden door. She feared they would reach through and take her. Would they kill her like they killed Blake?

Then she heard words that set her mind at ease.

"Mrs. Jillian Swaggerty," a voice shouted through the door. "This is Special Agent Jonathan Holbrook of the CIA. You are in terrible danger. You need to come with us."

She cautiously moved the old curtain aside and saw several official-looking men scattered about. The agent pressed his identification against the window and she opened the door as tears ran down her face. She was finally safe. Had they done the same for her husband?

She invited the agents in as she retreated to the inside of the room.

"I'm sorry guys. Please stay here while I change."

Agent Holbrook nodded at four of the men and motioned outside.

"Secure the area and keep an open frequency."

Riding in the back of the sedan, Jillian regarded the trees that hugged Route 20, noticing how different the scene appeared in daylight. They reached Benedum Regional Airport quickly; the Lear jet cleared for departure within minutes of arrival.

The flight time to Reagan National was only thirty-five minutes, and upon landing Jillian was escorted to a waiting car that drove directly to Langley. Throughout the entire process no one would answer her questions. Director Willard would speak to her personally, she was assured.

Once at CIA headquarters, she was rushed through the front doors, down a side elevator, through a long corridor, and down another three flights of stairs. A swipe of a card opened every door, and she was finally allowed to relax on a sofa in a very comfortable room. As she entered, two men approached. Steve McCallister hugged her.

"I'm so sorry Jillian, I'm sorry for all this," Steve said waving his hands in the air. "Thank God you're safe."

Turning to the man beside him, he said "This is Donald Willard, director of the CIA."

Jillian stared at both men indifferently. "I just want to know what's going on, where my husband is."

"That's our number one priority," Steve responded. "Let's get some coffee and talk."

"Not yet. Where's Pete?"

"Jillian. Let's move to the other room."

"Don't do this Steve! Where is my husband? Just answer the question." Her voice was raised, her face red, and her eyes were fixed on Steve, who conceded and began to speak.

"We are investigating a report at a service center in Pennsylvania. A trucker apparently picked up a man matching Pete's description in Vermont. The trucker said that he probably lied about his name, said it was Sam something. Anyway, a Buick was tailing and baiting them on the New Jersey Turnpike. The trucker slept while this man drove. When the trucker awoke, he was locked in the cab and it was parked at a rest stop. There was no sign of resistance, but the trucker thinks something happened. He seemed to think the man was in some kind of trouble, so he called the police."

"Are you sure it's Pete?"

"We are analyzing the 911 conversation, and we are interviewing people at the place. Trouble is, it's visited by thousands of people every day. Needless to say, we've been having problems."

"I don't care about problems, Steve. I want my husband. Have you heard the tape yet?"

"No I haven't. But my gut tells me it's him."

Jillian moved closer to Steve and fell into his large chest. She let her emotions go and sobbed uncontrollably as he awkwardly stroked her long hair. He put his cheek on top of her head for added support and whispered to her.

"I've got men all over the area. We'll find him."

Suddenly she pulled away and wiped the tears from her face, glaring at the two men stubbornly.

"No bullshit. What's going on? Tell me everything!"

Steve looked at Director Willard, who offered a reassuring nod.

"Let's move into the next room and have a chat," the director said.

Steve swiped a card and the door opened. This room was smaller than the other but just as welcoming, with plush carpeting, soft lighting, and comfortable furniture. There were deli sandwiches, chips, soft drinks, and fresh coffee on a nearby table. Jillian sat at the edge of the far sofa and stared at the two men in front of her. Director Willard was the first to speak.

"Most of what I'm about to tell you is confidential for now, but will no doubt be picked up by the media sooner or later. An information leak *now* could threaten the security of the United States. You understand that what I tell you cannot be repeated to anyone, not even another agent at this location. You also must remain here or in a safe house for the balance of our investigation, and obviously until we straighten things out with your husband."

"How long will that be?"

"Could be a couple of days or a couple months. We have quarters for you already, and can supply you with anything from your home. As things cool down, you can move to a safe house if you'd like, or have security at your home."

Jillian took a deep breath. "Tell me everything," she said, stretching her legs and finally accepting the sofa's comfort.

"I'm sure you've heard of the terrorist faction al Assad. We have reason to believe they are actively carrying out a terrorist campaign against the United States on our soil. We have limited information on the potential targets but we know that each has a separate team assigned to it."

"What targets?"

"I can't answer that, but we're also not completely certain."

Director Willard turned to Steve, who took a few paces toward the wall and examined a vase on a shelf.

"We do have reason to believe that the two senators that were murdered in their homes were an introduction to coming events."

Jillian stared blankly at the two men, believing the outrageous story but not fully accepting her place in it. Sure al Assad had been on the news, but what did that have to do with her and her husband?

The director continued. "The reason for Blake's death and the recent attempt on Pete's was, we believe, due to their recent conversations in Switzerland. We think the terrorists believe that Blake and Pete are linked to a U.S. intelligence agency, which isn't true, of course. They want to figure out what Steve knows. We were too late for Blake and just in time for Pete, but he took off. We'd been watching your home and were hours away from taking you both in when they beat us to it."

"You mean you *knew* they were after us and you did nothing!" Jillian fumed, glaring at Steve. "Your friend is dead and Pete's somewhere out there!"

Jillian was up from the couch in no time as she rushed toward Steve.

"You've put us in jeopardy, you son of a bitch!" she screamed, awkwardly swinging her fists in the air.

Steve easily caught Jillian in a bear hug and rocked her in his strong arms. She began to cry softly, as Steve whispered to her.

"We'll find him, Jillian. I *swear* to you, we'll find him."

After several moments, Jillian broke from Steve and found a nearby stack of tissues. She found no consolation in their story, but couldn't fight exhaustion any longer. She removed her shoes and fell farther into the sofa, eventually sleeping soundly for several hours.

Steve hoped she could get some rest. She would need it to face the reality of the situation. Steve knew that al Assad had Pete and he hoped he could find him within forty eight hours. After that, historically, the only thing to be found would be his body.

Chapter 25

PETE'S BODY JOLTED, awakening him from a near comatose condition. He felt light-headed but definitely aware of his surroundings. He immediately noticed the amputation of his right pinky finger, but showed little emotion in its discovery. He was at the center of a large warehouse, tied to a wooden chair facing large pallets of unrecognizable inventory tightly bound in green shrink-wrap. And he was alone.

He could remember little of his immediate past and couldn't piece together coherent thoughts, but he was alive and for that he was thankful. He recalled the questioning, the non-stop questioning. Questions about the CIA, Pete's involvement with Steve, his knowledge of any terrorist strikes. Did Pete know anything? Had Pete told anyone? Pete remembered their stories, their occasional phone calls assuring slow progress. He heard pieces of conversations as he drifted in and out of unconsciousness, enormously preferring the latter.

"He doesn't know anything," he heard at one point. "The bombing of the Golden Gate was on schedule," was heard at another. Then he blacked out and was at peace in a delirious sleep.

Pete looked around, wondering what time it was, where he was. Most importantly, where were they? As the numbness in his right hand gave way to a sharp sting, he decided his only option was escape.

He tried to stand but was instantly caught by the restraints that bound him. But he did hear the faint squeaking of the chair, hinting at its weakness.

The sudden burst of energy gave him a painful head rush, but also made him slightly more aware. He looked to his right and saw a table. Moving the chair slowly with small hops, he turned to face it. There were knives, metal objects, white towels, and a medical kit. On the far right was a large black pot flanked by what appeared to be chemical solutions.

Pete looked at the contents and then at the restraints around him. He let out a sigh and looked toward the rafters high above. He didn't know what the next couple of days would bring, but knew it couldn't be good. He eased his chair back to its original position and let his chin fall to his chest.

He thought of the kidnappings in the Middle East and all of the beheadings that had captured the headlines. Is that what they planned for him? He remembered watching the news after confirmation that a hostage was beheaded. He was always sickened by it, but thankful that he and Jillian were so far from the conflict. But here he was, possibly being held by the same caliber of men.

At least they left him alone for short periods of time. For although the dull, acidic lump in his stomach was constant, at least his mind could wander and offer a distraction from his plight.

Then he heard voices, followed by multiple footsteps. Three or four of them, he guessed. The sharp pain in his gut worsened, adding to the assemblage of fear, and he became overwhelmed by a fright he'd never known. The door slammed and Pete's head spun involuntarily to meet the eyes of his captors. They took their time in walking over, exuding a confidence that didn't sit well with him.

Simon bent down and looked him over. The killer reached into his pocket, pulled out a small flashlight, and shined it in Pete's eyes for a few seconds.

"He's okay," he said, lightly slapping Pete's cheek.

The man's gloved hand made an enhanced sound, echoing for a short time against the gray concrete surroundings. Confidently, Simon looked down at his prisoner.

"Are you ready for another round?"

Chapter 26

WITH A HIGH BLUE SKY and a subtle breeze, the autumn Sunday morning was warmer than it should have been. Sitting on the steps of the Lincoln Memorial, Steve was enjoying the bright sunshine on his face and the comfort of his outstretched body on the wide stairs.

He was early for his meeting with Dana, and used the time to reflect and gain some composure. In less than a week, his world had been complicated by the death of a friend, the kidnapping of another friend, and the task of stopping an invisible and very capable terrorist group from attacking the United States. He'd also been traveling extensively and had personally led the team that thwarted a terrorist strike in Cleveland. He questioned the validity of meeting with Dana at a time like this, but decided he needed a small break from his ruthless schedule. Still, he remained connected with his teams by both cell phone and beeper.

But as crazy as his life was, he was entering into a stranger situation by flirting with a women. Was this even a date or was he entirely off base? His only thoughts were of bringing al Assad down, but Dana was in the back of his mind; a small beacon of hope suggesting that all was not evil in the world.

He needed to find the truth. He needed to engage Dana in conversation and either put to rest the phantom flirtation, or proceed with extreme caution and open honesty. Could his career withstand a relationship? Could Dana accept his unwavering loyalty to his country? Delicate footsteps caught Steve's attention and he looked into blinding sunlight, halfway squinting.

"Hey there," Dana called. "Sunning yourself a little?" she chuckled.

"Yeah, beautiful day. Have a seat."

She swung herself around and sat next to Steve, crossing her hands across her lap and accepting the higher step as a backrest.

"Wow, this is nice," she began. "You know, I have to take advantage of this city more often. Look how the sky and trees reflect off the reflecting pool. I bet most of the people that work and live here never take time to notice. They spend all their time in their cars on the Fourteenth Street Bridge or in some office building."

"Watch it. I'm one of those people," Steve smiled, turning to see her for the first time since the interview.

She was wearing a long black skirt with a light purple sweater that hugged her figure. A petite woman in her early forties, she had shoulder length strawberry blonde hair and wore just enough make-up to accentuate her natural beauty. She had the look of an all-American girl, very beautiful to the eye but not overdone in any area.

"You're hardly one of those people, Steven," she said, lightly tapping his leg with her one-inch black pump.

"So what's up?" he started. "Like I said, I'm sorry about the interview."

"That's okay, I just wanted to follow up on some questions that I didn't get a chance to ask."

Steve settled back into the stair, a slight look of defeat crossing his face. Coming to the sudden realization that the slight flirtations were for nothing, he bounced back quickly.

"Okay, Dana. What's your first question?" he asked confidently.

"Well, would you like to go on a spontaneous date with me right now? Take a long walk, eat a light dinner, and who knows, talk about stuff that doesn't really matter?"

His face lit up and he grinned like an excited child.

"That would be nice. I accept."

They walked down the stairs and took a left past the Vietnam Memorial. Seeing the large walls with the names forever etched into the stone reminded Steve of his past. He knew it was an absolute miracle he was not among those men, and he promised not to burden Dana with any talk of his work.

Chapter 27

IN THE DARKNESS -- the complete darkness -- in silence and with the gentle touch of an angel, Pete felt the presence of another. It was in front of him, then behind him, and eventually beside him. Although his mind was swarming and his body felt numb, he retained his senses and the sweet smell of cologne overtook him. He heard the breathing and the gentle tiptoeing of someone moving around him.

Pete heard the sharp sounds of ropes being cut and felt the tight bindings fall away. He instantly fell limp on the cold floor, but an arm quickly lifted him to a standing position.

The stranger helped him to the side door and into an alley. A light wind blew and Pete smelled the fragrances of the night. Still, all his energy escaped him and he fell sideways onto the pavement and rolled over. He lay there for a few moments, unable to move, and focused his attention on a small puddle a few feet away.

The man knelt beside Pete and held a pungent cloth over his mouth, which forced him awake. Then the man ran down the alley and Pete realized he was free. Free from his captors, their incessant questions, tools, and drugs.

With all of his might, Pete got to his knees and crawled a few feet. Then, halfway standing, he walked a couple of steps only to fall again. A mixture of heavy drugs ran freely through his body, only adding to his disorientation. He felt nauseated, but a fire inside him slowly grew, and he was able to regain focus.

He could see that the alley gave way to a city street just a hundred feet away, and it quickly became his goal. If he could just get to the road, everything could be okay. He tried to stand once more, his head becoming clearer with every movement. As he walked sideways, his gait became brisk and he concentrated on his freedom.

Clothed only in jeans, he ignored the cold pavement and the chill in the air. He finally entered the road and found it vacant at the late hour. He looked across to find another alley and quickly made his way, hunching over and moving sideways to even his pace.

Walking through the alley deliriously, he noticed people lying in large heaps of trash, others walking like zombies. But the homeless of Philadelphia paid little attention to Pete, as he picked up his pace in an effort to put as much distance as possible between himself and his captors.

After several minutes of weaving through alleys and back roads, Pete's feet began to feel numb from the cold and he could walk no further. He was perspiring, but a chill was beginning to set in. Noticing some rubbish and a large box at the side of an alley, he gathered debris to create a makeshift bed to retain a hint of warmth for the night.

His shelter, although modest, protected him from the wind and rain in the hours ahead. He didn't hear the cars that drove by, or the homeless men and women who came near to investigate. He was finally at peace in his dreams, alone in one of the many anonymous alleyways of Philadelphia.

"Toss the whole city if you have to! How the hell could he have escaped?"

"I don't know Simon," the man responded. "But I will take full responsibility for this."

"You assured me he was close to death, all but paralyzed!" Simon shouted, pointing a long finger at his colleague.

"He should've been," the man countered. "We held him for almost thirty hours with no nourishment while pumping him with drugs. He can't be far."

Simon frowned with a scowl that forced the man to turn away. A recent addition to his team, Dr. Alvin Habib was supposed to be the best biochemist in town. He was a trusted ally to the cause, with several years dedicated to al Assad, and Simon found it difficult to yell anymore.

"Just start the search," Simon conceded. "Give the men your estimation of a radius. If we understand his mind frame and physical condition, we can narrow the hunt."

Simon left Dr. Habib and walked into the alley, plopping into his Lexus. He pulled into the street and eventually joined a multitude of other vehicles, as he turned onto Snyder Avenue and then Broad Street. He occasionally saw pockets of pedestrians in the late night. Instinctively, and to no avail, he studied each one of them in a futile effort to find Pete.

Within the hour, he came to the realization that Pete might never be recovered. He was lost on Simon's watch, and if not reacquired soon, Simon would probably find himself in front of Almedi Hahn Sahn explaining the situation. In person.

Chapter 28

EARLY MONDAY MORNING found Katie Wood in her Saab, weaving in and out of rush hour traffic with ease, more in an effort to elude boredom than to reach work on time.

She'd been living in Sausalito her entire life and knew the traffic patterns better than most. Descending the hill near the Golden Gate Bridge, she knew that traffic would slow and eventually stop, as the bay would come into view and downtown San Francisco showed in the distance.

As brake lights lit up, she accelerated into the far right lane, usually the fastest moving on the bridge. Horns blared and people yelled, but it was routine for Katie. As she slowed to a stop, she rolled down the driver's side window and held out her left arm. The salty breeze filled the car and she fell complacent, inching forward toward the blue Camaro in front of her.

From a boat a mile away, Falby watched the slow-moving traffic with binoculars in his left hand, a cell phone in his right.

"Everything's a go," he said, as he put down the binoculars and focused on the waves lapping gently on the side of the boat.

"Then continue as planned," the voice responded.

The conversation over, Falby took one last look at the bridge. In silent admiration, he took a moment to regard the two large towers and the sweeping cables between the spans. Then his line of vision dropped to the roadway and the motionless traffic; but more specifically to the eight rust-colored boxes attached every seventy feet to its underbelly.

It had taken considerable time and effort to place them perfectly, a lethal and balanced combination of Semtex, TNT, and C4, but he knew they were not strong enough to topple the bridge. So spanning in all directions from each of the larger manufactured explosives were many smaller charges attached to the more critical, load-bearing components. The spray paint that covered them all -- including the dual priming detonating cords that linked them -- was a perfect match to the bridge itself, and Falby doubted any were detectable even to the most trained eyes.

He walked to the front of the boat and started the engine, turning northeast at fifteen knots and enjoying the breeze on his face. Soon, he was in sight of a large marina, with a small outdoor café and fueling station. An old man was on the dock drinking coffee and reading a newspaper.

As Falby slowed to minimize the wake, he kicked open a black utility box at his feet. He saw the blinking light on the receiver, signaling that the system was armed and ready. He reached down, depressed a switch on the radio transmitter, and heard the muffled sound of multiple explosions a few miles away. Ahead of him, the man didn't flinch. The many levels of terrain and tree cover had proven effective in insulating the noise of the two tons of explosives.

In the plan, this was the one element that was unsure to Falby. The calculations came up ambiguous as to how far the sound would carry. He pulled the boat to the dock and cut the engine. The old man walked over and offered Falby a hand with the boat's ropes.

"How were they bitin' today?" he asked, excitedly.

"Pretty nicely," Falby replied, pointing to the open cooler to his left and the four Rock Cod, all over the season's minimum. "It was a good day for bagging a few fish," he added.

It wasn't a bad day to bag a bridge either, the killer smiled.

Falby walked off the dock to his car and started the engine. Tuning to the local a.m. news station, he drove out of the marina, watching it become smaller and smaller in the rear view mirror. He removed the fisherman's hat, gray wig and beard, and popped out the colored contact lenses. As he listened to the breaking reports of utter destruction, he hummed an old Beatles tune.

Where there was road, there was nothing. Where there were cars full of commuters, there was just dead air. Where a significant span of the longest high-level steel bridge in the world was just moments before, there was black smoke and confusion. The smell of death was overwhelming and it carried a deafening silence.

A traffic helicopter had captured the horrific event on film, a tape that had quickly been duplicated and been played non-stop on the major networks. Almost one thousand feet of the bridge had fallen into the San Francisco Bay!

Katie heard the explosives detonate and felt the bridge buckle beneath her. She watched in the rear view mirror as the road collapsed, cars falling like dominos into the bay far below. She heard the crashing sound of tons of concrete and twisting metal, not knowing what to do, not knowing what she *could* do.

Before she could react, her car shot upwards, forcing the front wheels in the air. She felt herself moving backwards slowly, and as she looked behind her, saw water through the dust. No bridge.

She was on the edge of a long drop and inching closer by the moment. When the car reached a forty-five degree angle, it stabilized. Still, Katie realized her precarious situation and tried to remain calm.

A neighboring car had been launched sideways into the cables on the side of the bridge, subsequently crashing into her and shattering her driver side windows. It now lay upside down, also on the brink of falling off the edge. Katie could see a lifeless man lying inside the car, not ten feet away. Obviously dead, his open eyes would not turn away from her.

Katie was paralyzed with fright. She almost envied the dead man. Although both hung from the same bridge, he had found his peace, while hers depended on the rescue efforts of strangers and more heavily on the San Francisco crosswinds that were gaining spirit.

A fireman inched toward her car. He could see the young victim pinned by the steering column and the twisted metal that had been her Saab.

The scene was chaotic. Helicopters swarmed overhead, rescue boats were positioned below, and a combination of curious on-lookers and emergency personnel gathered on both sides of the bridge watching the horror unfold.

The car teetered, along with its frightened passenger. As the wind strengthened and the weight of the car pressed on the cables, it continued a slow, backward descent. Captain Jacob Hershey, anchored to a truck, sensed the urgency and quickened his pace.

He mentally disconnected himself from the noise and centered on his goal of securing the vehicle with the cable and checking the condition of the woman. He then hoped to use a compact chainsaw to free her and the harness attached to his waist to carry her to safety.

As he approached the car, the deafening screeching of metal on metal forced him to stop. A brisk wind moved the car a few inches and then a few more, but it still held. The fireman inched closer. To his left were cables and metal debris that had fallen from the higher parts of the bridge. To his right was another car, its passenger side ripped open, giving a clear view of the interior. The man inside was covered with blood and Captain Hershey dismissed him for dead.

The front of the woman's car was now nearly vertical, exposing its undercarriage. He attached the hook to the front bumper and reached for his walkie-talkie to confirm that the cable was secure. While waiting for the large truck to reel in the vehicle, he approached the driver's side. Although she was trapped inside, he could see that all of the windows were broken and moved closer.

"Ma'am, it will all be over soon," he said in a reassuring tone.

She looked up and he saw her pale face, one of the first signs of shock. Small cuts covered most of her face and neck and fresh blood covered her clothes.

"What's your name?"

"Katie," she replied. "Katie Wood."

"Where are you hurt Katie?"

Calmed by the man's voice, she regained some composure. "I can't feel my legs and my head is clouded. I don't know… what happened."

"Try not to move," he warned. "Everything will be okay."

She cracked a nervous smile, then closed her eyes and waited for safety.

"I'll wait right here for you until it's over."

As the cable became taught, the car responded by suddenly wrenching upright. It squeaked, but began a slow ascent. As it moved upward, the very cables that prevented the car's fall, pressed against the tires creating more tension. The cable stopped and became taut, but before Captain Hershey could radio the truck to stop, the cable snapped and the car fell back a few feet. Looking at Katie, Captain Hershey's face was horrified. She made little attempt at communication as the car slipped further from the safety of the bridge and began to fall.

The fireman rushed to the car and pressed his hands on the hood in a helpless and desperate attempt to hold it down. But as it moved closer to the edge, he looked into Katie's eyes, which were fixed on his. The car continued to move and then swiftly hurtled over the edge, spending a few moments in a silent somersault before crashing into the bay.

Alone on the bridge, the fireman fell to his knees, pounding his fists into the pavement. He whimpered like a wounded animal, knowing she was certainly dead. His emotions controlled him and he rolled over in a rage. He would never forget her face as she went over. He had a daughter Katie's age. *This is America, dammit! How could this have happened?*

Chapter 29

JILLIAN PACED Steve's large corner office, looking around and admiring the expensive mahogany woodwork, the leather furniture and amazing décor.

"Looks like you do well for yourself, Steve," she said, examining him at his desk.

"I do alright," he said, not looking up from the report he was reading.

She studied a painting by John Powell, looking for the duplication number and how many were in its series, but there wasn't one.

"Is this an original?" she asked skeptically, inching closer to the piece.

He glanced up at her. "Yep. They all are."

"I guess this job pays nicely."

"Jillian. I work thirteen-hour days followed by sleepless nights and chaotic weekends. Believe me, no one wants this job."

"So you're the big macho guy that can handle it all, huh?"

One of the phones rang on Steve's desk.

"Steve McCallister," he announced, eyeing her incredulously.

"Mr. McCallister of the CIA?" a man questioned.

"Yeah, who's this?"

"Doesn't matter. You still searching for your buddy Pete?"

Steve sprang to his feet. "Yes, where is he?"

"Relax. I'm here to help you," the voice said, loosely. "He's in Philadelphia, in an alley at 19th and Bainbridge; at least he was ten minutes ago. Bring him in. He's been through quite a bit."

"Who is this?" Steve demanded, vaguely sensing the familiar voice.

"A friend. A *very good* friend. Quit wasting time."

The man hung up and Steve picked up a neighboring phone, dialing the Philadelphia branch of the CIA who had been briefed the night before.

"Armstrong," a faint woman's voice announced.

"This is Steve McCallister, listen up. I want a team of agents to surround and close in on the alleyways and tributaries surrounding 19th and Bainbridge ASAP! We have reason to believe that Pete Swaggerty may be alive and in that vicinity."

The woman didn't reply as Steve rattled off instructions. He sat upright in his seat and methodically barked orders between breaths. Jillian watched him intensely.

"I want the mobile team to call me within five minutes and to stay on line until the operation is complete. And I want no police interference!"

"Yes sir," the woman said. "We'll be in touch."

Steve turned to Jillian, who had moved next to him in an attempt to hear both sides of the conversation.

"What is it?" she inquired, excitedly. "What's going on?"

"It could be Pete. I think we may know where he is."

Jillian let out a yell and jumped around excitedly. She walked excitedly in small circles, a bundle of energy with no direction. She turned back to Steve, who remained calm. Inside, he was wondering in what shape Pete would be. Was he even alive? He had seen a lot in his tenure and caution always tempered his elation. He never jumped to conclusions. Everything was a potential trap.

"What's the matter Steve? My baby's coming home!"

The phone rang again and Steve picked up the receiver. "McCallister."

"Mac, it's Wilton. We're en route, E.T.A. six minutes."

Steve was quick to respond. "Go in fully armed. I want eyes in the sky to monitor the operation."

"Roger that. Two birds are already deployed."

Getting uneasy, Jillian looked at Steve. "What's going on?" she asked, nervously.

"We'll know shortly," he said, covering the receiver.

Without notice, Director Willard barged into Steve's office, ignoring Jillian and looking grave.

"They bombed the Golden Gate Bridge. Several hundred fatalities. Staff meeting in ten minutes."

Steve looked at him expressionless. "How?" he managed to say, still covering the receiver.

"Who are you on line with?"

"I think we may have Pete."

The director managed a glance at Jillian. "Staff meeting in ten minutes," he repeated stone-faced, and he walked from the room.

The corner of 19th Street and Bainbridge adjoins Philadelphia's famous South Street, and the expanse also doubles as shelter to many of the city's homeless. With the large trash receptacles and overflowing refuse, the alley could yield a nice meal and modest cover, and the constant flow of foot traffic is a panhandler's dream.

The monotonous sound of falling rain hitting cardboard had awakened Pete, who rolled over, wondering where he was. Several of the homeless noticed and walked over to him.

"Hello," an old woman said. "I'm Charlotte. Who are you?"

Several others gathered behind her, curiously watching Pete, and it was clear that she was a leader among the small culture. Pete looked at the people and then at the trash scattered around him.

Before he could answer, a well-dressed man appeared. He pushed the woman away and looked around cautiously. He had a gun in his hand and was talking into an invisible devise on his lapel. Still oblivious to his surroundings, Pete frowned with dry, cracked lips.

The man was direct and brief. "Get up Mr. Swaggerty. We have to go."

Pete was yanked to his feet and carried to a waiting van, its doors already open. As they approached, people appeared from everywhere and surrounded them.

"Get in Pete. We're CIA. It's all over."

Chapter 30

IT WASN'T AN AVERAGE MEETING. In fact, it was like no other meeting Steve could recall. It was attended by fifteen high-clearance individuals, mainly the directors of the NSA, CIA, Department of Homeland Security, and FBI, and their immediate officers. Secretaries and staff were not invited.

The room was small and sound proof, covered by layers of concrete and hidden by long, curving hallways deep inside CIA headquarters. Deemed a "clean room," it was swept daily for bugs and was the favored meeting place for highly classified conversations. Today, al Assad was the only subject. Tensions were high; they had to be stopped.

Steve looked around the room, eyeing each person inquisitively. He had previously met with each of the directors before, so he studied the others that nervously sat beside them. They were all elite members in their fields, all dedicated to national security, and each probably fronted a team of hundreds, Steve suspected. Director Willard was the first to speak.

"Alright people. I know we've had our disagreements over the years, but before we go to our respective agencies, we're Americans first. And as Americans, I ask that we form a single alliance. No titles."

The director paused and his words hung in the air. It was his intention to let the idea of teamwork sink into the thick egoistic skulls that were his audience. It was true that these agencies had little history of cooperation, though in the field they knew of each other's endeavors. He wanted to evaluate and defuse any skepticism early on. This was crucial if the team was to function properly.

"We've been stumbling over each other for far too long and it ends here. I've already talked to the president. He is asking for complete cooperation and teamwork among the agencies. This will be home base. All information is brought here. You now work at CIA headquarters and the packets in front of you contain all the information you'll need."

Director Willard had always been a powerful motivator and Steve found himself gaining more respect for his boss.

"Now I know we have separate intelligence on these bastards, so let's get it out on the table. CIA will go first. Steve?"

The director motioned to Steve, who stood and regarded his boss before acknowledging the group.

"I'm going to start at the beginning so I apologize if it's repetitive. It's no surprise that we've had agents in the field monitoring the threats from underground terrorist factions. Al Assad has obviously been the most elusive, but every organization must have a nucleus and exposing that nucleus is our number one priority."

Steve sipped his bottled water and surveyed the room. The group was at full attention and he continued with ease.

"Al Assad's members come from countries and territories that the United States and its allies do not recognize. Because of unstable governments and an aversion to peace, trade embargoes have been permanent, and these countries are starting to feel the pressure, especially now that we're closer to a world economy. We've tried to bring deserving leaders and democracy to these regions, but insurgency runs freely."

"Al Assad has declared war on the United States. We know this to be true. We believe that there are at least four targets on our soil; the first being the simultaneous assassinations of Senators Keeler and Molanovich. Another attack in Cleveland was thwarted, and the Golden Gate was the third. In front of you are the classified details of the three strikes and information about potential future actions. It could be a dummy list, but all sites are under surveillance as we speak."

Director Willard assumed control and nodded at Steve. "Thank you for that brief synopsis. What's the FBI have?"

In the back of the room were four men from the FBI, and they were in a deeply hushed conversation.

"Excuse me gentlemen. What's on your mind?"

A small, balding man stood and looked at the director. He wore gold-rimmed glasses and was dressed in beige pants and a brown tweed sport coat. A thin red tie dangled over a wrinkled white shirt.

"Hello everybody," he began, nervously. "I'm Special Agent James Gibson, FBI. My people call me Gibby."

He moved to the front of the room with small, hurried steps and turned to face the group. Another FBI agent began handing large binders to the others in attendance.

"I'm here to bring you up to speed on what we've uncovered on the first two acts of terrorism. Everything is in the binders in front of you. Al Assad undoubtedly carried out the two assassinations. Entry was gained by the rear of the homes in both cases, the alarm systems were disengaged, and there was little interference from there. Both spouses were left alive, showing that their only interest was the senators, but neither of 'em got a good look at the killer. They were both knocked out before they knew what happened; Mrs. Keeler in particular didn't wake up for several hours afterward. Copies of several newspaper articles highlighting the senators' outspoken views on terrorism were at the scene and there were no witnesses. We have a positive match of hair fibers taken from Senator Joyce Monahan's home to a terrorist within the al Assad organization. If you turn to page eight of the folder, you will see the face of the man that is responsible."

Steve turned to the page and stared into the cold eyes of Simon. He was taken back for a second, not only from the eeriness of the man's look, but from the fact that he knew who he was. Many years ago, when Simon's name was Jonathon Kelley, Steve had even saved his life.

Steve read the impressive amount of information the FBI had assembled on the decorated soldier turned terrorist. Still, Steve knew several important details that were absent, and for now he thought it best to keep them buried. Steve was instantly in deep thought.

Although not formally assigned to Steve's team in Vietnam, Simon was a Delta and had worked in a handful of tense seek and destroy campaigns that Steve orchestrated. They were night-time, surgical assaults on hot beds of Vietcong resistance. In one battle that lit the nighttime sky for over an hour, Simon was immobilized between two advancing groups of the enemy; further pinned geographically by dense forestation and high cliffs.

Steve went against all odds, ordering most of his team to flank the enemy while he ran into an open area to reach and provide cover for Simon and their eventual escape. When it was over, several hours later, the enemy was destroyed and the scene rivaled the horrific images of My Lai, Hue City, and Duc Duc. Still, Steve's unit hadn't suffered a single casualty, and he took satisfaction in knowing that they had saved American lives.

Thinking of the past, Steve was reminded of the horrific battles he'd fought; the many lives that were cut short so violently. He also thought of a key detail that was very interesting. When the battle was over, he remembered Simon seeking out the highest ranking officer for the Vietcong. Steve had looked on in contempt as he saw Simon take out a long knife and sever the dead man's right pinky finger, discarding it in the nearby brush. The sight was repulsive, but Steve let it go. He'd seen a lot in the field and he knew that some men reacted to the horrors of war differently. This was Simon's.

Gibby continued speaking and the group was at full attention. Steve listened intently; the FBI hadn't immediately shared this information because it wasn't immediately clear *who had* been responsible.

"Let's talk a bit about yesterday's action in San Francisco. The death toll may be as high as seven-hundred, but we don't have an exact number yet. Our experts have concluded that it must have taken about two tons of explosives and detonation was via radio signal from no more than a three mile range. We've been talking to everyone; from the fishermen that sail underneath the bridge to the commuters who drive overhead. A boat was found at a marina a few miles from the bridge. The place is owned by a man named B.J. Harris, and he remembers an older gentlemen getting off a boat about the time of detonation."

Gibby looked down at a notepad and began flipping through pages. He eventually found what he was looking for and resumed his summation.

"When the boat remained docked overnight, the man called the police. A small box was discovered, and it was determined to be the radio transmitter used for the explosives."

The description of the man is in the folder -- An older white man with gray hair and a beard, resembling a fisherman. He spoke with a slight European accent. We believe it all to be a disguise, so it's not much of an I.D. to go on."

Gibby went on for several minutes about the specifics of the explosions, the number of fatalities, and the composition of the bomb. It only confirmed Steve's own information and he became restless, yearning for anything new that could help bring al Assad down.

Then Gibby spoke about the psychological aspects of terrorists, their motivations and their dedication to their causes. He detailed how they were recruited and what made them tick. It was all very interesting and Steve entertained all of Gibby's ideas, but then the FBI man said something that gained Steve's full interest.

"Our profilers believe that there is a weak link inside the organization, not stemming from a lack of skill or determination, but from competition. We believe that there are multiple targets and operators, but each act is carried out separately by a team of only one or two individuals, and we think they may be competing with one another. We also believe that the group is very displeased with one or two of their top soldiers. Someone made a mistake in allowing an informant to send information to the CIA and Mr. Swaggerty somehow managed to escape from certain death. This person or persons is not in favor with the group."

Steve perked up. The idea of terrorists working alone intrigued him. If each incident could be isolated and analyzed, the terrorists could be compared to serial killers, and there were profilers that could assist in the analysis. Also, with animosity within the faction, it could be easier to expose them. Still, the idea of tracking so many individual cells working independently complicated things.

Steve appreciated the information, but he didn't know if things were getting better or worse.

———————

Manford Gillespie stood and introduced himself as the NSA's Officer of Intelligence on Terrorism. He was a tall black man with a thin mustache and light complexion. He wore a conservative navy pinstriped suit that hung well on his athletic frame, and confidently walked to the podium, shuffling some papers before turning to his peers.

"We've got profiles on ten of their soldiers," he began, enthusiastically. "I'd like to show you their faces and give you a brief overview on each one."

He opened a box, removed several bulky binders and passed them around the room.

"Each binder is broken down by tabs, starting with the history of the faction and ending with what we believe is their main agenda. Please turn to the third tab and you will see the faces of the enemy."

The group accepted the binders and turned to the third section with efficiency. Steve also turned to the designated section, sensing that the NSA had spent an unbelievable amount of manpower and time on the project. What he expected as a routine overview had turned into an in-depth report. While he was happy to synergize with other agencies, he was suspicious. How long had they been tracking the same terrorist faction?

"Let me begin by defining the words soldiers, loyalists, and affiliates of al Assad. Soldiers are on the front line. They are the most skilled, elusive, and definitely the most deadly. They are our number one enemy, carefully carrying out their vicious acts and then disappearing. They work alone or in very small groups and are extremely mobile. They make international borders appear transparent."

This was nothing new to the group. It was common knowledge that the soldiers were the biggest problem, but Manford's tone seemed to give the information a new tilt, and seeing the faces of the soldiers added to his credibility.

"The Loyalists are members, but exist solely in the background. Some are reluctant and join out of fear or duress. Their only fault is poverty, and they live a humble existence in countries or territories where the group flourishes, mainly Syria, Pakistan, and Afghanistan. Affiliates are not members, but belong to other neighboring factions. They sometimes have similar interests and prove to be valid resources for al Assad at times."

Manford began scrolling down the faces of the front line soldiers, spending time on each one. He was unsure as to how many there actually were, but ten was by all means a decent number. After an hour and a half, the NSA's presentation was over and a break was called and gladly accepted by the group.

Everyone stood and small conversations erupted. As they stretched their legs and moved to the rear of the room, Steve's voice boomed over the drone.

"Before we break, Mr. Gillespie. Is there anything else you've forgotten to mention?"

Steve was the only one still sitting, which emphasized his question. He appeared to be content to continue the meeting for the rest of the day if need be. His legs were crossed casually, but his eyes stared directly into Manford.

"That's all I have, unless there are questions," Manford replied casually, obviously irritated by Steve's outburst.

"My question is simple," Steve countered with matched arrogance. "Is there anything else?"

The other NSA agents stirred for a moment, frowning and avoiding eye contact with the others. They shuffled their feet and looked around the room with blank faces.

Manford broke the silence with a calm, reassuring tone. "There is something that I was saving for later gentlemen. You all may want to take your seats. Were gonna be a while."

Everyone eventually found their seats, some irritated at Steve's stubbornness; other's looking at him with approving admiration.

"In the late 70's, the president called for the most radical surveillance of our enemies in the history of modern intelligence. He approved the selection of twenty former Special Forces operators to break ties with anyone and everything they ever knew and move abroad to infiltrate and cohabitate with our enemies. They had two simple rules. The United States would not recognize their existence, and these men would do everything in their power to defend the interests of our country. They were told that small, short-term incidents were inconsequential, as long as the big picture remained in focus."

The group was now at full attention. No one had ever heard of such an extreme experiment. Manford sensed the tension and returned the stares defiantly. Gibby broke the silence.

"What kind of 'short-term incidents' are you referring to Mr. Gillespie?"

At times, to gain entry into certain groups, or to earn the respect of their superiors, it is suspected that one must carry out actions which are, shall we say, not in alignment with national security."

"Are you saying that we've financed our own men to be part of terrorist actions?"

"I'm saying that to gain entry into certain groups -- and especially at the levels desired -- these men were allowed to carry out acts that would have happened anyway. Gaining a foothold into these groups was the most important thing. Small casualties can be absorbed."

The group was taken back by Manford's uncaring attitude toward the killing of innocent people, and the bitter disdain quickly showed on their faces.

Steve silently regarded the group. He agreed with the idea of human intelligence. Simple photographs and generic intelligence would do little to stop their efforts. He did not share the opinion of the group, but saw little harm in letting his peers vent their aggressions on Manford. Steve was eager to see how the man would hold up to the negativity.

Gibby continued his assault on the project. "How do you get financing for killing innocent people?"

Manford discounted the insult and answered the question politely. "Each man was properly paid and asked to disappear. I assure you each was highly capable and their allegiance to United States was impeccable. Because of their amazing sacrifice and heroism, they were called 'Patriots.'"

Steve's face reddened and the temperature in the room seemed to increase. And for the first time for as long as he could remember, he was visibly shaken. He casually looked around the room to see if anyone noticed, moving his head smoothly. But all eyes were fixed on the speaker.

"How many of these 'Patriots' are accounted for?" Gibby asked.

"We believe that most are dead, but believe that several are in league with some of the most venomous factions. Due to their skills, there is little doubt that they hold positions of power and are bringing them down from the inside."

Manford spoke with such electricity and charisma that the others had nothing further to say about the "Patriot Operation." It was put in place by a president that was now dead, and covered up by years of political turnover and global change. Everyone was hoping that the plan would bear fruit, and soon.

"One more thing gentlemen," Manford said, looking hopeful. "We strongly believe that there is at least one Patriot inside of the al Assad organization. We think Pete Swaggerty may have met him as a means of escape."

The meeting over, Steve drank a bottled water as the others talked among themselves. He moved from the room and eventually found his office. Sitting at his desk, he took his head in his hands in deep thought. If he just heard what he thought he'd heard, there would be plenty of blood spilled, and it was clear that his life would change very much in the next couple days, if not end all together.

Chapter 31

STEVE MOVED SLIGHTLY in the rocking chair adjacent to Pete's bed, his shoes gently tapping the tiled floor in an even rhythm. Pete had been in CIA custody for two days, closely monitored by doctors in a room next to Jillian's, and this was the first time Steve was able to break away from his hectic schedule to see his friend. He sat with his hands clasped together, staring at Pete sleeping peacefully; a friend whom he had almost killed, albeit indirectly.

Steve had been battling several emotions. It was he who first drew attention to his friends by meeting with them in Switzerland, and he knew he was being blamed for what happened to them in the week that followed. Yet Jillian had seemed grateful for his quick response in finding Pete and for her own protection as well.

Jillian had been living comfortably at CIA headquarters in one of their suites. It was underground, so there were no windows, but the three bedrooms, two bathrooms, and living areas were nicely decorated and furnished with every modern amenity imaginable. Food was brought at regular intervals, and every book and magazine she could ever want was delivered to her doorstep. Since Pete's return, she had been more at ease and managed to relax a bit, giving in to the luxuries that surrounded her.

Steve studied the floor, tired of balancing his duty to country and his loyalty to his friend's well being. He had jeopardized both and people were dying. Looking up at Pete, he held his friend's bandaged hand as he whispered to him.

"I'm sorry for what I've done to you Pete, and please forgive me for what I have yet to do. I hope someday you can understand."

Then he rose and walked from the room. He was already late for another meeting.

———————

The smell of pancakes floated through the halls and into the ventilation system. It was sweet and familiar, and Pete had awoken to it several mornings since his marriage to Jillian. The room he occupied was next to the kitchen, and the freshness quickly overtook the antiseptic smells that had been all too familiar over the last couple of days.

He had spent his entire stay in bed, in and out of deep sleeps. The doctors were tending to his many injuries and burns, and monitoring his condition, aided considerably by the many tubes and wires connected to him. His pinky had been severed and a white bandage now covered his right hand. The cut had been clean and there was little the medical staff could do.

Jillian had been at Pete's bedside every possible minute since he was found. She sang, prayed, and gently caressed the hair on his head, waiting for him to come back to her. *The monsters are gone now baby.*

She hated the thought of anyone hurting her husband and couldn't stand seeing him this way. Still, the doctors assured her that a complete recovery was expected. He was merely suffering from extreme exhaustion.

Pete opened his eyes to see balloons and cards everywhere. He smiled at the festive scene and took in his surroundings before speaking.

"Honey," he called out in a scratchy tone. "Are you there?"

His eyes darted across the room, trying to gain a sense of where he was, but at ease knowing he was probably safe. His voice sounded strange, as if it wasn't his. His throat was extremely dry and it hurt to speak.

Jillian rushed from the kitchen and knelt beside her husband. "Oh Pete, you're awake!" she exclaimed.

She brushed his hair and he managed to speak in a soft whisper. "How are you, sweet heart?"

She could hardly contain her joy as she smiled, exposing perfect white teeth. She stroked his hair and stared lovingly into his eyes, which were fixed on hers. She had cried every day since they separated four days prior, and it took its toll on her face, which was red and worn. But Pete looked her over, smiling.

"You look beautiful," he managed.

She looked down in embarrassment and then returned her eyes to his.

"Where am I?" Pete asked.

"CIA headquarters. There are private doctors here and we're safe from all the craziness. They bombed the Golden Gate Bridge!"

She instantly regretted telling him; the doctors had told her that he needed rest without excitement. He didn't seem to care much about it, though, and kept looking at his wife.

"The Golden Gate Bridge? Yes, for some reason I knew that." Pete propped himself up and used his left arm as a crutch as he concentrated.

"And there will be others. I remember bits of, of something..."

"Try to get some rest Pete, I'll call the doctor. Can I get you anything?"

"Water. Can I have some water? And something to eat, I'm starving."

"Of course," she replied. "I'll bring over some pancakes."

Tears began to well in her soft brown eyes and she sat on the bed, hugging him tightly.

"I love you so much."

But Pete was already deep in thought, troubled by something he couldn't quite understand.

Chapter 32

THE PATRIOT sat silently on the floor, completely naked and in absolute stillness. Performing the ritual as he had every morning for the past thirty years, he found solace from all of the craziness.

He was a soldier for al Assad, a killer for a group bent on hate and destruction. Was he still the man the president had appointed to the most secretive fighting unit the United States had ever assembled?

Years had clouded his recollection of himself. What did the politicians know of his existence? How many other Patriots were left? They were individually selected and withdrawn from society, killed on paper and never missed. He had met other Patriots in the field, but he knew them all to be dead, forgotten in shallow graves in countries that most Americans couldn't even locate. Yamir had been the last he'd seen alive, and *he'd* been killed in London the week before.

And for what? Had he made a difference? Had the countless innocents he'd destroyed help him rise in al Assad to a trusted position? Almedi Hahn Sahn confided in only a cherished few, and until then, even after more than two decades of reluctant but proven service, The Patriot could not act.

Now in his fifties, he yearned for a sense of stability; the comfort of a suburban life. Could he ever go home? Could his lifetime mission *ever* end?

On the table across the room, his cell phone came to life.

———————

Simon sat in his room at the Hotel Intercontinental consumed in darkness, swirling a glass of brandy. From room 2112, he had a splendid view of the Chicago skyline and was enjoying it from the small table. His suit and tie had long been discarded, his shoes lay dormant in the corner. Those items had quickly been replaced with baggy black sweatpants and a Hard Rock Café t-shirt, a souvenir from his recent trip to London. He retained his black silk socks, and the rough carpeting felt good as he moved his feet along the floor. He stretched his legs and tapped his left hand on his leg.

He didn't like the uneasiness in his stomach. September 11, 2001 had shaken the United States and astonished the world, and as he looked at the Sears Tower just a mile away and thought about what was to happen in just a week, his throat became dry.

What concerned him more was that he was in complete control of the planning, with total discretion except for the time and date. He was a loyal member of the cause, but the thought of an estimated eleven thousand dead bothered him, and he didn't like caring.

His cell phone rang and the darkness seemed to magnify its intrusion. He reached for it and after a few brief words, took one last look at the skyline, threw his few belongings into a bag, and made his way to the door. He had to take the red-eye to Alabama.

Another assignment, another death.

Chapter 33

THE MID-DAY SUN shone brightly, in sharp contrast to how Simon was feeling at the moment. It was harsh and unforgiving, even in early November, and the beads of perspiration had long begun to form on his face. Still, he had to be here to write tomorrow's headlines. The event was hours away, but he wanted to study the layout in daylight so he could better maneuver in the dark.

It was Thursday afternoon and Simon was in Pittford, Alabama, in a park that would soon play host to its annual observance of Veterans' Day. The town had begun a formal celebration in 1943 and the annual event had grown in popularity since.

The day now consisted of a traditional parade, speeches by local media celebrities and politicians, a full symphony orchestra, carnival games, rides, and a fireworks display. Excited children ran through the crowd while watchful parents gathered early to talk with neighbors and to secure a favorable spot on the grass.

Simon sat on the wooden bench taking in the day. He heard the droning sound of distant lawn mowers and could smell the sweet aroma of the freshly cut grass. He looked at the gazebo, with its dramatic red, white, and blue streamers, and the stage with its balloons and bows perfectly attached in place. A lone microphone at the center would be where the honored guests would greet the crowd.

On the bill for tonight were Alabama Senator Nelson McNeely and the town's Magistrate, Amy Ponch. They would deliver uplifting messages and patriotic speeches throughout the evening, facilitating the celebration for the estimated crowd of four-thousand.

Once upon a time, Simon would have loved a gathering like this.

A middle-aged couple made their way across the park toward Simon, who carefully studied them from the bench. Both were barefoot and walked casually across the grass without a care in the world.

The woman was stunning, wearing a flowered summer hat and a full length red summer dress with white polka dots. In her right hand she carried a wicker picnic basket, and her left arm was wrapped around a man who matched her carefree demeanor. He wore light cotton trousers and a yellow collared button-down.

It seemed as though Simon were in a movie. Was this the perfect town out of the 1950's? He began to reflect more on his childhood, and the drastic turn of events that gave birth to "Simon," one of the deadliest and most skilled terrorists in the world.

Sitting in the sun took Simon back to his high school years, and the countless football practices he had endured in similar southern heat. His name was Jonathan Kelley then, and the fall of 1969 had changed him forever.

He was a tall, naturally athletic boy with amazing speed, energy, and strength. He made first string varsity quarterback as a freshman; his coach had never seen an arm like Jonathan's.

He was an only child, raised by loving parents in the sleepy town of Clifton, Texas. The population of the county was about eight thousand and high school football was an important focus.

With good looks and an electric personality, Jonathan made friends easily and connected with people of all ages on multiple levels. He had dark, straight hair with long bangs that stopped short of dark brown eyes. Boyish dimples appeared when he smiled, which was often. Jonathan had the world in his hands.

October 11, 1969 was Jonathan's last football game at Richmond High School. It was their Homecoming game against Fairfield, the conference champions three years running, and he'd thrown for almost two hundred yards with five touchdowns, an unheard of statistic for a high school quarterback.

Winning the Homecoming game was the biggest rush in young Jonathan's life. Hearing and seeing hundreds cheer for the team that he led yielded an incredible high. Afterwards, there was a celebration party at the coach's farm, with a barbecue, bonfire, and plenty of beer.

When his parents greeted him, he was still in full uniform.

"Congratulations son," his father said from twenty feet, closing the distance in a brisk walk.

His mother had tears in her eyes as she received him into her arms. A small, delicate woman, Jonathan held her easily, looking like a giant next to her.

"There are scouts here from the Big Ten, Jonathan. Everyone is talking about you. Just remember to stay humble and mind your manners."

"Okay momma," Jonathan replied in his typical sheepish voice. "Is it okay if I go to the post-game party? Everybody'll be there."

His parents looked to each other, smiling silently. Jonathan was such a good boy, well mannered and without the curious tendencies that drove the typical teenager to trouble. He would come home after every game, never drink alcohol, and seemed incapable of lying. It seemed odd that he would want to attend the party, but with the excitement the game generated, it was certainly understandable.

"Of course, son," his father said. "Have a good time and call us if you need anything. We'll see you at home."

With a quick hug, his parents slowly walked off, his mother's head leaning against his father's strong arm. They resembled two teenagers themselves, off for a walk in the cool air.

But Jonathan would never see his parents again. On the way home, a drunk driver in a pick-up collided with them head on, killing both instantly. Being an only child with no other living relatives, Jonathan was suddenly alone, and he abandoned all that he knew.

Soon after the funeral, Jonathan quit school and went to Vietnam. Being thrown into such a violent life weighed heavily on him, and the aggression began to build slowly. Always dedicated to the duty at hand, Jonathan became an expert at the art of war, learning anything and everything he could, and never turning down an opportunity to prove himself.

Most of the assignments he chose were high risk, one-man missions, and it seemed to many that he was committing slow suicide. After several years in Vietnam, he was the perfect soldier. Uncaring and highly motivated, he was a product of the United States military and the murderous environment around him. He became a Delta, one of the more covert Special Forces units, and his past became a very distant memory.

Simon glanced at his watch. The festivities were still hours away. The children's cheerful laughs and yells echoed in the park, as the birds chirped in turn. Both provided a serene backdrop as he closed his eyes and thought through the plan of the day.

Someone was going to die.

Chapter 34

DR. HERBERT TWINN, a top hypnotist and psychiatrist, was accompanied by a medical doctor in Pete's bedroom inside CIA headquarters. Recording equipment was ready, and wires covered Pete's exposed chest to monitor his heart rate. He was being hypnotized of his own volition, so that the government could better understand what he could have subconsciously learned while being detained by al Assad.

"Just lie back and close your eyes, Pete. You're safe here and among friends," the doctor said. "Just breathe deeply and relax."

Pete did as he was told over the next several minutes and soon his breathing leveled.

"Pete," Dr. Twinn began in a soft voice. "I want to talk about the place you were held a few days ago. Can you picture it and look around for me? What can you tell me about it?"

Pete didn't respond immediately. Instead, his head jerked back and forth in many small movements. His face became flush, and a glaze of sweat began to cover his face. Although Pete was physically safe, his mind was under great trauma. He truly believed that he was being held prisoner.

"I see darkness. But I hear and smell the surroundings."

"Tell me more about that, Pete."

"It's cold and dark. It's damp. I'm in a large room, a warehouse I think. I'm alone for now, but they'll be back!"

Pete's voice began to rise as he talked about his captors. Dr. Twinn did not match his tone. Instead, he continued in a soothing voice and led Pete into the next question.

"Have you met these people Pete? Can you picture them and hear their voices?"

"Yes," Pete responded, dryly.

When it was clear that Pete had nothing more to offer, the doctor moved on.

"What are they like Pete?"

"Mean. Controlling. Determined. They want to know what I know. But I have no answers for them. They're mad. They're doing things to me."

"What are they doing Pete?"

"They've injected me with drugs. I feel light-headed and weak."

Pete's face flushed even more as he consistently shook his head back and forth.

"I keep falling asleep and waking up. Time is foreign to me. I have no control."

"Are they speaking to you Pete? Are they discussing anything amongst themselves?"

"The Golden Gate Bridge will be bombed. Thousands will die. They'll never know what hit them."

Pete's voice was flat. It was evident he was repeating what his captor's were saying. Dr. Twinn was taken back at the drastic change in conversation and sat speechless for several seconds.

"That's good Pete, go on," he said, flipping to a new page in his notebook and crossing his legs.

"There are explosives in the van. It'll fall like a house of cards." Pete began to smile and his frame eased in the leather chair. "The van can jump the curb in a moment's time."

Quietly, Dr. Twinn straddled his chair and moved closer to Pete. The bombing of the Golden Gate had already occurred, but this new terrorist action was something new.

"Go on, Pete. When will this happen?"

"It'll be a huge demonstration for the cause. It'll stun America."

Dr. Twinn looked at his colleagues and then his eyes met Steve McCallister, who had entered the room in a hurry. Steve made a quick movement with his hands, instructing the doctor to probe further.

"Pete. I uh, I want you to tell me more. What is the van's color?"

"It's white. It'll be beautiful!"

Chapter 35

THE PARK had taken on a different look since late morning. Flags had been planted into the ground and now outlined the entire perimeter. Bright lights illuminated the well-manicured lawn and emphasized the night sky with its bright flickering stars.

Excited children ran with sparklers blazing, and adults greeted each other with enthusiasm. Simon made his way through the crowd and stopped a few yards from his prey. The target for the evening.

As the orchestra played "Grand Ol' Flag," the crowd tightened, conversations stopped, and everyone focused on center stage and the large flag towering above. Some swayed and sang to the music.

Fervent clapping poured out as Amy Ponch walked on stage and approached the microphone.

"Hello, hello, hello good people of Pittford!" their Magistrate sang out. "How are you on this *beautiful* evening?"

She waited a few moments for the crowd's cheerful response and continued in a softer, guarded tone.

"This evening is a time for celebration, but also a time for remembrance. Often we forget what our war veterans, both living and deceased, have sacrificed for our country. With a natural separation from the conflicts, both past *and* present; and the diluting effects of time, things are forgotten and messages are lost. But we *are* at war everyday with those that want to destroy our way of life. There are no better examples than the actions of September 11, or the recent bombing of the Golden Gate Bridge. Tonight I hope that you enjoy yourselves, but do not forget the people that have perished in battle or in terrorist actions. And with that in mind, I'd like to begin four-hundred and eighty six seconds of silence. One second for every life that was lost this past Monday in the bombing of the Golden Gate Bridge."

The Magistrate stepped away from the microphone and lowered her head. The crowd silenced themselves, many looking down in deep prayer or personal reflection. A light wind seemed to be the only movement in the crowd of thousands, and the flag high above the stage moved majestically.

After several minutes, Amy Ponch's voice sounded once more, this time more upbeat and energetic.

"Thank you everybody. We are so glad you are here; each and every one of you. Welcome to our annual celebration of our war veterans. We will be playing the fight songs for each branch of the military, including the Coast Guard. We would like anyone who has served or is currently serving in any branch of the military to stand when your song is played."

The orchestra began playing "Anchors Aweigh" and several Navy veterans, old and young, some dressed in full uniform, stood proudly, saluting the flag.

The "Air Force Song" was played next, followed by "The Marine's Hymn" and "Semper Paratus." Simon held his stance.

When "The Army Goes Rolling Along" rang out, Simon slowly moved closer to the target. Just in front of him, a very old man rose from his wheelchair, aided considerably by his teenage great grandson.

The old man was the only five-star general still alive and Simon watched him intently. His chest stuck out to expose several medals and honors, accumulated over his illustrious fifty-year career with the Army.

Appointed by President Lyndon B. Johnson, retired General Henry Wesley Spencer had served in three wars and had become an integral part in the nation's wartime efforts. Now old and withered, he needed help with the most common of tasks. The good general was finally going to meet his maker, and Simon was all too eager to facilitate the encounter.

Chapter 36

THE PATRIOT STOOD before Almedi Hahn Sahn, his supposed master, hands clasped behind his back, his head bowed in humbled respect. They were near Tumal, Afghanistan, in a small shelter camouflaged by large sand-colored tapestries. There was much to discuss.

The Patriot had never been to this location and was hardly comfortable. Almedi, however, was quite used to being on the move. Things were heating up, and the United States would be focusing its attention towards him very soon, if it hadn't already. He hadn't spent more than a few nights in the same area for years; he knew he had to be careful when initiating war against the world's most powerful nation.

The Patriot shifted uncomfortably, wondering the purpose of the meeting, but masking his uncertainties behind a permanent frown. The man towered over Almedi, a weathered frame of a man, but both knew who was really more powerful.

Was Almedi upset? He hid his feelings so well it was difficult to tell. The Patriot had given more than twenty years to the cause and had always outperformed expectations, whatever was asked of him. And now, as he received the call to drop everything to meet one on one, the terrorist that was feared amongst friend and foe alike, became humbled beyond description.

"Thank you for coming on such short notice, my long-time friend," Almedi began. "It is such a pleasure to see you again. How are things?"

The Patriot eased slightly, but remained guarded. "We are all in place and awaiting your instructions, but to be honest, many of us are in doubt about our assignments."

Almedi sat down carefully, an old yellow chair easily receiving his small body. He shot a quick glance at The Patriot.

"Secrecy is our most important weapon. Only the individual soldiers know of my strikes."

"Certainly sir," The Patriot nodded.

"But I would like to share a vision with you."

"Yes sir."

"You know of Falby?"

"Only by reputation."

"In three days, Falby is going to unleash Sarin gas in New York City."

Almedi rose and stood, grinning like a young boy. After a few seconds, he peered into his comrade's eyes, seeking approval. The Patriot's soul seemed to shrink, and for a moment he felt as though he would be physically ill. Still, he had to maintain himself; not allow Almedi to know that he wasn't loyal to the cause.

He processed the information instantly. Any real amount of Sarin gas could kill thousands of innocent people! It would be extremely difficult to manufacture and transport the volatile poison, harder still to position, but it seemed as though these obstacles had already been eliminated. Could it be possible?

The Patriot wasn't sure if he could steady himself. Inside he felt drained and was reminded of the extreme hate he felt for the man in front of him. Almedi held his gaze, awaiting a reply from his friend.

"That's quite a strike, sir," The Patriot responded. Despite the hollowness he felt he remained stone-faced, unmoved. "How can I help deliver the package?" he asked indifferently.

As the humidity dissipated and a blanket of crisp air settled on the small town, the band played its final piece, the last ring of smoke merged into the darkness, and General Spencer was pushed by his great grandson on the winding path across the park.

Along the adjacent street, Simon followed them, peripherally tracking his prey like a hungry predator. This was Simon's favorite part of the kill. It was when things could take a sudden turn and add a bit of unexpected excitement. But Simon didn't anticipate anything unusual about this hit. The van was parked in the corner of a dark lot, shadowed by thick trees and dimmed further by a shattered light, which was conveniently broken earlier in the day. The perimeter showed no signs of compromise, and the only people to overcome were the driver, the boy, and of course the main attraction, General Henry Wesley Spencer.

Simon continued his walk, now humming an old show tune and kicking a pebble with alternating feet. A quick glance to his left revealed the unlikely pair slowly making their way to the parked van, now no more than two-hundred feet away.

Simon broke his walk and briskly jogged ahead to flank them from the opposing side. As he approached, he saw the driver leaning against the side of the van, smoking a cigarette. He was a black man in his early thirties, wearing baggy jeans, an un-tucked shirt, and Nike Airs. The driver checked his watch, took a drag of his cigarette, and gazed at the blackened sky, unaware of the danger that was so near.

Why did these people make it so fucking easy, Simon thought to himself as he closed his distance to within fifteen feet, a thick set of bushes the only obstacle.

Chapter 37

THE PEOPLE in the small village stared at The Patriot as he walked through the dirty streets of Tumal, staring blankly ahead but seeing nothing. It was early morning but the streets were busy.

A few peddlers approached him but were pushed aside without a glance or a moment's hesitation. His complexion was dark but he was an unlikely native, and his clothing -- jeans, boots, a green t-shirt, and a light, flowing trench coat -- screamed for attention. In fact, he looked American, and was therefore unwelcome. Still, he walked the streets with confidence, and although he had no real destination, his pace was fast and direct.

Many of the Arab men took notice as he walked through them and a few began to follow. Unsure of a desired outcome, they sought to occupy some time and satisfy a bit of curiosity.

When The Patriot reached the end of the square, he turned right and strolled past several blocks of poor shelters with whole families sitting on the streets silently watching him walk by. He looked into the sad brown eyes of the young, and noticed the deep, sun-baked cracks in the faces of the elderly. Life was hard here. The country was war-torn and unsteady and he wondered how they even survived. Thank God he would be leaving soon, but not without a heavy heart.

After so long, he had finally infiltrated al Assad and gained the trust of their leader. He had waited so long for this day. Would it all be over soon? The Patriot program never spoke of an end. It was a lifetime undertaking. But what happened once the mission was complete? Could he come home to an accepting America? Did anybody even know he was still out here?

He could have killed Almedi Hahn Sahn, the most wanted man in the world. He could have put a couple of rounds in his brain before his bodyguards even knew what happened. He could have killed them with ease as well. But The Patriot knew that although rewarding, it would only be a short-term win. He needed more information. Where were the targets? Who was assigned to them?

Almedi controlled many men, all highly trained and determined, and they were well-positioned in the United States. With separate assignments, no one knew the consummate strategy except for Almedi. With him dead, the missions would still be carried out. New leadership would emerge. It could be even worse with inner power struggles creating multiple factions. Decentralization could be a security nightmare!

The Patriot began to reflect on his life, and wondered how he came to be who he was. Was it worth it? Was he really who he hoped he was? Would he finally be able to complete his lifetime mission? And would anybody care?

In the beginning he was eager to become a Patriot, part of a secret society to bring down the United States' worst enemies from the inside. He had been in the Special Forces in Vietnam, had seen things that most could not even imagine.

They were told from the start that they had been re-born; of no relation to the United States. Invisible. Their lifetime mission, quite simply, was to infiltrate terrorist organizations or governments and prevent their anti-American efforts. Kill at will, as long as it saved American lives or defended American interests in the long-term.

As a Patriot, he soon found himself a mercenary for hire, seizing weaponry from neighboring Middle Eastern governments. Then he was recruited by al Assad.

He had been a hired gun for the better part of his life and often wondered who he truly was. Was he still a good man, or had his integrity been compromised by the many assignments he had completed in the name of hate? Would anyone ever know the many sacrifices he'd made for his country?

The reasoning behind his secret visit with the leader of al Assad troubled him. Did Almedi know that he wasn't loyal to the cause, that he was a mole trying to bring the faction down?

Nothing of consequence was spoken. If anything, Almedi gave him more information about the organization's direction. Almedi Hahn Sahn was a brilliant man; he seemed to know everything and be everywhere at once and The Patriot didn't take the man's actions lightly.

He heard the footsteps behind him as he reached the edge of the street and looked into the bright desert. Turning, he untucked his shirt and stuck two thumbs in his front pockets. He stared at three young Arab men, all holding weapons, and they stared back, matching his gaze. A moment of silence passed and the man in the middle spoke.

"Who are you?" the man snarled, in broken English.

The Patriot had other things on his mind and wasn't in the mood for anything but deep reflection. Smiling, though, he spoke in perfect Arabic. "Go home and live another day."

In a smooth movement, The Patriot flared his trench coat to reveal two guns and a belt of carefully aligned knives, all neatly hugging his waistband.

The men remained defiant, but unconsciously revealed their weaknesses. One took a couple of steps back, while the other two hid within themselves, unable to move. They all stared at the American, who stood his ground grinning.

"Let's go," one of the men said, as he turned and walked into a side alley.

The Patriot turned on his heel and walked into an opposing alley. As he turned the corner, he flattened against the wall and took out two 9 millimeters, quickly checking the clips and yanking back the slides.

Within seconds, the men ran into the alley and fired wildly into emptiness. The Patriot, now perpendicular, fired two shots into two of the men's heads, and a third into the other's shooting arm.

The surviving man dropped his weapon and fell to the ground, shaking. He looked at the bodies of his friends, their bright red blood being absorbed into the sandy street, and then his eyes turned to the American, who stared down at him.

"Please, please I... didn't. Please!" The man pleaded.

The Patriot scooped up the three weapons and hung them on his shoulder. He looked at the frightened man who had crumbled into a pleading boy. He knelt beside him, checking the superficial wound on his arm.

"Your hate killed your friends," he began, slowly. "You should be dead right now."

The man blinked several times and moved to better see the American.

"Thank you," he whispered.

The Patriot quickly walked out of sight. He threw the weapons in a nearby trash heap, and continued on. He had to get in touch with the one man he could tell about the pending Sarin attack in New York. Many lives depended on it.

Chapter 38

AS THE GENERAL came into sight, his driver flicked his cigarette into the street and hit a button in the van. A mechanical platform descended, and Buddy moved behind his employer to move him in to place.

"Good evening, sir," he sang, over-enthusiastically. "Did you enjoy the festivities?"

"It was alright," the man barked. "Let's get on with it. I've gotta take a whiz!"

"Yes sir."

Buddy secured the general and hit the button once more, ascending the old man to his seat. In no time he was secured and his great grandson was strapped in beside him. Buddy shut both doors and was about to get into the driver's seat, when something caught him off guard.

Simon made no attempt to disguise himself. He walked to the van and opened the back door, peering in. The size was about right. He could carry out his mission within the given area, but three prisoners in a van would be too much, especially when they were alive. He hadn't planned on it, but he decided on killing the driver to reduce the risk of exposure. While Simon continued his on-sight appraisal of the hit, Buddy glared at him, unsure of what to say.

"Can I help you?" Buddy asked, sarcastically.

Simon was motioning inside the van and the driver eased, looking to where Simon was pointing. When Buddy neared, Simon pushed him against the van, took out a twenty-two with a silencer, and fired two bullets into the man's skull. Buddy landed with a terrible thud against the concrete and Simon quickly moved him underneath the van and out of view. Next, the killer moved into the front passenger seat, shut the door, and turned to the two curious passengers that were now his prisoners.

"What the hell is going on?" the general demanded. "What's this about?"

Simon smiled at the old man, and then turned his attention to the young boy. "How are you, son?"

"Shut up! What's going on?" the general fumed. "Where's Buddy?"

Simon produced a rag and duct tape and quickly moved to the general. He shoved the rag into the man's mouth and made several quick revolutions around his head with the tape. The general resisted at first, but then relaxed as his eyes focused on Simon.

"I'm sorry, sir, but Buddy won't be joining us. Forever." Simon chuckled.

Simon took out a six-inch bowie knife and quickly cut off the general's right pinky finger, letting it fall to his lap. The old man's face turned bright red, and his pale blue eyes doubled in size and started to water. He made several high-pitched whimpers, and then defeatedly slumped into his chair and looked toward his bloody hand. The young boy was in a trance.

"My name is Simon," he began slowly, cleaning the knife with a handkerchief and taking time to admire the blade. "I'm here to educate your great grandson on the ways of the world. The way it should be. The way a few friends of mine would like to make it. You led the United States' campaign in several wars, people hailed you as a hero in many ways. But you are nothing more than a killer, and you did nothing but advance turmoil in the Middle East."

The retired general stared blankly.

"From the beginning your government has promised democracy but practiced genocide. How did you get Florida? From the Spanish. How did you get the American West? By exploiting the French. How did you get the South-West territory? By murdering Mexicans. Then you took Alaska and Hawaii. You supported the Afghans against the Russians and then pulled out. You helped the Kurds in northern Iraq, but again pulled out. You have a hand in everything around the globe, but when other countries practice what you've done, they are embargoed or attacked."

The general shook his head, not understanding. He made an effort to speak but created only muffled noises behind the tape.

"What's that, sir?" Simon asked. "Oh, the tape, of course. Let me help you with that."

Simon forcefully yanked on the tape and removed the rag from the man's mouth, allowing him limited communication.

"What's going on?" the general managed.

"*You* are sir," Simon said, surprisingly upbeat and jolly.

"You have no doubt heard of the two assassinations of Senators Keeler and Monohan? The bombing of the Golden Gate Bridge? You're about to become strike three in what I like to call 'kill the bastards who think they can fuck with anyone they want.' My employer, of course has a more professional name. Al Assad. The Lion."

The general stared in disbelief as a few moments of heavy silence passed. Finally, he put his arm around his great grandson, looked down, and spoke in a very compassionate voice as the reality of the situation gripped him.

"I am a simple man, not the ugliness you are trying to portray."

"No! You *are* the ugliness!" Simon hissed. "Up to tonight you *were* a living hero, a *living* testimonial to this country's war-time success."

Simon again removed his twenty-two, the silencer still attached, and rested it on the seat. Before the man could react, two shots were fired into his head, and the dead man slumped away from his great grandson, resting against the car door as if asleep. Simon turned his intentions to the boy.

"Now, son," he began, evenly. "You have the opportunity to be a hero. I'm going to tell you something very important, so listen carefully. There is a white van loaded with explosives, somewhere in Washington D.C, and it's on its way to a very important place."

Simon stopped to check his listener. He had to remind himself that others were not as accepting of cold-blooded murder. Looking into the young glassy eyes, Simon was reminded of himself as a boy. The boy stared back and blinked, bringing Simon into the present.

"Are you with me, kid?"

"Yeah, I guess," he replied in a small voice.

"Good. It'll be a white van, packed with explosives. The game is getting boring and I'm giving your government a head start to even the playing field a bit."

"So when's this gonna happen?" the boy asked, surprising Simon.

"By the time you get outta here and to the authorities, they'll have about thirty minutes."

"Who are you?" the boy blurted, again catching Simon off guard.

"Great question," Simon nodded accordingly, checking his watch. "But unfortunately not one I can explore at this time."

Simon poured out of the van and stopped to survey the area. A symphony of crickets sounded from the enveloping darkness, and there was no one in sight. He stepped between a row of bushes and eased out of view.

His cell phone rang and he rushed forward a few steps before reaching for it.

"Yeah," he said into the small receiver.

"This is Falby."

"Yeah, so?"

"Go to Montgomery Regional Airport and take the 10:40 flight to Reagan National. I'll pick you up and brief you on your next assignment."

"You're not my boss pencil dick," Simon laughed into the receiver, unknowingly increasing his pace.

"Do as I say Simon. There is something I need to discuss with you and I'll be in a better mood tonight."

The line went dead and Simon flipped the phone shut. Torn between his allegiance to the cause and his bitter disdain for being told what to do, he reluctantly made his way to a waiting car.

You & I are going to have to have a little chat, Simon thought to himself as he merged onto 331 North.

A little chat, indeed.

Chapter 39

ONLY A LIMITED FEW knew Steve's official cell phone number, so when an unexpected voice came on the line, he knew he was dealing with professionals.

The level of technology the CIA utilized in its telecommunications was not available in the private sector. With changing phone numbers on multiple frequencies, Steve rarely even knew his own number. He just knew it was secure. Until now.

It was just after eleven p.m., and Steve was sitting in the study just off his master bedroom. Still in his work clothes, his tie was loosened around his neck, his shirt un-tucked.

He held his face in his hands as he thought through the information on al Assad. Shutting his eyes, he rubbed them forcefully, seeing different shades of purples, blues, yellows, and reds, each color appearing and disappearing at random, not unlike the grand finale at a fireworks show. The pressure provided short-term alleviation from the stress, but as he rolled his head from shoulder to shoulder stretching his neck, he again felt deflated and eventually slumped further into the chair.

Through a combination of Yamir's letter, Pete's hypnosis, and the government's own surveillance, the CIA knew that al Assad had acted on three targets. But what were the others, and more importantly *when* were they? Pete had recalled hearing something about a white van blowing up an undetermined target. Then he'd escaped, aided significantly by an unknown ally within al Assad. Could it have been a Patriot that had called Steve and helped Pete?

Steve hoped that Pete's abduction was an act of desperation. It showed that al Assad was uncertain of what the CIA knew. Or were they omniscient? They seemed to be so well connected.

Steve had thought of nothing else for the better part of the day as he planned his next move. Innocent Americans were being killed, and everyone was looking to Steve for answers. The meeting with the NSA, Department of Homeland Security, and FBI had been very telling, uncovering something that Steve could never have imagined. Had anyone sensed what he had learned, his ensuing uneasiness?

When his cell phone rang, Steve made no attempt to answer it. He casually glanced in its direction on the dresser, its green light signaling an incoming call. *Probably the director or the president,* Steve thought to himself. *Not the kind of people to keep waiting.* Steve walked to the dresser and reached for the small unit, expecting to recognize the voice. But he didn't.

"Steve McCallister," he said into the receiver.

"Hi Steve," a voice responded, calmly.

Taken back, Steve stared straight ahead and spoke again, more formally. Even wrong numbers happened sometimes.

"Who is this, please?"

"Good, it is you. Sometimes even *we* mess up."

"Who are 'we'?"

"You should know who this is, Steve, but don't ask while your still inside. Take a walk in the woods."

"I was wondering when you were going to call again. It's been so long."

"Yeah, it *has* been. Go outside."

"No one has bugged my home, I can assure you."

"Steve. Leave your home and we'll resume our chat."

Steve quickly slipped on the closest pair of shoes he could find, old Keds that clashed with his suit pants. He hurried down the back stairs and into the dark kitchen. He saw the large sliding glass door, which looked opaque due to the heavy blackness on the other side.

In his left hand he held the phone, in his right his trusted Glock. He never assumed anything, though he was almost sure he knew who the stranger was.

He slid the door open and ran across the backyard in the cool wet grass. The uniform hissing of locusts and crickets welcomed him as he entered the woods and crouched behind a large tree. Looking around, he was satisfied that he was alone in the starry autumn night.

"Okay, I'm here."

"Be at New York's Rockefeller Center, tomorrow at noon. I'll call you a few minutes prior, and we'll arrange a meeting. I'll be in the area."

The voice seemed very familiar to Steve, and he smiled at the thought. His suspicions were confirmed. He immediately eased; finally assured that this was not a hit. He knew the man on the other line and was thankful he was still alive. Maybe together, they could finally bring al Assad down.

"I thought the Patriot system was dead."

"Tomorrow at noon, Steve."

"My number will have changed by then. Is there another way?"

"I'll have the number. See you tomorrow."

The line went dead and he was left alone in the darkness. Without time to think about the brief exchange, the phone came alive once more, and he immediately flipped it open.

"Steve, this is Director Willard. We have another terrorist action, this time in Alabama. It's retired General Spencer. Remember that guy?"

"Yeah, he's a great man."

"Well he's dead. We're certain it's that terrorist suspect Simon. He talked a good bit to the great grandson, who witnessed the execution. The kid's in protective police custody. We have a team on the way for an early morning interview. I'm faxing you the summary from the incident. Nothing much, except for the last paragraph. He mentions a white van being involved in a terrorist action somewhere in D.C., probably what Pete was talking about."

Steve walked into the kitchen, the rubber soles of his shoes squeaking on the dry hardwood floor. He slipped them off, steadying himself against the adjacent wall, and eventually made his way upstairs. He was greeted by the local news, the anchorperson's voice becoming louder as he drew near.

"You still there, Steve?"

"Yeah. But you better turn on the television, it's going down right now. I'm gonna have to call you back."

"Hold up Steve. Have you come up with anything?"

Something in the way the director spoke ushered in a wave of uneasiness in Steve. Pausing, he tried to act normal.

"I'm taking off for a couple of days, Donald."

"Where? What's up?" the director blurted.

"New York City. It's just a short getaway."

"Come on, Steve. What's up?"

Steve made no attempt to answer and the director's last words were emphasized by the long silence.

"Okay," the director conceded. "But check in. This better not hamper the White House State Dinner on Saturday night or both our asses will be in a sling! I'll get with the others and talk with you tomorrow."

Steve folded the phone and sat at the edge of his bed, listening to the news. Although briefed about it several months earlier, Steve had almost forgotten about the upcoming White House State Dinner. Security was being handled by the Secret Service and FBI, but the CIA had been notified because of the international implications.

Other than the State of the Union address, it would be the only time the president and his entire cabinet save one would be assembled in the same place. They would be joined by leaders from at least forty counties; with many more ambassadors and diplomats. Could the two be linked? What could the van have to do with a function that was still a couple days away?

On the television, there was a live picture of a white van at the base of the Washington Monument with two unmoving people lying nearby. The only other visible image was the quick flashing of the van's yellow hazard lights reflecting off the base of the monument.

As he listened intently, Steve began packing a few bags. Within minutes he was on his way into D.C.

The director quietly sat in the large leather chair in his plush office on the seventh floor of CIA headquarters. He methodically unfolded his cell phone and held it to his pursed lips in deep thought.

Alone in the silence, he dialed a number as blood rushed to his head. When the voice answered, the first signs of perspiration appeared, and he noticed that he was visibly shaking.

"He's going to New York tonight. Take him down there."

———————

The conversation over, Falby closed his phone and directed his attention back to his half-eaten apple. He'd arrived at Reagan National moments prior and stretched his legs as he walked in search of Simon.

He weaved in between people in the terminal like a seasoned running back. The single suits rushed for the exits after a long workday, or to perhaps find an empty seat at a smoke-filled bar. The tourists, often in groups of four or more, walked much slower, mostly in search of bathrooms and restaurants. Tired children lagged behind exhausted parents, slowing them even further.

Staring straight ahead, Falby's line of vision seemed to part the crowd as he narrowed in on a large, hostile-looking man walking toward him. Likewise, Simon's eyes found Falby's, his casual and uncaring glance showing obvious bitterness.

Simon quickened his walk and moved directly toward Falby, his demeanor changing dramatically as he remembered their talk earlier in the evening. Nobody spoke to him like that. He was after all, the self-proclaimed baddest motherfucker of them all.

Chapter 40

THE WASHINGTON MONUMENT, from the Key Bridge looked normal, if not peaceful. The highest structural point above D.C., it was brightly illuminated, stretching into the black sky as if challenging gravity itself. The only evidence of life came from the lazy flickering of the two red lights near its top.

Glancing East, Steve could only see the top two-thirds of the structure, knowing full well, though, that at the base there was a flurry of activity. Unfortunately, this could be the next terrorist strike by al Assad, and so far their acts had been so well calculated, so precise. How many more people had to die?

Turning right into Georgetown, he was greeted by the typical evening crowd. Groups of twenty-something Generation X'rs hurriedly walked the streets to get to their next favorite hot spot. Others carried bags from the now-closed boutiques that hugged the narrow roadway of M Street and its many tributaries.

Without hesitation, Steve flicked a switch, bringing to life a flashing blue light on the dash. He turned his Mercury Sable into oncoming traffic and accelerated through Pennsylvania Avenue and into the heart of the District. He was slowed by three police barricades, but soon found himself near Seventeenth Street, looking at the Washington Monument in its entirety.

At its base was the solitary van. A couple hundred yards back was a loose perimeter of police vehicles and wooden barricades. Busy men and women talked among themselves and everyone was watching with fearful anticipation. Two helicopters were shining circular white lights across the scene and flashing blue lights from a mounting police force lit the immediate area.

Just behind the perimeter, a makeshift tent had been erected and officials entered and exited at random. At street level, there were several pockets of the media gathered, many with large vans that held high antennas that seemed too disproportionately high to be supported. All provided a colorful backdrop to the main attraction, a single and seemingly innocent van parked at the base of the tall structure. A personal delivery by al Assad.

At Seventeenth Street, Steve's car slowly jumped the curb, each tire patiently taking its turn with the sharp incline. He started up the grassy hill to where the balance of the authorities were gathered, parking next to several other vehicles.

A man in a beige trench coat approached his car, stopping short of the door and waiting for its occupant to exit. Steve recognized him from the meeting as Special Agent James Gibson of the FBI. The two shook hands, Gibby's grip much tighter and purposeful.

"Hey Steve. Glad you're here! We've got quite a mess on our hands," Gibby said, quickly turning and walking toward the others.

"I assume you're in charge?" Steve asked, considering the scene and walking with Gibby up the hill. "What do you have so far?"

"We've secured a perimeter of about two-hundred yards. We have eye witnesses that saw the van speed up the hill and crash into and through the concrete barricades at the base."

Gibby was motioning to the curbside at Seventeenth Street, directing Steve's line of vision with a short, pointed finger.

"The consensus is that there are two men in the van. A spray of gunfire erupted shortly after reaching the monument, and it's been relatively silent since. That was about an hour ago. We have visual confirmation there are two people down, unmoving. Probably civilians. There's been only one communication from them, saying they have a couple tons of explosives and are ready to detonate unless we reach their demands, which have been none so far."

"What's the max the van can carry?" Steve asked.

"The van's fully capable of the load and our engineer's have all agreed it's enough to topple the monument."

"Any visuals of the men in the van?"

"This happened well after sunset and there are curtains in all the windows, but we've detected some movement inside. Our shooters have seen shifting in the tires."

"I wish we'd get a list of demands," Steve began, grim-faced. "I get really nervous when there is no immediate motive, no reasoning. Maybe they just want to go out with a bang and are waiting for the right time and the right amount of media attention."

Gibby, a much smaller man, looked to Steve and nodded in respectful agreement. His hands were clasped in front of him, and if Steve hadn't read up on him, he would never have guessed the man was as accomplished as he was. One of the FBI's finest.

"Look Gibby. This is your deal, and I don't want to come here and piss in your Cheerios," Steve said cautiously, the palms of his hands in front of his chest. "But just to be safe, with the amount of explosives we're talking, and the very real possibility of a suicide strike, I'd move this perimeter back. I'd also be very proactive in establishing a dialogue. If nothing other than a distraction, at least it'll give 'em less time to think."

"I agree," Gibby said, solemnly. "I was really impressed with you at the meeting. You were the only one without anything to prove."

"I've got no problem working inter-agency to bring these guys down," Steve said.

"Likewise," Gibby said. "I appreciate whatever the two of us can do together. No bull shit."

"I just may take you up on that offer, and sooner than you think," Steve said with a sudden smile, and then his look turned serious.

"You know this is al Assad, right?" Steve said, waving at the activity all around them.

"I figured that but I wasn't told," Gibby admitted. "How do you know?"

Steve informed Gibby about the recent developments in Alabama and the warning of the coming strike.

"It happened so fast," Steve said. "Only a few minutes of realistic reaction time to prevent it."

"So what do you think this means?" Gibby asked, obviously deferring to Steve's experience.

"It's not in their normal pattern to just blow something up. Although this monument is a national treasure, this strike wouldn't be too productive, other than to show us their capabilities, which we know already."

Suddenly, Steve turned away from the monument and faced Gibby.

"I'm going to New York for a couple of days. I'll call for updates."

Gibby handed a business card to Steve, who reciprocated.

"Thanks for coming, Steve. I'll keep you appraised."

Steve turned and immediately noticed the downward, awe-inspiring view of the White House, not two miles away. He stopped and looked at Gibby, who hadn't moved, a look of concern on both faces.

"I know," Gibby said. "The Secret Service has been all over me on this. The White House State Dinner is on Saturday and this shit happens. Do you think it's a coincidence?"

"Doubtful. Too far away. They'd know that this would be over in a couple of days. Maybe they just want to throw a wrench into things and keep us guessing."

Steve eased into his car, gripping the roof for added support. He sat for a moment before turning the ignition, reflecting on the recent exchange and staring ahead to the monument. As he looked to Gibby, he saw him radioing his team to expand the perimeter.

Steve picked up his cell phone and called Andrews Air Force Base to secure a ride to New York. Hopefully he'd get there and be settled in by two a.m.

———————

Simon rushed toward Falby, stopping just short of the smaller man, who didn't budge or flinch. He threw his duffel bag onto the ground, allowing it to slide a bit on the worn floor.

"So what's this all about?" Simon hissed. "Drop everything and meet you here?"

Falby chuckled and shook his head at Simon, taking his time to reply.

"Good job in Alabama, Simon. Of course you blabbed a little too much to the kid. In monitoring the police scanners, you all but told them the license plate number of the van!"

"I don't need this from you, you piece of shit," Simon swore in a hushed whisper, his fists clenched at his sides. "I've got no problem taking you out right here."

Simon's face was bright red, sweat gathering on his forehead. Conversely, Falby held his ground and looked around to monitor the outburst. When satisfied, he looked Simon squarely in the eye.

"You're not going to do anything," he began in a subtle German accent. "Any defiance will be dealt with immediately. Almedi has granted it. You are, as they say, 'disposable.'"

"What are you talking about?" Simon managed, speaking for the first time from a point of defense.

Falby began a slow, deliberate walk. "Let's reflect on your recent resume, shall we? You failed to kill Yamir, who was able to detach from us and inform the CIA of who knows what. Then you brag to the general's great grandson, barely allowing time for the van to get to its designated area. And now you're giving me flack when I try to inform you of your next hit."

"I take orders only from Almedi Hahn Sahn," Simon stated, regaining his confidence.

"Not this time. He's rather upset and doesn't want to be bothered with you."

"If you're lying, you know I'll kill you."

"I assure you that I am not lying and you *better* watch your mouth."

A few seconds of silence existed between the two. Simon hung his head, his chin hitting his chest. Falby, followed Simon's gaze with cool, gray eyes.

"Anyway," Falby began, "Steve McCallister must be killed. He's getting too dangerous. He's on his way to New York, late flight from Andrews into LaGuardia."

Falby handed Simon an envelope. "Here's your contact in New York who will give you more specifics. Also included is your flight information and ticket. You leave in forty minutes."

Simon accepted the envelope and placed it in his breast pocket.

"One more thing," Falby said. "I understand that you worked with McCallister in Vietnam. Is that going to be a problem?"

Simon nodded a definitive 'No,' and without a word Falby turned and walked away.

"Where are you going?" Simon all but shouted.

"I've got a later flight to New York. Separate business."

And he was gone.

Chapter 41

STEVE DROVE through the gates of Andrews Air Force Base with a quick salute to the guards, driving another mile and taking a left into a gated area where he parked his sedan. He was greeted by an M.P. who produced a narrow smile and opened the car door.

"Hello, Mr. McCallister. You're clear for New York City whenever you're ready. The Lear is right over there."

The man motioned to where a black Lear Jet was waiting just outside of a hangar. The bright lights shining from the building's roof made it appear to be made of plastic, but the humming of the running engines, the pulsing lights on the rudder, and the large American flag on its side made it appear very real.

"Just need you to sign right here, sir," the officer said, moving a clipboard and pen in front of Steve.

Minutes later, Steve was airborne, one of four people on board. As the plane steadied at its cruising altitude, Steve rested his forehead against the airplane window, the coolness very real and welcome.

Steve had flown with the crew before, the routine not at all foreign. This time, though, he had been cool to them, going through protocol with an air of aloofness. Based on past trips, the crew should be offering him a magazine or a cold drink. But now they remained at bay, two in the tiny cockpit and the other in the rear busy with paperwork. They had obviously sensed Steve's guarded demeanor and he was thankful for the privacy.

Steve looked through the darkness to what he knew was the Chesapeake Bay. He saw a galaxy of lights that ended in absolute blackness, where the bay had carved out its rigid boundary with centuries of effort.

Al Assad had consumed him. Their motives, their actions, their possible weaknesses. Could they have a frailty he could expose and exploit? He was supposedly on his way to meet a Patriot. Or could it be a trick? He knew the man, or *did* three decades ago. But time changes things.

The only good news of late was that Pete would make a full recovery and Jillian was safe after being on the run. From what Pete had told the CIA, al Assad had nearly completed their interrogation of him, and had indeed discovered the truth that Pete was ignorant of their plans. Still, it was obvious that they were not pleased with his unexplained escape. Although Pete was surely meant to have been killed, it was considered doubtful that they would risk another attempt on his life.

It was decided that Pete and Jillian were safe to go home and resume their lives, limited to necessary trips out, and three shifts of men watching the house around the clock.

Steve leaned back from the window, still maintaining a distance of mere inches. The glass had fogged into an almost perfect gray circle, about five inches in diameter. Steve traced a smiley face and two eyeholes, allowing himself a short moment of contentment. How long had it been since he had smiled? When would he smile again?

He looked around the cabin, noticing the rows of high, empty black leather seats, the plush red carpeted floor, and the curves of the bright white ceiling. He finally received the plane's comfort, leaning far in his seat and allowing the natural drone of the engines to relax him.

Still, he couldn't stop thinking about al Assad. The media was frantic over the surgeon-like precision of the Keeler-Monahan assassinations, eating it up like hungry predators and writing descriptive stories, some real, some works of fiction for a country that couldn't get enough. They speculated about the common denominator, the motivations that would fuel such a drastic, unheard of measure. Duplicate murders exacted at the same time hundreds of miles apart!

Then the two senators were forgotten, only to be replaced by the four hundred and eighty six Americans that had perished in the bombing of the Golden Gate Bridge. *People Magazine*, who only a week earlier had run a story about the two senators, had dedicated an entire issue to the attack. After studying the methodology, timing, and especially the intricate positioning of the explosives and wiring used, it was actually considered good news that the dead numbered hundreds and not thousands, a credit to single-occupancy rush-hour vehicles and virtually vacant north bound lanes.

The media produced story after story, dedicated at first to the lives of the dead, but then settling on a more newsworthy target. Were these people dead because of the ignorance of the United States government? Shouldn't they have been able to prevent this monstrosity? The American people wanted blood and their leader had assured it.

In forum after forum, the president of the United States had promised an exhaustive investigation and retaliation for the people who had perished. "America will not rest," he had said, "until those responsible are brought to justice."

But time had passed and the sentiment of the American people had changed from anger and aggression to self-preservation. Al Assad had brought a one-sided war into the homes of every American, into their very lives. It was universally accepted that the threat was valid and the United States government was powerless to prevent it.

Still, the CIA *had* learned about the planned Cleveland action and *had* been able to prevent the strike. The men had worked at their two objectives well, the shooters silently stopping the would-be killer and the quick evacuation spoiling any amount of public awareness.

But al Assad was invisibly at work, their effectiveness evident.

Steve couldn't shake the empty feeling in his stomach. Something was not right and it was gnawing at his very being. At the recent inter-agency intelligence briefing, he had uncovered something that had to be dealt with immediately, but there was something else.

Suddenly his phone rang and he turned in his seat, allowing easy access to the small device on his waistband.

"This is McCallister," he announced into the receiver.

"Steve," a low voice countered. "This is the president."

Steve's expression revealed nothing new, but he closed his eyes and inched upward in his seat.

"Yes, sir. How have you been?" Steve asked, as if speaking from a script.

"You know how I've been, Steve. I've got a damn circus outside my window! Are they gonna blow the Washington Monument?"

"I don't think so sir, but I can't be sure."

"Where are we on this al Assad thing?"

"Working day and night, sir. Doing the best we can."

"People are dying, Steve. The country is scared! Your best is obviously not good enough!"

Steve could picture the man on the other line, feet kicked up on his desk in the Oval office, giving the obligatory speech to try to bully him into action. Steve didn't ask for this, nor did he appreciate it. He was one of the few higher-ups at the CIA with direct decision-making ability, even to the point of creating policy among the field force. Nothing the president could say could motivate him to work harder or with more vigor. On this point, Steve did not work for money. He was as loyal to the United States as they came, and he took al Assad and their actions very personally.

Sensing Steve's mind frame, the president loosened his verbal grip. "Are we any closer to finding out where these bastards are housed, their main concentration? If so, we'll bomb the shit out of 'em."

"NSA is mapping their movements, which are mainly between six areas in Pakistan, Syria, and Afghanistan. Any strike now would be premature. The problem lies within the U.S., where they have multiple cells working at different targets independent of each other. Killing the brain will not stop the tumors. They will live on and possibly flourish."

"I can't see that. You ..."

Steve cut the man off curtly. "Keep your finger on the button. I may be coming into information in the next several hours that could considerably define the target areas. And when you act, do so quickly and on full faith."

"How long?"

"We may be ready to strike within twenty-four hours."

Over the next ten minutes, Steve was open and honest. He and the president had sparred in the past, and it was clear that they didn't get along. But to his regret, the president respected Steve more than any other in the country's Defense Department.

Steve put his feelings aside for the good of the country, politely refuting all inquiries with courtesy and professionalism. When the conversation ended, not much was gained by either, but the president had at least attempted a dialogue and Steve appreciated the effort.

Steve opened his phone once more. He thought of calling Dana, but decided against it. She was probably at the scene of the latest terrorist scare, and even if he were to reach her, she would possibly want information from him, and that was not the kind of conversation he was looking for.

They had connected the day before in a way that was unfamiliar to Steve, but very exciting. He said he would call, but the day's events had thwarted any attempt. He punched in a number and waited only seconds for a voice on the other end.

"This is Special Agent Gibson," the voice announced.

"Gibby, this is McCallister. I need you on an early morning flight to New York. Meet me in the Waldorf Astoria lobby at 8 a.m. tomorrow. I have an idea."

"I can do that. Do you want an update here?"

"Let me guess. More media attention, no demands, and an anxious FBI negotiating team?"

"I'll see you tomorrow morning," Gibby said, and the conversation ended.

Chapter 42

STEVE WOKE UP NERVOUS, the unsettling in his stomach instant. Although he always stayed at the Waldorf Astoria when visiting New York City, his surroundings seemed foreign. Glancing around the sun-lit room and still wrapped in covers, he studied his quarters for the first time, taking time to see things he'd missed in the near darkness upon arrival.

The room was small but well decorated, its size doing little injustice to its natural ambiance. The paintings hung at eye-level on the two walls flanking the double windows that looked out across Park Avenue. A dark wooden bureau housed a television, and the desk beside it held a small plant with large leaves that extended to the windows.

It was just after 6 a.m., and being accustomed to early rises, a wake-up call or alarm clock was unnecessary. Steve firmly planted both feet on the rough carpeting, still sitting in bed and bandaged in blankets. He rubbed his eyes and slowly massaged his neck to release the stiffness he felt. His eyes eventually rested on the television's remote control and the screen soon came to life.

He scanned the morning programming; most of the channels carrying the familiar reverberations of pleasant talk show hosts, up-beat info-mercials, and exaggerated cartoon sounds. He eventually settled on CNN, which carried a live image of the Washington Monument.

The camera panned from top to bottom, and although appearing very close on screen, Steve could tell that the picture originated from about a mile away, due to the slight jiggling and haziness hugging its edges.

The scene hadn't changed much from the evening before. The number of people at the makeshift command center had dramatically decreased and the human perimeter was replaced by wooden barricades and more permanent, armed personnel. But the van remained unmoved at the base. Like the terrorists, the authorities had dug in; the overall scene much more concentrated and sedate.

On the screen, next to the CNN logo and a time of 6:08 a.m., was a banner that read "Terrorist Standoff." An energetic reporter was explaining the current situation, which Steve knew all too well.

It was confirmed that the two dead bodies were tourists, enjoying the monument grounds after the usual crowds had left. The terrorists, communicating via cell phone, had allowed the bodies to be removed during the night, contingent upon a one-man recovery team.

Steve lowered the volume to a moderate level, high enough to hear, but low enough not to dull his concentration, as he moved to his laptop computer to check his email.

After dialing into the network through a secured cellular line, he spent several minutes reading and responding to several messages, mostly updates on happenings around the world. Nothing though, was as newsworthy as the pending terrorist action in the middle of the nation's capital.

After the immediate action, very little had transpired, and for a very capable and action-oriented group that had proven themselves as such, tensions were at an all-time high. The world was eyeing the monument from mediums across the globe, anxiously waiting for the structure to either explode or produce a paralleled spectacle.

Standing in the center of the room, Steve worked his tired muscles. Other than a rare uneasiness, he *did* feel well rested. The hot shower that followed completed the job, and as he stepped from the steamy bathroom and into the much cooler air of the room, he was ready for the day's events.

Please God, he thought. *Don't let me die. At least not for a couple of days.*

––––––––––––––––

Gibby, true to his nature, was early for the 8 a.m. meeting, sitting in the majestic lobby of the Waldorf Astoria reading a newspaper, most of which had already been perused and discarded on the large chair to his side.

He was dressed in a worn brown suit that hugged his body too closely, but fit his image all too well. Reading glasses were pushed to the front of his nose as he peered through them and on to the pages. Other than a slightly wrinkled shirt and a dated tie, which defined his way of dress, Steve saw a man that seemed very fresh and alert, an unlikely product of the early morning flight from D.C.

"Hey Gibby," Steve said, moving toward him confidently.

Gibby slowly and methodically folded the newspaper, looking up and into Steve's eyes.

"Mr. McCallister," he began, as he stood to receive his new compatriot, tossing the paper on the stack with the others. "What'd ya know?"

Steve maneuvered Gibby to a group of chairs away from the lobby traffic, and sat down after a quick, mandatory glance around the large space. He told the FBI agent about the call he'd received the night before and the intended phone call at noon. A plan was hastily assembled, and after a pointed discussion, they left the comforts of the lobby for the benefits of a traditional New York City deli breakfast.

Unfriendly eyes followed their every move.

Chapter 43

AT NOON, Steve stood above the Rockefeller Center ice-skating rink, which was closed in early November, temporary white plastic fencing maintaining a boundary for future use. A chill caught him off guard and he tightened his trench coat against his body.

It was a crisp fall day and the high sky revealed only a few transient clouds. The sun burned brightly but seemed to only provide light, as the cold air won the battle of the thermometer.

His senses heightened, Steve heard the distant sounds of unseen automobiles, all hidden behind the tall, thick buildings that neatly lined Fifth Avenue. At his feet, a stray plastic bag made its way across the street, and he took time to notice the more permanent debris: flattened cans, scattered food wrappings, blackened gum, and cigarette butts that clung to the ground, almost as enduring as the concrete itself.

Hurried pedestrians passed Steve as he waited for the promised phone call that could help destroy al Assad. Gibby promised he was "around," and Steve was passing the time ineffectively trying to locate him. He thought he saw the FBI agent leaning into a phone booth, but his train of thought quickly escaped as his cell phone rang. He found a small nook of privacy and reached for the small unit. Turning his face away from the busy sidewalk, he spoke calmly.

"This is McCallister."

The voice was direct. "I thought I requested that you come alone."

"It's okay. If you trust me, we can…"

"We are *both* alive because we don't trust anybody," the voice responded quickly, a hint of hostility evident.

"Where are you? We'll both come."

"Too dangerous. Al Assad's swarming the area and even *I* haven't met most of them. We'd be sitting ducks."

"How were you going to meet me if I were alone?" Steve inserted, clearly on the offense.

"I was *going* to leave a handwritten message somewhere, but it's okay. I may have use for your FBI friend. I'll call you back in fifteen minutes."

The call over, Steve loosened his shoulders and walked to the corner, where he stood for a few seconds. He then made his way back to where he started. Gibby was waiting for him, his deflated composure mimicking Steve's.

The two men shuffled their feet and looked around suspiciously. They were in the open, naked to the world and they were noticeably uncomfortable.

"At least we're not dead yet," Steve joked.

"Maybe that's a good sign this isn't a trap," Gibby added.

The call came sooner than later, and Steve was thankful. Gibby anxiously moved to his side.

"I'm staying at the Ogden, room 252. If you are followed and we are found out, this is all over. We are dead and thousands will suffer. Make sure you're not followed. Do not underestimate them. They're everywhere. Room 252 in two hours."

Gibby and Steve agreed to separate to minimize the risk of a tail, each employing a successful and tiresome combination of subway, taxi, elevator, and old fashioned double backing down one-way streets. The two hours lapsed quickly, and when individually satisfied, each made their way to a solid wooden door on the second floor of the Ogden Hotel. Gibby had been early and was sitting on the bed eyeing the so-called 'Patriot' with obvious interest.

Steve was quick to follow and the three men stood in the small room looking at each other, wondering if the door would be blown open at any moment. Steve, a powerful intelligence officer of the CIA, hell bent on al Assad's downfall, Gibby, a decorated FBI career man with a mind for detail hoping for the same, and a 'Patriot,' an excommunicated, highly decorated Special Forces operator that no law-abiding council knew anything about.

Steve and The Patriot looked into each other's eyes, regarding each other for a long moment. The effects of time, although taking its toll, had left the rigid features alone and allowed for quick and easy recognition.

Steve, who thought The Patriot was dead long ago, found it hard to take his eyes off his long-time friend.

"How many are left?" Steve managed, his voice strained.

"I don't know. Maybe three or four."

"How'd you escape?"

The Patriot moved to Steve with a large hand, which he placed on his friend's shoulder. "If we live past the next seventy-two hours, I'll buy you a drink and fill you in."

Looking beyond Steve, The Patriot's eyes found Gibby. He smiled and outstretched his hand.

"If Steve trusts you, so do I. Together, we may be the only hope to destroy al Assad and prevent what I'm about to tell you."

Gibby nodded but moved past both men to the television. He needed an update on the terrorist standoff that he was still heading, albeit it from several states away. He was in constant communication via cell phone, but appreciated the visual from the television. The scene still appeared stagnant.

The men settled into the middle of the room, the task at hand holding their complete attention. The Patriot was the first to speak.

"I've been in al Assad for over twenty years, but only until recently, have I been entrusted with information that could save the lives of thousands."

The Patriot's eyes searched Gibby's and Steve's, finding absolute concentration and total attention.

"I'm going to tell you what I know, and I trust you to use the information well. Being who I am, I can only deliver the message. I cannot be involved in its physical prevention."

Steve had told Gibby that The Patriot had been absent from any formal United States defense unit for quite some time, but that he was one of the best and to forgo any prejudices. Treat him like any high-end officer in the Department of Defense. Still, Gibby looked apprehensive and only listened.

"In two days, I am told that Falby, an al Assad soldier… You know of Falby?" The Patriot interrupted himself.

"Yes," Steve replied solemnly. "He did the Golden Gate, right?"

"Yeah, he did, so I don't have to remind you how lucky we are to have this information."

Steve and Gibby nodded.

"To be direct, he's gonna spread a shit load of Sarin gas somewhere in New York City, and you're gonna stop it."

The Patriot stopped talking as quickly as he had started and just looked at the two men, the words emphasized in the ensuing silence.

"How much are we talking?" Steve asked, exasperated.

"Can't be sure but it'll be lethal and just as big if not bigger than San Francisco."

Gibby jumped into the conversation for the first time, and Steve couldn't tell if the man was more astonished at the information, or the fact that he was listening to a person that technically didn't exist.

"Could it be a trick?"

"Who cares? Everything could be," The Patriot blurted. "But it has to be confirmed or denied regardless. We have to believe it's legitimate. Falby is *very* capable of this."

Gibby looked preoccupied and Steve focused on him. "What's up Gib?"

"We've recently traced three separate movements of suspicious materials on the East Coast.

"Couldn't be us," The Patriot was quick to say. "We'd be invisible, receiving the materials, manufacturing the poison, housing it, transporting it, and unleashing it. Maybe two others besides Falby could be involved, but he's probably on this one alone, knowing him."

"So you *know* him?" Gibby inserted, expectantly.

"No, only by reputation."

"And what is that?" Gibby asked.

"That he's a perfectionist loner, extremely motivated, and he can't be caught."

Gibby was perplexed. "Why can't he be caught?"

"His nickname is 'The Chameleon.' He's a master of disguise, illusion, weaponry, and escape. You wouldn't know it if he was standing right next to you."

"What other info do you have?" Steve asked, suddenly acting the moderator.

"Nothing. Saturday evening. New York City. I'd be scanning everything and you'd better do it transparently. One hint of abnormality, and it'll spook him. He'll unleash the next day in some other city, guaranteed."

"You seem to be glorifying this," Gibby said.

Steve looked between the two men, the only one who knew both. He rubbed his eyes with the tips of his fingers, waiting for the heated exchange that was sure to follow.

"You think I'm enjoying my life?" The Patriot whispered, angrily. "I haven't had a home in decades. I've watched innocent people die and been powerless to stop it. I live every day thinking it could be my last, and sometimes I wish that it is!"

Gibby made no attempt to look at The Patriot as he continued.

"I've killed innocent people trying to gain entry into al Assad. My only hope is vindication and this is the first time I'm in a position to achieve it. I have information that very few know, and if accurate could prevent an attack that could save thousands. This is my saving grace. If they're defeated, I may be able to reenter society and salvage a life for myself."

Gibby now found The Patriot's eyes, revealing a broken man showing himself for the first time. Helpless to prevent the strike himself, The Patriot entrusted his own salvation to Gibby, a man whom he'd never met.

Gibby knew he had been too quick to judge the man. After all, The Patriot had dedicated his life to national defense, sacrificing without recognition. Gibby thought of his own world, his two daughters, his wife, even his '67 Corvette. Could he have been a Patriot if called upon? The answer was evident in his response.

In a hushed whisper, barely loud enough to escape his lips, he said, "I'm sorry. Let's do this."

For the balance of the afternoon, the men talked strategy. Finding and isolating the Sarin would not be easy, but it would be done.

The two men told The Patriot of the al Assad soldiers that were known to the authorities, and The Patriot added more to the list. Still, he warned that secrecy was of utmost importance in the regime, and even the members had little contact with one another. No one but Almedi Hahn Sahn knew the consummate plan and the true population of the group, and even killing him would do little to hurt the cells already in place.

But The Patriot did confirm that Almedi Hahn Sahn traveled in a relatively small radius, in and out of Pakistan, Syria, and Afghanistan with considerable help from their shaky governments and local insurgents. A strike would have to be very specific and absolute, if initiated at all.

Throughout the conversation, Steve was patient, allowing the information to flow. But soon he couldn't wait any longer. He looked squarely at The Patriot.

"I have a suspicion that needs to be validated."

"What is it?" the man replied, hungry to help in any way.

"Simon. Have you met the man?"

"Yes, on two occasions, unfortunately. He's not a man to be taken lightly, but then again not like Falby, thank God. Simon's been working in Chicago for several months now, and that could be something extremely lethal as well."

Steve made a mental note to follow up with the information later. He had to ask something that was eating at him.

"Is there competition in this faction, and is Simon on the outs?"

The Patriot received the question, thought about it with a few blinks of the eye, and shook his head affirmatively, confirming Steve's suspicions.

"Yes, there is competition. And yes, Simon is out of favor, as I've heard. A couple ego-driven mistakes have recently hurt al Assad's position. Falby and Simon are at each other's throats."

"Well then," Steve said, leaning back in the room's only chair. "I have an idea."

Chapter 44

A DISGUISED SIMON sat in the small bar inside the Waldorf Astoria, sipping Crown Royal and reflecting on the day's events. Independently of each other, he and two others had followed Steve and his new friend across town and back, but all had failed to trace them to their final destination.

Simon was stewing in anger, finding solace in the near empty glass he cradled in his large hands. He had given more thought to this kill than any other, mainly due to the fact that Steve McCallister was no stranger to him; but perhaps more importantly, the CIA man's skill matched his own.

Tonight Steve McCallister would die, in the open if need be. An al Assad associate was watching the CIA officer from the lobby. But the lookout concerned Simon.

The younger man was too eager and wanted to kill McCallister himself. He wanted the CIA man's head as a trophy and was over-anxious to the task at hand. A newer member to the cause, Simon had not trusted him from the beginning. The man had never known the target and had never seen him in action. "He is just a man," he had said. "Let's just kill him and get some dinner."

Simon's phone had buzzed minutes earlier to reveal good news. Steve was having dinner solo, in the hotel restaurant merely one hundred feet away. The FBI agent was no where to be found, and the perimeter was being monitored for any sign of him. Open lines of communication were to be maintained and Simon had a green light to take McCallister at will.

The killer finished his drink, left a generous tip, and walked out of the bar to do just that.

From a corner booth, his back to a wall of dark paneled wood, Steve peered through the restaurant foyer and into the hotel lobby, watching the comings and goings of a variety of interesting people. Eating alone and with nothing to read, he observed the foot-traffic with great interest.

A young man in his early twenties caught his attention more than once, his eyes resting on Steve for a little longer than they should have. His demeanor was unsettling and rushed. He hurried here and there, made several pointless laps through the hotel lobby, but always returned to the same place.

He was light skinned, with high cheekbones that gave way to sunken blue eyes. A thin smile played on his ruby lips, and Steve guessed that the man was not just another tourist.

A New York Jets ski cap was pulled over his forehead, but stray white strands of hair peeked through, resting in slight curls above nonexistent eyebrows. A dark trench coat covered the bulk of his height but allowed a look at his large heeled black boots, the likes of which were not indigenous to the area. The young man looked Norwegian, his clothes out of place, even for New York. His composite appearance begged for attention.

Steve became more apprehensive as the moments passed. He wouldn't be surprised if al Assad was watching him, but were they ignorant enough to have the tail dressed so colorfully? Melting in with the environment would seem a more logical alternative.

Steve wiped his mouth after a fine meal that included a large salad, lemon chicken, garlic-mashed potatoes, and a medley of vegetables. He was enjoying his second cup of coffee, the caffeine giving his body a well-needed boost.

The young man crossed the lobby once more, eyeing Steve for a long moment and then maneuvering near the twenty-four hour convenience shop. Steve's cell phone rang and the director of the CIA was on the line.

"Steve. What's up in New York?"

"I'm at the Waldorf, finishing up with dinner. I'm about to get some gelato at Grotto's"

The director laughed. Steve and Director Willard had spent many nights at the Waldorf Astoria, their favorite hotel in New York when visiting there. And every time Steve was in Manhattan, he had to have Italian ice cream at Grotto's.

"Are you wearing your body armor, Steve?"

Steve thought about the odd question, valid but out of place. He also wondered about the man's tone, but replied nonchalantly.

"No, you know I can't stand that stuff Doc," Steve lied.

"Have it your way. When'll I see you?"

"I'll be back tomorrow night."

"Keep me updated."

"Will do."

When the conversation ended, Steve pocketed his phone and looked toward the suspicious-looking man, the display cabinet still holding his attention. Steve saw him receive a cell phone call, shuffle his feet, and walk out of sight.

The bill paid, Steve placed the napkin on the table and walked through the restaurant and into the lobby. A quick glance revealed nothing new, and he walked down the stairs, through the large revolving doors, and into the night air on his way to Grotto's.

The small cafe was about seven blocks away from the Waldorf, and although alone, Steve felt comfortable with the weaponry he carried and the body armor covering most of his body. He was ready for an ambush and scrutinized everything with great detail.

———————————

Simon mirrored Steve's route just one block south. To reduce the risk of detection, the killer chose a wider course to the same destination.

Breaking into a modest run, Simon was confident that he could get to Grotto's before his target. But an overwhelming sense of uneasiness grabbed at him, and although he knew Steve's intended location, and being assured that his adversary *wasn't* wearing body armor, Simon had never felt more unsure in his life.

Indeed he did reach Grotto's before Steve, moving into a small brick enclosure under a stairwell and flattening himself into the dark area. It was more than perfect, and Simon's discomfort quickly gave way to absolute confidence as Steve came into view.

"Here piggy piggy," the killer whispered, checking his 9 millimeter.

Chapter 45

STEVE SENSED DANGER before the pounding footsteps alerted him to it. Until now, he had enjoyed his evening stroll in mid town Manhattan, maneuvering the city streets in a lazy walk that lent itself to self-thought. But something didn't feel right and unfortunately his suspicions were justified.

The night was foreboding. A heavy fog settled well below the tops of the buildings, creating a low blanket of complete gray. The cloud cover emitted a persistent mist that was too light for an umbrella, but real enough to dampen clothing in a minute's time. Thick white steam rose from covered manholes as far as the eye could see, the light winds forcing a quick dance before dissipation into the night.

Steve felt unusually claustrophobic. The low sky seemed to press down on him, the concrete buildings personified unbending barriers, and visibility due to fog was greatly compromised. He felt as if he were a character in a snow globe, swirling around in an environment that was foreign and unreal.

The running footsteps caught his attention immediately. Even the most resilient joggers wouldn't venture out in this weather. He didn't hesitate in reaching inside his trench coat for his two Sig Saur handguns, cocking both to their three pound pull. But he didn't look back. He wasn't prepared to meet his attacker and the distance, he estimated, was too far. Instead, he maintained a steady walk, readying himself for the confrontation that was sure to come.

He looked ahead and to the sides of the street in search of possible cover. A bench, a trash can, a vehicle, even some sort of landscaping or grouping of bushes could provide a makeshift stronghold to at least buy some time and perhaps counterattack.

But he saw nothing. The empty two-lane street didn't allow vehicular parking, and was lined with wide buildings that merged with each other without allowance for an alleyway. Steve was in the open and feeling it.

An arm-locked couple exited Grotto's, which was just ahead and across the street. He eyed them keenly, hopeful for a quick glance in his direction and maybe to the possible attacker coming from the rear.

But they were lost in each other, deep in conversation and oblivious. They immediately passed a row of upward stairs with a small enclosure underneath. That space, Steve thought, could provide some form of cover, if he could just get there. But it was too far away. The footsteps indicated a proximity of no more than two hundred feet. This hit could happen in less than ten seconds, Steve knew.

A speeding taxi emerged from the fog in a burst of movement and sound. The running footsteps were lost in the passing drone, and Steve's attacker now had an extreme advantage. Invisibility *and* silence.

Just before Steve was to swing around with both weapons in hand, his attacker made a move. Still looking ahead, Steve saw the passing taxi's rear window shatter simultaneous with a gunshot behind him. The car skidded to a sudden stop several buildings ahead.

Steve knew the shot was meant for him but the shooter missed! Instinctively, he hit the ground flat to the sidewalk as another shot was fired well above his head. Both of Steve's handguns fired alternating rounds, all of them finding their intended target in his attacker's chest, not fifty feet away.

Complete shock was evident on the man's face as wide eyes saw Steve take complete control in an unlikely turn of events. The man fell backward, a single pistol thrown from his right hand and into the street. His head hit the pavement with an eerie thud, and Steve found him lying in a strange, contorted manner that was not at all natural. It was the young man from the hotel lobby.

His face was white, his breathing coming in short gasps. Heavy clothing hid the blood that was pouring from his mid-section, but the many bullet holes in his coat evidenced the man's grim condition. Quick words gave way to gurgling sounds, and Steve looked at quivering blue lips and frightened eyes.

It was obvious he was suffocating in his own blood. His lungs were punctured and blood was filling them quicker than he could spit it up. Steve knew he had only a matter of seconds before the man would go into shock and ultimately leave him.

Steve knelt above the man, placing both weapons to the side. He cradled the fallen man's head in his hands, not noticing the people who had cautiously gathered around, the cars that had slowed and stopped.

"Just whisper. Don't talk," Steve said, calmly.

The man blinked rapidly as he looked through Steve. The falling mist gathered on his face, joining the assemblage of perspiration that was already apparent.

"I guess you can get your gelato after all," the man whispered, and Steve detected a nervous smile.

"How did you know that?" Steve asked, unconsciously tightening his grip on the dying man's head.

The man jerked suddenly and coughed blood that rolled down both of his cheeks as he turned. No attempt was made to wipe it away as he focused on Steve.

"You haven't figured it out yet have you?" he managed. "*We* are everywhere. *We* are everything."

"Where are the next strikes?" Steve asked, and then something caught his eye.

A piece of paper peeked out from the assailant's coat pocket and Steve grabbed it, taking a second to check on the fallen man before reading it aloud.

"What's this?" Steve asked, as he read the nine letters and numbers slowly.

"'NY3T3C1A1.' Does it have to do with the Washington Monument?"

The man looked at Steve, and even for his grave condition, a puzzled expression crossed his face.

"That's still going on?" he asked, fixing his eyes on something far above Steve's head.

It wouldn't be long now, Steve knew.

"Tell me something," Steve yelled, shaking the man. "Do you want your last words to be of hate? Tell me about the Washington Monument."

Steve's hands were clasped on the man's shoulders, his face red, and his blue eyes peering into what soul the man had left.

"The monument thing's nothing," he started in a liquid gurgle. "Compared to what's gonna happen in that city next."

"What's that mean? What'll happen?"

With a slight movement, the man nodded toward the note. "The answer," he started, with a substantial amount of effort, "...is in your hands."

Steve glanced at the piece of paper before placing it in his own breast pocket. A quick cough interrupted the hurried exchange, and the man's body shuddered as he spit blood. His feet involuntarily kicked to the side, and he froze in a forced position reserved only for the dying. His breathing slowed and Steve knew death would come quickly.

Steve resumed a kneeling position, holstered his weapons, and surveyed the scene. A police cruiser arrived and the flashing lights lit the nervous faces of the curious onlookers who had happened on the scene. With identification in hand, Steve waived at the officers as they emptied their vehicle. After assuring his cooperation in writing a report, Steve moved down the street, punching several numbers into his phone. It would be the first of many calls he'd make before the night was over.

If Steve were to look behind him, he would have noticed the only person to leave the area. The man appeared to be homeless, about sixty years of age with dirty gray hair a matted down beard and torn clothing.

With a look of disgust, the man made his way through the fog, a slight limp to his labored walk. The bulkiness of his coat hid an expansive and deadly array of weaponry that would not be used this night.

Like Steve, Simon had a great many phone calls to make.

———————————

From the darkness, crouching far against the wall, Simon could see Steve McCallister getting closer and closer.

But then he saw a man running behind him, wielding a gun, and closing at a high rate of speed. Curiosity turned to anger as Simon recognized the man as his partner, his lookout from the Waldorf Astoria.

Simon could see Steve's eyes search, peering into the darkness that *was* his hiding place. Was Steve aware of Simon's presence? He couldn't be!

A young couple walked by and a taxi appeared out of nowhere. A shot rang out and the cab almost skidded into the stairs that hid Simon, coming to rest only a few feet away, above him at street level.

Then several more shots were fired. Peering underneath the stopped taxi, he could see Steve hunched over the man, leaning down in conversation. A note was taken from the man's coat and Steve held it as he talked further.

Still camouflaged in darkness, Simon openly cursed his partner, not believing his arrogance. His only job was to shadow Steve, to provide another set of eyes. He had no right to make an attempt on the man's life! This was *his* hit and he'd been mere seconds away from victory.

The young lookout was lucky he was dead, Simon thought. If he lived, Simon surely would have killed him. Nobody stole his thunder. He had only met the man that day and had no knowledge of any other operation he was connected with. What did the note say? How would this look to Almedi Hahn Sahn?

Timing his exit perfectly, Simon emerged from the small space and slowly walked away, every step creating a comfortable distance between him and the failed murder attempt.

He flipped open his cell phone and dialed Falby's number. He couldn't remember ever needing someone more but wanting to talk to them less.

Chapter 46

THE BOAT HAD BEEN DOCKED at the dilapidated pier for years; completely neglected like the town near it.

It rested in a small inlet, technically within the borders of Steeples, New Jersey, a sleepy industrial town dedicated to the production of a variety of metals, chemicals, and general manufacturing staples that kept the local economy going. The town's sky was a blanket of white, gray, and black smoke; the air full of the pungent stench of burning plastic and refuse.

The general workforce entered and exited through Route 4 in a monotonous flow of depression, comprised of three eight-hour shifts Monday through Friday. Falby found the location perfect for his needs, though, so the most deadly terrorist in the world found anonymity among the approximate six thousand residents. As they mechanically went about their lives, he was fervently planning his next strike against humanity.

The private dock, a generous term for its appearance, was accessible only through a two mile unpaved and narrow path through dense woods. Years ago the road was barely wide enough to allow vehicles through. Now it was riddled with deep holes and high root systems, a testament to the thick trees that created the uncompromising walls flanking it.

Finding the way at night was quite a challenge. At daytime it was easier, but one still had to find the entrance from Route 4, which had become more difficult with the recent planting of several Leland Cypresses. Even if someone negotiated the path, booby traps would alert him to their presence and allow a lead-time of several minutes. Heavy tree cover limited a potential sighting from above, and the very small house was nearly encased in ivy and covered by more trees.

Months earlier, in searching the New Jersey real estate listings, Falby had found the place, owned by an eighty-year old recluse named Benny Smith who rarely ventured out. It was listed "as is" by the owner; a small, neglected home on an expansive and private piece of water front land. The boat came with the property, but it hadn't run in years.

Days earlier, Falby had come to the site, surveying every aspect of the run-down place and asking questions that the old man deemed personal, but felt obligated to answer. The visiting man was nice enough, reminding the old hermit of himself half a lifetime earlier.

After an hour of conversation about the privacy of the land and the man's very few acquaintances in town, Falby was satisfied with his choice. The man apparently had no friends or family, and except for a monthly trip to the store for food and supplies, it appeared as though he had no ties to the neighboring town or the community. He was living on a forty-acre parcel of waterfront land, and although the water was shared by the factories directly upstream, the place was an island of exclusivity, remote from the outside world.

Getting up from a chair on the porch, Falby stretched and turned to the old man. "This will do just fine," he had said.

Smiling, the man shook his head excitedly, and Falby watched him enjoy a moment of self-content.

Then Falby removed his Beretta and fired a single shot into the man's head. Finishing his stretch, Falby moved to the edge of the water, the only noise coming from the brown water lapping at the oil-stained rocky shoreline. It was not privileged waterfront property, but it was forty minutes from New York harbor by boat and would do just fine.

The boat turned out to be an old wooden Dead Rise and it took Falby less than three hours to fire up the engines and make it seaworthy. Removing its contents took another hour.

Falby rested on an old cot, one of the few items allowed to stay on the boat. In deep thought, he reviewed the logistics of the strike that was now only a day away.

He reflected on his recent past, including the assassination of Senator Keeler, the bombing of the Golden Gate, and most recently, the mixing of the Sarin that was held in the four large bins across from him.

Was it even fair? Did the authorities even present a challenge to him? His thoughts were discarded when his cell phone rang. He reached for it with frustration, remembering that he had requested an absolute detachment from the cause. He needed to concentrate on the task at hand.

"Yeah?" he spoke in to the receiver.

"It's Simon," the voice said.

"Is it done?"

"There were complications. My idiot partner -- who wasn't chosen by me -- showed up and tried to kill McCallister himself. He compromised everything and McCallister's still alive."

Falby sunk into the cot and rubbed his eyes.

"You can't make a simple hit? You *are* useless."

"Look," Simon shouted. "This guy was *your* pick not mine. I'll take McCallister out tonight!"

"No." Falby replied. "I'll take care of it."

"I can do it," Simon challenged.

"You've done enough and I'm not in the mood. Get back to Chicago."

Both parties hung up. Falby held the phone in his hands for a few seconds before dialing a number.

"Yeah," Hortence said.

"This is Falby. I need you in New York right now."

In the early morning hours, in the financial district of lower Manhattan, two very capable men met in a parking garage in a car. The engine was left running to effect a quick escape if need be.

Both were apprehensive about the task at hand; the public killing of a CIA agent was no easy thing. A plan had to be assembled and executed flawlessly. Their very lives depended on it.

Chapter 47

STEVE HADN'T SLEPT all night, deciding instead to trade the much-needed rest for a tumultuous night of reflection. Al Assad was the only thing on his mind.

He rehashed everything, separating each piece of information, analyzing it, and then reassembling it hoping to find a pattern. Was there *anything* he may have overlooked? He'd been in contact with a variety of key people throughout the night and early dawn, all planning a defensive against the terrorist faction.

Fueled by strong coffee and cellophane-wrapped pastries, he worked diligently on cell phone and computer, trading messages and ideas with other intelligence agencies and the Pentagon. The most detailed conversation was with the Secretary of Defense, a man he got along with exceedingly well, considering the buearocratic nature of the office. Steve was a man of action, and all too often the war department had heavy legs.

Ten minutes prior, he had called the FBI field team in D.C., and acting in tandem with Gibby's orders, it was decided to move in on the van at the Washington Monument. The information and reaction from his would-be killer the night before was very telling, and Steve's better judgment told him that the whole thing was a facade.

The van had to be empty, the reported movement in the tires attributed to wind or some remote-controlled device moving inside.

It could be wired to explode, Steve knew, but he thought it doubtful. If his suspicions were confirmed, the van would be empty and that was even more disturbing. Why would they take such a huge risk with no immediate gain? The game had stepped up a notch. If this was a simple diversion, what was the main attraction? Chemical warfare in New York City? Some other random target? He expected to know very soon.

Steve increased the volume on the television as a reporter interrupted the normal broadcast. She hurriedly explained the movements of several teams of men running up the hill to the base of the Washington Monument. Then her face was replaced by a live picture of the scene, the slight bobbing image of the van.

Steve watched in a concentrated stare as the first of the FBI team members reached the van, stopping short. The three men held up a large metal shield as they inched closer.

A hand was placed on the door handle, and with a quick jerk, the van door slid open to reveal nothing. The others joined the first group, weapons ready, and a large spotlight was used to peer inside and search the surrounding area.

Even from the distance of the CNN cameras, which had amazingly zoomed into the van, Steve could see that there was no activity and his hunch was realized. It was empty.

He picked up his phone and pressed several numbers, and then several more. After a few moments he was put through to his intended audience and the president of the United States was on the line.

"What's this mean, Steve?"

"Sir, I can't speculate as to the motives of..."

"Dammit Steve! In your opinion, what the hell does this mean?"

"I think there's something much bigger on the horizon and we've got to stop them right now. This was some sort of diversion and that's very disconcerting."

"No shit. But what did they gain from this? Why didn't they blow it anyway? It would have still been a diversion."

"Because sometimes the knowledge that they could have done it is just as bad as doing it. They could have brought the monument down, but they also know that the U.S. would respond with swift force in absolute totality. They're not ready for that, at least not yet."

"What do you have so far?"

"Mr. President," Steve began slowly and methodically. "You must hit them within the next couple of hours as if they actually *did* destroy the monument. I urge you to contact the Secretary of Defense, whom I've been talking with already. NSA has mapped several movements and has verified five camps in Pakistan, Algeria, and Syria that are known to house Almedi Hahn Sahn and act as training facilities. We've named them Echo's one through five, and the lats & longs have already been recorded, awaiting your order."

Steve cut himself off, and in the silence the president didn't make a sound.

"But there's something else," Steve started again. "I think I know where he is and where he'll stay for the next several hours. I'm going to assemble a Delta team; an air strike will do no good there. I think he's in Syria, and I'd bet my life on it."

"Okay," the president said. "I'll initiate the air attacks on the camps, but if you're wrong, I'll kill you myself."

"Sir, if I'm wrong, I'll probably be dead through *other* channels."

The conversation ended and the dial tone seemed louder than it ever had before. Steve's face was flush, and placing the phone back on the nightstand, he noticed the wetness that had transferred from his sweaty palm to the small black unit. Not one to easily be shaken, Steve placed his hands to his face to steady himself.

Minutes passed and Steve opened his phone once more to contact Gibby.

"Gibby, it's Steve, what do you have on the Sarin attack?"

"We've estimated a time of detonation between 5 p.m. and 10 p.m., and have pretty much scoured the entire New York City area. If it is indeed Sarin we're dealing with, the best conductor is dead air, and the most effective environment would be a very confined area with a crowd of unexpecting people."

"Do you think it'll be a subway attack like Japan?"

"I don't think so, but we're looking into it."

"What'd ya think then?" Steve persisted.

"I think there will be a crowd and I think it'll be on camera. Our profilers think they want to draw the American people into this one. We've concentrated our efforts on the main stadiums and sporting complexes. This includes all schools and YMCA-type places."

"I wouldn't rule out malls, the docks on the south east side, the theatre district, hotels, Penn Station and both airports."

"I thought you weren't going to tell me how to do my job," Gibby jested.

"I know, I'm sorry. Anything turn up yet?"

"We've scoured everything you've mentioned, plus Central Park, its perimeter, all of the government buildings, and the underground."

Sensing Steve's ensuing question, Gibby answered the question before it was asked.

"...The underground is a series of tunnel systems that run under Central Park. There's also a system from just under the Brooklyn Bridge to the Financial District."

"Whatever."

"I've had to call in almost every field agent from Maine to Michigan, and southeast to Virginia."

"Do they all have those cool navy jackets with 'FBI' printed in gold?"

"Shut up Steve. I heard you had some excitement last night. Did you pack an extra pair of shorts?"

"It was close. Have you thought about what the number could mean?"

"No, have you told our new friend about it?"

"He's been briefed, but he's laying low for now. Quite understandable considering some of his boys are in town, and he doesn't even know most of them."

"Hey Steve," Gibby began. "In all seriousness, I think you're gonna need some protection. I mean, if they've tried once, they'll probably try again. How about I send a couple of guys to your hotel to shadow you for the next few days?"

"That's very nice of you, but…"

"This *isn't* a game, Steve, and I don't see any CIA exposure here. They'll be in the lobby waiting for you at 7 a.m."

"Thanks Gibby. Keep me appraised."

Steve returned to his work, looking at an incoming email and then returning his attention to the television. There was now much more activity at the base of the monument; it seemed that every authoritative body wanted a first-hand view.

The reporter was back on screen, communicating with another anchor at CNN studios and summarizing the situation.

Steve's phone rang and he muted the television.

"This is McCallister."

"Steve!"

"Who's this?" Steve said, loosening his shoulders.

"It's Pete. I didn't think I'd reach you!"

"Hey Pete," Steve sang, enthusiastically. "Are you home? How's Jillian?"

"We've got a couple of goons outside. I think they're the same guys who came with you to California for Blake's funeral. I'm glad they're on my side!"

"Yeah. Look Pete, I'm real sorry about that. I didn't…"

"Steve. It's cool. I just wanted to call and hear your voice. I know everything's crazy, but let's get together sometime and talk everything through."

"I don't know, Pete. This is going to sound cold and strange, but I think we should just meet at the designated time and place, however far off you may think it is."

A moment of silence loomed and then Pete spoke again.

"Alright, that's cool I guess."

"Pete," Steve said, dejectedly. "I'll see you in Chile, okay."

"I thought you said not to mention the name ever?" Pete said.

"I've gotta go, buddy. I'll see you in Chile."

Chapter 48

AT TEN MINUTES before 7 a.m., on a morning that had been busier than most days he recalled, Steve left his hotel room to meet the promised FBI agents.

He walked into the cool hallway and was reminded of how long he'd been cooped up inside, engulfed in hot, stale air, and four very close walls.

It was his nature to immediately scope the area and appraise the scene. The hallway was lengthy and well lit; ending about one hundred feet away with a large mirror that looked back at him, though his reflection could not reach him. The carpeting was a combination of purples, reds, and yellows, and was very thick under his feet. Two laundry carts, one on the left, another to the right, were stationed in front of a couple of rooms. Both doors were open and a busy vacuum sounded from one of them.

Steve slowly moved down the long corridor, both hands inside his oversized coat pockets, firmly gripping the two 9 millimeter handguns that had saved his life on more than one occasion. As he walked toward the elevators, a door behind him opened and two children ran past him in a noisy game of tag. The parents were soon to follow, and they apologized without looking at Steve, quickly hurrying past him to the children, who had already found the elevator buttons.

Caught off guard by the sudden action, Steve let his guard down and slowly walked toward the small family and past the first cart and open door. From the second room, he heard the television and recognized the common sounds of crisp sheets being applied tightly to a bed.

At Steve's passing, a man emerged from the room and moved behind him, not making a sound and certainly not concerned with the family up ahead. He had but one goal and nothing would stop him from it. Nothing *could*. He held a small handgun with a silencer attached, and he pointed it at Steve's back as he mirrored his target's walking pattern.

Two shots were fired and Steve fell to the ground, gripping his chest, which was instantly stained bright red. He gasped for air and his entire body convulsed, his right foot kicking the wall. Standing above his victim, the man fired four more shots and the fallen man moved no more.

The man continued his walk to the end of the hall. The children, who saw the entire exchange, screamed at the sight and moved to their parent's side.

The killer paid no attention to them, nor did he slow his pace as he pulled the fire alarm and entered an adjacent staircase. The alarm had been an afterthought, but he knew the ensuing commotion could only help his escape.

Within moments he was outside and punching numbers into a cell phone.

Chapter 49

GIBBY LOOKED INTO THE DISTANCE, hoping for a little luck. The FBI was one of the most skilled and technologically enabled intelligence organizations in the world, but all too often they simply stumbled upon evidence and were able to solve a puzzle, long awaited.

But he placed little faith in al Assad making a mistake that would compromise their position. Gibby's web was spun across New York City, and albeit thin, he was hoping to catch a little dinner, maybe even the most deadly terrorist in the world.

Gibby was standing against a waist high concrete wall at Fisherman's Wharf in lower Manhattan. Ahead of him and to the right, the Statue of Liberty came in and out of view as if playing hide and seek with him. It peeked through a low haze only to be shadowed by a passing boat. It had to be at least four miles away, and Gibby marveled at how it could appear so small and magnificent at the same time. To his left was an eye-catching view of the Brooklyn Bridge, with its large underbelly of rusted steel under-workings. Traffic on top was slow but continuous, and other than an occasional muted horn, the bridge was silent and only added to Gibby's solitude.

In front of him, excited children played, couples walked hand in hand, and "the suits," as he called them, rushed in and out of the fast food joints, involuntarily checking their watches every couple of minutes. Others walked leisurely, many on cell phones and in no rush to be anywhere at any time.

Gibby liked people-watching and enjoyed his time in the autumn sun. He knew he should be one of those people checking their watches and talking on the phone, but he was close to losing his mind. He'd just pissed away the last forty hours and the FBI was no closer to finding Falby than they were days ago when the hunt began. And tonight was the supposed night of the terrorist action!

Over one thousand agents had inspected every hole in New York City, many two and three times, and other than finding the bulk of the crack-head population, they'd come up empty.

Gibby's first angle was to locate the terrorist by tracking the ingredients used to create Sarin gas. The chemicals, however, proved difficult to trace, as they were so commonplace. It was their methodical assembly and evolution into the handful of deadly pre-cursors that were the true threat, and the pre-cursors were mixed behind closed doors.

Gibby had sent agents to countless ports on the eastern seaboard where they had traced large shipments of the possible components. They found invoices for all sorts of chemicals and their corresponding purchase orders from manufacturing plants, hospitals, and major universities to legally account for every bit of it. Their follow up to each of the intended locations was fruitless and time-consuming. Many of the agents were becoming noticeably irritated, their energy levels and enthusiasm at an all time low.

Gibby's second avenue was to rely on the expertise of the FBI profilers and bomb technicians, who had communicated the ideal environment for mixing the gas, its transport, and the perfect target, which had proved elusive thus far. They knew Falby all too well and spent very little time in analyzing his motivations or proficiency. They were well aware of his genius and extensive, lethal past.

Sarin gas, although extremely volatile and difficult to transport, could be mixed in any cool and stable environment. This left things so unbelievably open that Gibby concentrated his efforts on the unknown target, which was still believed to be an open area with a large audience. The attack was supposedly only hours away and Gibby had men stationed at well over one hundred events with intended audiences of ten thousand or more. Employment records for the last five years had been scrutinized at each location, but other than finding illegal aliens, nothing surfaced.

Gibby looked through the foot traffic and saw an agent briskly approaching. Dressed casually in relaxed pants and a button down, he still had an imposing presence that Gibby picked up on right away. By the look of the man's face, the news couldn't be good. But what news had been good lately?

"What's up John?" Gibby asked.

The man nodded and slowed.

"McCallister's dead, sir."

Gibby's face muscles tightened, his body shifted, and he unconsciously returned to the view of the harbor.

"How?" he managed.

"Multiple gun shots at close range, just outside his hotel room."

"Witnesses?"

"A family was waiting for an elevator. Each is giving a different description. The assailant was quick and methodical."

"Al Assad," Gibby said, almost to himself. "Had to be."

"I take it the killer has not been apprehended. Probably escaped into thin air?"

The agent took this as rhetorical and thought it best not to answer. Instead, he examined the pavement with utmost curiosity, not wanting to speak.

McCallister had quickly become a good friend of Gibby's and a leading figure in the campaign against al Assad. Respected throughout the intelligence community, Steve was a great loss. And if *he* could be eliminated so easily, were all of their lives in jeopardy? Both men couldn't help but think it and the assignment had suddenly taken a much newer, personal, and very real consequence.

Gibby held his stare into the harbor, unsuccessfully looking for the Statue of Liberty. The scene seemed different now that Steve was gone. He looked at his watch, which showed a time of 10:45 a.m. The Patriot assured him that the strike would be this evening, which left about six more hours, conservatively.

Special Agent James Gibson sighed deeply. "How about a little dumb luck?" he mumbled to the unresponsive New York harbor, and again silence ruled the air.

Gibby's phone chirped in his breast pocket and he suddenly snapped into FBI mode.

"This is Gibson," he responded into the receiver. "Are you sure? How long has he been there?"

Empty moments passed as Gibby listened to the agent, and then he spoke very deliberately.

"Do not approach. I'm on my way by chopper. I'll land at a nearby field that you'll designate en route. Have a car waiting and call me in ten minutes."

He flipped the phone shut and looked at his fellow agent. "We may have something in New Jersey. Suspicious activity at an old house."

Chapter 50

ONLY FOUR COMPOUNDS -- following a five-step procedure -- are needed to create Sarin, one of the deadliest and most concentrated poisons known to man. But it isn't their simple combination as much as the intricate assembly. Precise allotments, perfect temperatures, and exact timing are essential to create the deadly gas, which has to be mixed with other intermediaries for increased purification. The higher the purity, the more deadly and concentrated the poison.

The rural homestead that Falby selected was perfect for the task at hand. Open and private, there was more than enough space to work. It had taken only a few hours to form and heat the dimethyl phosphate into methyl methylphosphonate and another day to purify and mix it with phosphorous pentachloride to form DC. After recovering the DC and mixing it with hydrofluoric acid to form DF, Falby isolated the DF and mixed it with isopropyl alcohol to form the most purified form of Sarin he'd ever seen.

It was nothing short of perfection.

The main house had served two purposes. The first floor was a sea of bottles, beakers, Bunsen burners, and tubes that flowed from one another with a certain exactness that couldn't be immediately understood. Several clear liquids were scattered about and timers were set at different intervals, each methodically counting down. The west wall held several clipboards, each with a series of journal entries and mathematical calculations. Against the adjacent wall were three fume hoods, with separate tubing punched through the walls to the outside. There were three makeshift tables lined against the other wall, each holding a vast array of round bottom boiling flasks, heating mantels, hotplates, weighing balances, and laboratory thermometers. For two days, the room had been quietly bustling with activity, with several different components working independently to create the largest amount of Sarin gas Falby had ever seen.

Falby liked the irony of being charged with creating the Sarin gas. He was after all, from Germany, the birthplace of the deadly poison. He knew its history well, its very name coming from the four German researchers who discovered it in 1938: Schrader, Ambros, Ritter, and van der Linde.

Almedi Hahn Sahn had selected Falby long ago as a skilled and unremorseful killer. But if Falby were to author his own resume, he would be a biochemist, perhaps one of the best in the world. He had attended the most prestigious schools in Europe, excelling in all sciences, specifically chemistry. He absorbed the material easily, the information almost innate within him.

Upstairs were his sleeping quarters, with a small bed, desk, two dressers, and several alarm clocks. Falby had slept in four-hour allotments for the last couple of days, having to wake at specific times to tend to his project. The desk held an impressive array of firepower, and six monitors eyed the front entrance, the inlet, and north and south corners. The vast woods surrounding the property had been left unchecked, but wired to detect intruders.

Falby glanced at his watch and smiled. Almost lunchtime; his last meal at the place. It had served its purpose well, but the time was drawing near. In nine hours, Madison Square Garden had a big surprise on their hands. The rest of the United States wasn't far behind.

An outside noise took him by surprise and his eyes immediately darted to the monitors and the large black receiver, the heart of his defense. Everything was as it should be; the television screens empty, the single light a reassuring green. Still, he picked up two handguns and headed downstairs to investigate. Nothing was going to ruin tonight. *Nothing could.*

Chapter 51

GIBBY AND HIS ENTOURAGE quickly arrived at LaGuardia and were immediately whisked away by helicopter. Each man was given a headset with a direct feed to another team in neighboring New Jersey. On line was Special Agent Christopher Woods, a veteran agent that Gibby trusted implicitly.

"Okay, Woody. What do we have?" Gibby began.

"Suspicious male in his forties at a farm house in Kincaid County. He stopped in the local store to purchase food items and supplies about five days ago and was seen on the road leading to the house. He's definitely not from around there. A couple of hunters were near the woods, saw something suspicious and called it in."

"Is it confirmed that he's there now?" Gibby asked.

"Not confirmed. But they haven't seen him leave. You know the locals. They know everything that happens."

"Copy that. Where is our rendezvous?"

At an elementary school about ten miles out. Your pilot has the coordinates and you're coming from the north-west so you won't be flying over the suspect. I've got men surrounding a perimeter of one mile, waiting for your order."

"Any police involvement?"

"None. We picked it up on a police scanner and headed off any participation."

"Good. Maintain radio silence until I arrive. I don't want any police activity. Those scanners could ruin what could be our only chance at this bastard. Have you heard about McCallister?"

"Yeah, we all have. I'm sorry, Gib."

"Yeah. He was a good man."

"One more thing, sir. We have CIA here, sent by the director himself. About fifteen of 'em."

"That's fine," Gibby replied. "I'll see you in a few."

Gibby stopped the conversation but kept an open frequency. The drone of the powerful blades just ten feet above his head put him at ease, allowing his mind to wander.

A farmhouse in New Jersey made perfect sense. Far enough to be unnoticed yet close enough to have proximity to New York City.

Gibby couldn't fault the CIA for sending personnel. After all, al Assad had killed one of their own; and given the international implications, Gibby didn't understand why they'd been out of the game thus far. Then he thought of Steve and his determination to work alone. To be alone.

The helicopter slowed and made a slight downward turn. Gibby saw the pilot press buttons and move several levers with ease, as the noisy machine that encased them made the intended moves.

The brown, choppy waters below gave way to trees and a landscape of rolling green hills and Gibby questioned whether they were in New Jersey. The helicopter made a series of long, high pitched sounds as it began a rapid descent at the designated location. To his left, Gibby saw three blue sedans and a group of men awaiting their arrival. He saw an agent talk into a headset, and suddenly a voice sounded in Gibby's ear.

"Alright, sir. The latest is that we have visual confirmation. The subject is home."

"Then let's go get him," Gibby said.

Chapter 52

THE HOUSE came more into view with each step and Gibby's heart rate elevated. He was one of sixty agents, some CIA, most FBI, converging on the farm house through the dense forestation.

"Okay. Report in, gentlemen. Shooters?"

Ten voices sounded and six confirmed visual contact of the man in the house. The shooters were the backdrop of the operation, with trained marksmen at the trigger, waiting for a hint of aggression that would be their automatic order to drop the suspect.

"Front team?"

"We're ready sir, awaiting your order."

Gibby took in the scene one last time. The forest was quiet and still, except for the scurrying of distant squirrels and the mocking sounds of its inhabitants. He saw about ten of the field force; the others so well camouflaged that even he couldn't detect them. But they were all linked to the tiny headset that hugged his sweaty face. All eyes were on the house.

"We're a go," he stated, calmly.

Dozens of men rushed in, all stopping in front of the designated doors and windows they were assigned to earlier. Others took positions behind large trees and underneath low brush, their guns pointed steadily.

With surgical precision and impressive choreography, the agents shattered four windows and used blunt hammers on the two doorways to gain entry into the house. In less than ten seconds it was over.

The man was a drifter who had wandered into town. His immediate explanation, one that Gibby took as truthful, was that he had learned of the farmhouse from a neighbor who owned the place as a summer retreat. When the trespasser's wife filed for divorce, he just drove into the night, eventually settling at the empty farmhouse in the woods.

Gibby called the local authorities to take the investigation over. He had no desire to be involved with local law enforcement or waste his time with a wayward drifter. The clock was ticking.

Surprisingly, a lone sheriff was quick on the scene. He noisily parked his rusted police car in the driveway, quickly killing the engine. Showing its age, the old car didn't stop rumbling until the sheriff was out of the car, slowly making his way to Gibby and the large grouping of men. He approached the FBI from a point of curiosity, not respect.

"What the hell's going on here?" he snared through stained, crooked teeth.

"My name is James Gibson, FBI. We just apprehended a man that was admittedly trespassing in a house in your county."

"How come you got so many of your boys out here? He a wanted fugitive or something?"

"Actually, we thought he could be linked to something much bigger. Do you mind if I ask you a few questions?"

The man regarded the area without saying a word and Gibby automatically continued.

"Have you seen anything unusual lately? Anyone or anything suspicious?"

"Can't say that I have. What's this all about?"

"I'm sorry but we can't go into that," Gibby said, flatly.

"You government pricks are all the same. All secretive. Bet you think I'm just another dumb hillbilly with a gun don't you?"

Gibby smiled and looked around at his men, all of whom were enjoying the exchange. He certainly couldn't tell the man the truth, but decided to concoct a story to gain his trust.

"Alright," Gibby lied. "We're looking for someone who may be running guns from the New York City harbors. They may be stockpiling them in Jersey. We've been onto the syndicate for quite some time but haven't been able to pinpoint their ever-changing location. It's Russian mafia. Have you seen anything strange out here in the past month?"

Feeling accepted into the group, the sheriff loosened his shoulders and enjoyed the sudden attention from the agents gathering around him. He smiled confidently, shaking his head as if he knew all about the Russian mafia and other international conspiracies. Then he frowned as something sour jogged his memory.

"Well. Actually, there is... no, nothing really," he blurted in a mumbling of words.

Gibby studied the man's face and came to the realization that he was genuinely uncomfortable and rattled by something. The sudden pinkness in his face was from embarrassment, not hypertension.

"What is it?" Gibby asked, directly.

The man shifted and avoided eye contact. Gibby grabbed the man's shoulder to steady him, then he turned the man's face toward him, as if chastising a small child.

"Do *not* fuck with me! What is it?"

"There's a friend of mine, a few counties away. Every thirteenth of the month -- we consider it our *lucky* day -- we meet at the ridge where we have a little shack in the woods. We make our own stuff, you know, moonshine, I guess. But we don't sell it to anybody. We just keep it to ourselves when we go fishin'."

More agents surrounded the man, examining him as though he was on display.

"Look. I ain't a criminal. I just..."

"I don't care about the shine. Go on with your story," Gibby interrupted.

"Okay, I went to our place to meet him yesterday and Benny wasn't there. He ain't got a phone and his place is about thirty miles out. I was going to check on him now, but I came here first."

"And you've met him *every* thirteenth of the month for how long?"

"About forty years."

———————

Within the hour, the team held a near-exact position from their prior operation. They approached the target house much slower, however, after detecting cameras at the south end of the property, and trip wires in the immediate distance. The sheriff had assured Gibby that they were recent additions. Benny would never think about home security, much less video surveillance. It looked as if they had found Falby's hideout.

When the first team came into view of the clearing and the small home, they brought in the "microwave," a heat seeking x-ray device used to see through most walls. It responded to the heat of living tissue, showing a bright orange image on its attached monitor.

Preliminary scans showed only a very small occupant -- possibly a rodent or small pet -- and the team slowly advanced to the house. This time, though, Gibby was at the front of the pack, approaching with an intensity that he'd never known. He entered the home without incident and stopped within three steps, taking in the scene.

Looking to his left he saw a blue parakeet, happily chattering in a large domed cage. Then he took in the entire room as he lowered his weapon. He put his hands to his mouth, as muted words escaped pursed lips.

"Oh my God," was all the veteran agent could manage to say.

Chapter 53

LOOKING IN THE MIRROR, even Falby couldn't recognize himself; but as scary and unreal as it was, even for him, he was not at all new to the feeling. For he was a master of disguise -- a human chameleon -- completely at ease with its elaborate design and intricate detail. And however foreign his outside appearance, his thoughts remained unchecked, often evidencing the only trace of his true self.

Today was his last day in New York City, at least for a while. And just as he had done every other weekend for the last several months, he spent the balance of the morning sculpting his face with a long-perfected combination of facial putties, false teeth, contact lenses, cosmetics, and a wig he'd made himself. He then stepped into a body wrap that made him look portly and out of shape. Next, a wardrobe of old clothing dulled his appearance, exacting the look of a simple working man; someone who could fade into the background and subsequently do as he pleased. The whiskers were his own.

Studying his weathered face, he marveled at his work. A blend of carefully placed wrinkles, several shades of make-up, a random scar, and dark circles under his eyes helped create Reginald Abrams, a quiet but dedicated employee of Elway's Refuse, Inc.

The waste-management company had won the recent bid to maintain forty of New York City's largest attractions, including

Madison Square Garden, and Falby had secured part-time weekend employment there the day of the agreement. Although not reaching any formal news-reporting agency, he had looked forward to the announcement with great anticipation for months. Only then could he act.

Reginald Abrams was a resident alien with a valid passport, driver's license, and social security number. He paid his taxes and even agreed to give the three dollars to the presidential campaign fund as a joke. As far as the United States government knew, he was a silent member of the fifteen-percent tax bracket; a typical hard working grunt.

Only he knew his true motives.

Falby exited one of Madison Square Garden's restrooms, listlessly walking to the concourse level where he could see the entire arena floor. He saw several of the day crew mopping the floor and going about their daily tedium with time-practiced movements. But he also saw men he knew to be FBI agents.

They'd been hanging around for a couple of days, talking on cell phones, smoking in non-smoking areas, and trying to look important.

Falby wondered if they had somehow been informed of the terrorist action, but he knew that was impossible. Only he and Almedi Hahn Sahn knew of the attack, and Almedi didn't even know the methodology. Falby worked alone and didn't make mistakes.

He discounted the FBI men, continuing his perusal of the floor and surrounding areas. All of the trashcans were in place, forty-two in total, all with permanent concrete bases supporting the standard ninety-gallon container. But Falby had added something else to the bases stationed on the concourse level, just within the arena.

Each housed five gallons of purified Sarin, twenty pound shaped C4 charges, trembler switches, and transmitters linked to a single source that he carried in his pocket.

The detonator itself was heavily coded and riddled with booby traps. Even if he was found out, only a wit that matched his own could prevent a detonation, and that was very unlikely. Tonight there would be an explosion. Falby was absolutely certain of that!

The bombs had been in place for over a week now. The Sarin gas, which was hidden in strengthened triple layered plastic balloons, had been carefully tucked away over the last two days. A slow and painstaking process, it forced Falby to work all hours of the night, sometimes on the clock, other times as a ghost.

Falby the chameleon.

He had orchestrated the strike over a six-month period, calculating the outcome to the smallest detail. He knew the consequences and reveled in both the complexity and simplicity of its delivery: simultaneous explosions in an arena packed with people!

The bombs, though, were only the mechanism that delivered the true threat and were not intended to kill. He used small, shaped charges that were large enough to breach the concrete basin, but not hot enough to consume the poison. The bombs could account for some deaths, he knew, but the real count would result from the release of the Sarin into an environment where desperate people rushed to the exits, only to find them cut off by hordes of others. The safest place would be on the arena floor, but human nature would move them to the exits where the air would be most concentrated with the poison. A couple of breathes were all it took. He got chills thinking about it!

He had worked very diligently in manufacturing the poison, spending considerable time in mixing the compounds into the precursors to create what he estimated as over 93% pure. His mixture, he prided, was unlike the Sarin used in the Tokyo subway attacks that was less than 30% pure.

He glanced at the FBI agents once more and smiled. *You're so close but so far.* This was getting interesting, even comical to him. Even bomb-sniffing dogs were useless, as no smell could penetrate the concrete basin, which had a false bottom. And Sarin itself was odorless.

Falby still had a full hour before his shift, another five until detonation. He walked down two flights of stairs to the nearest exit, instantly joining the minions in the late afternoon air. He pondered their simple agendas, their purposes. Were theirs as glorious as his? How could they be?

Reaching for his cell phone, he hesitated, noticing the heavy foot traffic. He cursed himself for not calling Almedi earlier, but time had gotten away from him and he put more emphasis on his mission than Almedi's enlightenment.

He took a right on 31st Street heading toward 8th Avenue and the crowd dissipated considerably. As he walked further from Penn Station, he was almost alone on the street and he reached for his cell phone.

"Yes," a voice responded, and Falby recognized the familiar tone of his friend.

"Greetings from New York," he said, as he turned to confirm his privacy.

A moment of silence took over, and Falby noticed the familiar drone of international calls, the random clicking sounds that reverberated in the intercontinental void.

"Why do you wait so long to call?"

"You'll be pleased," Falby began, dodging the query and pressing the receiver closer to his lips. "McCallister is dead."

"I know. Simon told me."

"When did you talk to him?" Falby shouted automatically, quickly searching the area for anybody who might be looking his way.

"This afternoon," Almedi replied in a thick accent. Then his tone changed.

"Falby, do you trust Simon? Do his loyalties lie with us?"

Falby was taken back by the question, its bluntness and unlimited breadth. He did not like Simon for more reasons than Almedi knew, but he wasn't about to put his opinion in the open. Almedi Hahn Sahn was a complicated man and always had an agenda. Every conversation had a reason and even Falby's sense of awareness was heightened in his company.

"Well, sir," he began. "He talked too much to the general's great grandson, failed to kill McCallister the first time around, and he does have an attitude problem, but I've never questioned his allegiance to the cause."

"Thank you for your honesty," Almedi was quick to say. "How's your assignment coming?"

"Everything's in place. I'll call you in about six hours when it's over. May I ask why you inquired about Simon?"

"Something is not right, Falby. If his assignment in Chicago was not so important, I don't know. I would…"

Almedi cut himself off and in the ensuing silence Falby heard explosions and screaming on the other end. Scattered gunfire erupted and then silenced itself. Men shouted in unrecognizable tongues and Falby heard Almedi's breath come in short, hurried gasps.

"What's happening there?" Falby inserted, quickly.

"They've found the camp!"

A high pitched whistling sound drowned out his voice and a subsequent explosion cut the line, shaking Falby where he stood over eleven thousand miles away. He was confident it was a missile, quite possibly a direct hit.

Almedi Hahn Sahn, the holy leader of al Assad, was almost certainly dead.

The heart of al Assad beat no more -- the lion's roar was silenced -- and for the first time in his life, Falby was visibly shaken. Although on a different continent, he had experienced the end first hand.

Falby slowly closed the phone and rejoined the sounds of New York City, the passing vehicles, distant horns, and the footsteps of countless pedestrians walking in zombie-like stares to their intended destinations.

He started toward Madison Square Garden, searching the eyes of those he passed. He held nothing but disgust for them, the citizens of the United States of America. They were so absorbed in their own intemperance and self-preservation. So pitiful.

His thoughts returned to the evening's events. Tonight he would strike at their hearts. Ten minutes before half time at the New York Knicks game. An estimated six thousand dead!

With the future of al Assad undetermined at best, he still had a mission to accomplish and would think of nothing else until the end.

Chapter 54

GIBBY WAS IN THE DRAGON'S LAIR; there was no doubt about it! As early as this morning, he knew Falby had been in this very room. He felt the presence of evil, targeted hatred.

Overall, a total of over one-hundred feds were scouring the area, independently going about their specific duties, all searching for clues as to the terrorist's current whereabouts, more importantly his plans for the evening.

What Falby left behind was very telling, and Gibby took it as another confirmation that tonight was indeed the night of a major terrorist strike. Falby, he decided, would never have left behind so much evidence if he knew there was the remotest chance of discovery prior to the attack. But as important as these items were, there was still considerable doubt as to the location of the strike.

The inside of the home was quickly sealed off and agents in chemical suits were slowly analyzing and inventorying all of its contents. Several liquids and powders had been identified as purified Sarin, and all of the chemicals and hardware used to manufacture the poison were there. In plain view were gallons of colorless liquids with hastily-written names on their sides. What caused the most alarm were the containers of dimethyl methyl phosphanate, hydrofluoric acid, isopropyl alcohol, and the jugs labeled DC and DF.

The facility was crude, but the biochemists on-site reported that all of the pre-cursors and related compounds used to create highly purified Sarin were present, and that as much as a ton of the liquid gas could have been produced.

Unfortunately, they reported, Falby knew *exactly* what he was doing.

The parakeet, they knew, wasn't a pet, but rather used for early detection if any lethal fumes breached the protective containers. The bird's respiratory system was much faster than a human's, and as long as it was alive the environment was relatively safe.

The body of Benny Smith, the old recluse and ejected resident, had been found in a shallow grave just inside the tree line. The security system and monitors were still in place, and in studying the complicated electronics involved, Gibby was again reminded of what he was up against.

Fingerprint dusting of the entire area, both interior and exterior, was underway, but nobody was optimistic at finding a single print. Still, the forensic team went about their duties with the greatest of determination, ready to fax any findings to the FBI central processing unit in Washington. There, it could be linked to any number of international possibilities that could narrow the search.

All of Falby's personal effects were gone, except for the items remaining in the refrigerator, which in all probability belonged to the previous occupant. The FBI cataloged a vast array of fruits, vegetables, and high-fiber dietary supplements. The trash, which hadn't been taken from the property, contained several apple cores, banana peels, and V8 cans. There were no signs of anything unwholesome. Falby, it seemed, was a health nut.

Gibby reported his findings to the other team members, and called for a heightened alert from every law enforcement agency in Manhattan. This wasn't a time to be shy or carry an ego. Tonight there would certainly be an attack within the city, quite possibly an act that rivaled the actions of September 11th and at least as lethal as the bombing of the Golden Gate earlier in the week.

Gibby knew a public broadcast would be futile, bringing only panic and quite possibly rioting and looting throughout New York City. He knew it could possibly stop the attack in the short term, but probably only suspend it until a later date. Falby wouldn't be deterred so easily. Gibby understood he had little time to counter the ensuing action, but what could he do?

Looking out the kitchen window, he took a mental vacation from the stress of the day. He studied the water leading to the bay, and eventually south east to the Atlantic or north to New York City and the Long Island Sound. The afternoon sun cast random sparkles on the tips of the small waves. Beyond that, the water was calm and glass-like, olive in color. A group of sea gulls flew low to the water, and the slight breeze moved the trees that hugged the shoreline. Such natural beauty in the midst of complete chaos.

Turning his attention to the inside of the house, he studied the faces of the people around him. Was it worthless? Were they just killing time while Falby counted down to his next deadly action? Falby had probably been working on the strike for months, if not years. Gibby and his team had been on the case for only two days and were admittedly tired, feeling the sting of the lopsided contest.

He stepped through a back door and into the soft, thinning grass of the yard, which was heavily shaded by tall trees. Several agents to his right were digging for possible clues. Gibby turned left for privacy and dialed a number on his cell as he walked. Within moments, The Patriot was on the line. Steve had told Gibby to trust him implicitly. With Steve dead, Gibby was out of options. The man answered within one ring.

"How are you holding up?" Gibby started.

"As well as can be expected. I'm watching CNN right now. Every station is reporting the attack on al Assad's camps. Did you know about it?"

"I was not informed prior to the strikes, but I've been in contact with the Pentagon since."

"I've been to those camps so many times. Is everything gone? What about Almedi Hahn Sahn?"

Gibby chose his words carefully. "The strike was a total annihilation. There were no survivors and nothing was left standing. Almedi Hahn Sahn's body has been recovered and over two hundred others in six camps are also dead."

Gibby stopped talking but The Patriot didn't say a word, so he continued.

"The missiles hit several targets in Pakistan, Syria, and Algeria. A deployment of Delta's followed up and finished the job in the camp where Almedi was located."

"So it's over?"

"No. You said it yourself. Al Assad soldiers are still working on our soil. We killed the brain, but whatever Falby has planned for tonight will happen regardless."

"What do you have so far?"

"Confirmation that it's Sarin gas... probably to be unleashed in a packed, public place. Definitely tonight."

"You've been to every scheduled evening event in town, I'm sure?" The Patriot asked.

"Everything's been picked apart," Gibby said, and then he became more direct and rigid.

"Do you have any other info that could help? Anything you've forgotten? Exactly what do you know of Falby?"

"He's a master chemist, keeps to himself, and gets off on killing people in an elaborate fashion. He feeds on it."

"We already know that. Anything else?"

"No. But I know Simon's up to something in Chicago."

"You've mentioned that, too."

"Secrecy is of the highest priority, and these individual cells you're hunting may only be two or three people each."

Someone shouted in the distance and Gibby glanced down the hill, where the terrain dipped to the shoreline.

"We've got something here," Gibby said. "I'll call you back."

An agent was waving something in the air and several others were running in his direction. From the excitement, Gibby knew it was a major break.

Falby may have made a mistake after all.

Chapter 55

THE PATRIOT didn't know what to think as he reflected on his conversation with Gibby. He just sat in his hotel room despondently watching CNN. He couldn't go back from where he came; there was simply nothing left of his recent past or of the terrorist faction he had been a part of for so long. And staying in the United States could be a death sentence, with Falby, Simon, and a host of the others still alive. How long would it take before they knew he was a mole, a traitor to al Assad?

Could he just give up and assimilate back into American society? Surely he could talk with the State Department, but he knew they had wiped his slate clean. He didn't even exist!

He turned to a different news station and watched another reporter tell the same story from a different perspective. They described the capabilities and firepower used in the attack. Total and absolute annihilation!

The television report was showing file footage of an F-14 Tomcat firing missiles at a target several miles away. The sleek jet looked so domineering with its brightly colored American flag and numerical decals.

Then, in a sudden moment of enlightenment, The Patriot almost fell off the bed. He ran to the hotel dresser and to the small piece of paper that rested on top; the note that Steve had taken from the would-be terrorist assassin three nights before. He read it excitedly.

'NY3T3C1A1.' He knew what it meant!

Picking up the phone, he dialed information, quickly asking for the customer service department for Trans Continental Airlines.

"Thank you for choosing Trans Continental Airlines, how may I help you?" an eager customer representative stated in a rehearsed but appealing manner.

"I'm checking on TCA flight #3311, possibly departing from or arriving to the New York area in the near future."

The Patriot patiently waited as he heard the clicking sounds of a busy computer keyboard.

"I've got TCA flight #3311 from New York LaGuardia to Reagan National, leaving at 7:25 p.m. this evening."

The Patriot tightened his grip on the telephone receiver. His whole body seemed afire and he realized he was sweating. He then glanced at the digital clock beside him, which showed a time of just after 5 p.m.

"Is there something that I can help you with, sir?"

In an even tone, The Patriot asked for a one way ticket to D.C. and subsequently provided information to pay for a first class reservation.

Tonight, his lifetime mission would be completed. He would silently save the lives of hundreds, maybe even thousands of unknowing Americans, and possibly kill a handful of the remaining al Assad soldiers in the process.

He knew exactly what al Assad was planning to do. Two terrorist strikes, one in New York City, the other in Washington D.C. Gibby had his hands full in New York. The Patriot, he decided, would take care of D.C.

This evening was the White House State Dinner. The president would play host to leaders and VIP's of over one hundred governments and organizations. His entire cabinet except for the Secretary of the Interior would be in attendance.

It made so much sense! Al Assad was simultaneously operating on two fronts. Even if the government was semi-aware of their operations, their efforts to counter would obviously be diluted.

Al Assad was going to show up at the White House in a plane. They were going to crash into it!

He played out the scenarios in his head over and over and finally decided that only *he* could thwart the attack. Exposing the plot too early would just suspend the action. It was all up to him, but he knew if he were to fail, U.S. aircraft would have to blow the plane out of the sky.

The Patriot quickly scribbled his suspicions and folded the paper neatly. He would leave it at the front desk in an envelope and contact the FBI moments after take-off.

Chapter 56

A SATISFIED LOOK played on Falby's normally expressionless face and a rare smile formed at the corners of his small, rounded mouth. A tingling feeling came over him and embraced him with a warmth he rarely felt. Never had he been this charged and he loved the thrill!

When he bombed the Golden Gate, he wasn't witness to the detonation, and even with the minimal amount of departure, he didn't feel an absolute part of the experience.

Tonight, though, he would be among his victims and see their faces. He would be party to the very chaos he would create; his most intimate terrorist strike yet. Everything was in his favor and he knew it.

There was only an hour before game time and the terrorist eyed the concourse level intently, watching as hordes of excited fans rushed to their designated seats in anticipation of the night's game. The New York Knicks were gaining in their conference and the playoffs were on everyone's minds. Tonight they hosted the Toronto Raptors and the fans were showing up to bear witness.

Groups of families were led by stressed parents; many carrying cardboard platters bending from the weight of drinks, fries, pizza, and other mass-produced slop. Others, dressed completely in Knicks attire, carried in newly purchased, colorfully branded banners, pennants, and other merchandise boasting the team's logo.

The players had just finished their pre-game warm-up, leaving the court, no doubt to hear the coach's last minute ideas, or maybe lend an ear to a motivational speech and obligatory pre-game prayer.

Falby and his fellow custodians were charged with a final sweep of the floor. Everything had to be properly cleaned and dried at least thirty minutes before tip-off. But unlike the others, he put little effort into the mindless task, his eyes again floating up to the concourse level and peripherally to the forty-two trash bins. *His* forty-two trash bins. *I have a surprise for all of you,* he thought. *Come on in and have a seat. The **real** show will begin just before half time!*

As usual, the floor was clean in less than ten minutes and the group quickly made their way to the exits at court level, which were now lined with police officers and the arena's own security. Any bustling of activity was now limited to the stands, where the fans kept pouring in with obvious anticipation.

Falby gave a final glance at the increasing crowd before going underneath. Most of the other custodians would take a freight elevator to their elected areas and join more than a hundred others in maintaining order until game's end.

Falby was one of ten janitors designated to the private "staff-only" areas and he was thankful to not be among the crowd in the minutes before game time.

He left his coworkers without a word, walking through a door and into a long corridor with a worn, gray-painted floor. The hallway connected the visitor's locker room with the administrative offices at the west-end, before it forked and stopped at two exits, one interior to the arena, the other to the outside. In analyzing the arena's blueprints several month's prior, he'd determined it to be the most strategic place to be.

There were a series of doors on the right side, the top sections of which were made of smoked glass. With time to kill, he stopped at the first door to check his appearance. The bright fluorescent ceiling lights created an opaque effect due to the darkness on the other side of the door, and he took a few moments to look himself over, again admiring his disguise.

Next, his eyes moved to the door which he'd just come through and upward to where a small painted box perfectly melted into the cinderblock wall. Then, looking down the corridor, he saw the other block demolition charges placed every twenty feet. The curve in the hall ended his line of sight, but he knew that the bombs were all in their intended positions, left unmolested since their placement the day before. There were two dozen in all, the last of them just outside the exterior alley door. They would help to effect a hasty exit if need be. Falby always planned for contingencies, often having several escape routes planned well in advance. The nickname his comrades had chosen long ago -- The Chameleon -- was well suited.

Satisfied, he put his broom to the floor, going through the motions of the dedicated employee. A quick check of his watch revealed another fifteen minutes to game time. That, he decided, was the point of no return. As improbable as it was, even if his intentions were discovered, there was nothing anyone could do after tip-off. He would simply detonate earlier than expected, be a little less successful.

As he made wide sweeping movements with the broom, he entertained thoughts of al Assad, Almedi Hahn Sahn, and his own future. He had intently watched the news in the employee break room, studying the television with an icy, concentrated stare. Every trace of al Assad -- the camps, the supplies, the soldiers -- were destroyed; the only remains of the faction being the handful of soldiers that were operating on American soil. Would they carry on after tonight? Would he? Or should he flee and live a comfortable life?

He'd been well paid for his mercenary efforts and the duty allowed him to explore the outer reaches of himself and mankind. He had seen it all and done it all. Was it time to retire?

He decided to couch the thought until later, turning his attention to the broom he was gripping so firmly. But he couldn't concentrate. One question kept tugging at him and he knew he could not make any material plans until he knew the answer. Loose ends were simply not tolerated. How did they know where Almedi Hahn Sahn was and what camps to hit? There must have been a mole! Then he remembered his leader's last inquiry. *'Do you trust Simon?'*

Was Simon a traitor? As much as he hated the man, he didn't want to believe it. He knew Simon was in Chicago and working on another terrorist action, with Falby hoped as much thought and methodical detail as he. But that was the extent of his knowledge regarding the man.

Falby *did* know that another action would be coupled with tonight's, but was unaware of its nature or exact timing. He would have to watch CNN later, and of course hear the talk of his own strike. Both attacks, he knew, would make every newspaper in the world!

His watch chirped, signaling a mere ten minutes before game time.

But then he heard the footsteps, several of them, resonating against the concrete surroundings. He couldn't see who it was, but he knew it couldn't be good. Not at this hour.

Still, he automatically pushed his broom toward the sounds, walking deliberately toward the unknown foe. With his right hand, he fingered the detonator, which was just inside his breast pocket. Feeling its bulk lent him confidence and he quickened his pace.

When they came into view, they were about forty feet away, stiff-arming pistols and taking cautious but steady strides. Two men wore the customary blue suits, starched white shirt with quiet ties, and cheap black shoes. They each wore their hair high and tight, not unlike Marines, and they looked at him with confident stares that only came with age, experience, or ego. Judging by their young faces, Falby decided on the latter. The man in the middle was dressed casually, with khaki pants and a loosely buttoned blue shirt. He was small and wore wire-rimmed glasses, but he appeared to be the agent in charge and his stance communicated a greater presence.

Falby knew right away they were feds, and although he'd never met the small, balding man in the middle, he recognized him immediately. Studying the enemy was something he always did.

With visual confirmation, both sides came to an abrupt stop, considering the surroundings and quickly calculating all favorable outcomes. Falby straightened, squaring himself against the group, who already had their weapons leveled. Two of the FBI agents assumed a rigid textbook stance, their elbows at right angles, their fire-arms a very extension of their long, thick arms.

Undaunted, Falby tossed the broom to the side, letting it fall with a loud crack against the concrete wall. The small man in the middle spoke first.

"Hello Falby," Special Agent James Gibson said. "What are you planning to do this evening?"

Chapter 57

AT THE END it was so simple, with two things happening almost simultaneously to bring the authorities directly to Falby.

The agent at the water's edge had uncovered a small, discarded portion of an event ticket. It was for a concert at Madison Square Garden a couple weeks prior and had probably traveled inadvertently on the sole of someone's shoe. Falby's shoe. The terrorist had some reason to be at the event, and the authorities suspected that he'd taken a job at the arena.

Minutes later, the old recluse's boat and Falby's likely mode of transport into lower Manhattan, had been discovered in an area marina. No prints or physical evidence were found, but the owner of the marina described a very strange man who would come and go at odd times, usually in the evenings and very late at night. Always on weekends. The times and dates easily corresponded with recent events at Madison Square Garden, and almost every available agent converged on the arena and its perimeter. The police were finally brought into the know, and the thousands of gas masks that Gibby had requested days earlier were dispatched to The Garden.

It was decided that if Falby would unleash Sarin into a crowd, he would almost certainly wait until the crowd was at its largest. Gibby's first call was to the men he already had at the arena. They immediately went to the security room that monitored almost every area.

The night manager was given a vague description of the suspect, but positive identification wasn't established until they described his likely personality: humble and friendly, but in the last few days, introverted and distracted. This, the manager revealed, fit one of the weekend crew's demeanor exactly, and they located him sweeping a secluded hallway under the arena floor.

Keeping an open frequency, Gibby was informed of the suspect's location and a rudimentary strategy was assembled. Without any further information about the strike itself, he still felt at a loss to effectively counter Falby's efforts. Should he keep the terrorist isolated and evacuate? Or should his men neutralize him immediately?

With an estimated ten thousand already in attendance and more than half that in the immediate area awaiting entry, he decided to partially initiate both plans, quickly and quietly, until more information became available.

By the time Gibby and his men arrived, almost thirty minutes had passed and Falby was still alone as a slow evacuation continued. Agents were positioned at every exit, security had cut off all entry to the building, and a steady flow of bewildered, sometimes-angry people were rushed out.

Another crucial decision came into play as five thousand gas masks arrived at the delivery docks and were moved near the arena floor. Disbursement, they knew, would evoke panic and breed chaos, the noise alone alerting Falby to the evacuation. The diminishing crowd would force him to deliver the poison and Gibby couldn't take that chance. He decided to keep the gas masks out of sight but readily available.

Although about a third of the people were still in the arena, Gibby made the decision to move on Falby. Game time was only minutes away, and although Gibby believed otherwise, he feared that tip-off could very well be Falby's strike time.

When Gibby first saw the terrorist, he noticed his eyes, and they were looking right back at his own. They were cold and direct, showing no sign of concern or the slightest suggestion of discomfort. Falby apparently feared nothing and that concerned Gibby immediately. How could he feel in complete control? It just wasn't reasonable.

The second thing Gibby noticed was what Falby was holding in his right hand. Realization came quickly and the unknowns came together in an instant of enlightenment and horrific understanding. Falby had a bomb -- or more likely several of them -- linked in some way with Sarin gas. And the detonator was in his hand!

Despite what he felt, Gibby eyed Falby confidently, speaking in an even tone.

"Hello Falby. What are you planning to do this evening?"

The man stood for a moment, taking time to contemplate the inquiry, outwardly enjoying the exchange. It gave Gibby a moment to check the status of the arena and he lightly tapped a microphone on his lapel, speaking in a hushed whisper.

"Status on the populace?"

"About three-thousand and decreasing," a muffled voice responded in Gibby's ear piece.

Gibby grimaced. They may have moved too soon. "Deliver the packages," he shot back.

Falby allowed the interruption, watching the agent's faces hint at something unfavorable. He chose his words carefully and then spoke slowly, making no attempt to hide a thick, German accent.

"Tonight I make history. You will feel my brunt and it's just the beginning!"

The FBI men maintained their positions, the two agents flanking Gibby holding their aim. Gibby eyed Falby carefully, searching every part of his being and looking for anything that he could use to counter. Time seemed to stand still.

What worried Gibby most was the air of absolute confidence that emanated from Falby; his feigned control of the situation. Surely the terrorist knew that every exit was blocked and that he was as good as in custody already. But the killer showed no sign of worry or of the FBI having compromised his strategy. It seemed as though Falby had his hand on a detonator, two trained guns aimed at his head, and he was not even thinking of an escape route! What was The Chameleon thinking?

Al Assad was a force to be reckoned with and Falby was an icy, highly accomplished and motivated killer. The thought of more of his kind chilled Gibby to the bone. Sure he had Falby in his sights, but what of the others that were operating in an unknown number of U.S. cities?

Gibby loosely determined how to accomplish as many goals as possible within the smallest of time frames. He had to stall Falby so the evacuation could continue, prevent the madman from detonating any bombs, and protect his men while attempting to take the killer down.

Gibby decided to leverage what Falby didn't think him capable of knowing.

"Falby," he began, palms extended. "It's all over. The entire place is surrounded."

"Nothing's over, Agent Gibson. The game has just started and you are mere players. Even *you* must know that."

Hearing his own name flow so easily over Falby's venomous tongue made Gibby weak, but no outward manifestation was apparent.

"You *know* it's over." Gibby repeated. "Al Assad is gone. You have no home."

"I don't live there and I'm certainly *not* doing this for them. This one's for me, a personal favor granted by the man himself."

Gibby decided on another direction, taking a moment to construct his thoughts. He had one piece of information that could shake Falby. The Patriot had informed him that Simon was operating in Chicago, and the recent events of al Assad's demise -- being so absolute and timely -- begged for answers that couldn't be immediately known.

"You know Simon told us of your little plan tonight. Almedi Hahn Sahn informed him of it this morning. Sarin gas, a large crowd. This, of course, was just before he eluded us for Chicago. Man he loves to talk!"

Gibby studied the man in the ensuing moments, and although Falby still held a concentrated stare, something within him stirred, suggesting a weakness behind his hostile gaze. Gibby knew he had chipped away at something crucial and he took advantage of the distraction while thinking about what was likely happening just above them at the arena floor.

The packages Gibby referred to had been the gas masks and butyl rubber protective suits; but also the thousands of syringes and boxes of atropine sulfate and pralidoxime salts, which would be used as an immediate on-site countermeasure if anyone was exposed.

"Falby, it's over," Gibby started again, this time in a much more casual tone. He allowed his eyes to wander, taking them off his foe for the first time in the highly energized exchange. "You have nothing to gain."

Falby absorbed the words, letting out a deep sigh and closing his eyes. But when he quickly reopened them, a menacing look came over his face and Gibby knew the killer would detonate the bombs and/or release the Sarin.

"Take him!" Gibby shouted, and gunfire sounded in the tiny corridor.

Falby fell against the wall, covering his head with quick hands, and it wasn't immediately known if he'd been hit by any of the spent rounds. As sulfur and smoke filled the air, a larger eruption sounded from far above.

The bombs had detonated.

The FBI men instinctively crouched, covering their heads with one hand, while maintaining a tight grip of their weapons. The sound was deafening and they feared the ceiling would come tumbling down. Worried expressions were evident but nothing happened, save the unified sounds of muted screams and the rumbling movements of the thousands above.

Falby still lay motionless as an increasing bloodstain appeared on his left shoulder. Both hands were in easy sight and his body snaked at a curvy angle. He still held his head in his hands. Now with three guns concentrated on him, the terrorist made a final statement

"Now it's half over," Falby said, and he tapped the detonator once more.

Instantly, a series of louder explosions erupted in the long hall and the three FBI men were thrown against the wall with a force that rendered them helpless. Falby had prepared for the blast and crouched away from the explosions. Now standing, he glanced in both directions, noticing several fires and a swiftly moving wall of white smoke.

Applying pressure to his shoulder, the killer ran; jumping over debris caused by the forty pound shaped charges that had cleared a path to the outside alley. There, he assumed there would be several other dead FBI agents, the unfortunate fools who thought they could simply cut off the exit. The heaviest of the C4 had been placed in the exterior alley wall.

As he reached the door, he found it open and on fire. He pushed it with his gun and saw the bodies of several men, most dead, others awake but incoherent.

He stepped over them with ease and looked outward to the street, some fifty feet away. There was a mass of people and yellow tape was strung across the outer buildings, but there were no other signs of authority in the space in between, and even Falby thought this odd.

He began a brisk walk toward Penn Station. From there The Chameleon was as good as gone.

Chapter 58

THE PATRIOT RUSHED from the hotel in a furious bundle of energy. The evening air was crisp and refreshing, strangely unaffected by the exhaust fumes from the grouping of taxis nearby. The air bit mildly at his face, which was flushed from the mad dash from his second floor room.

Although hurried, he slowed to regard the evening sky, studying it as if it were the first time. Knowing this may be his last night alive, it took on a different posture and he cursed himself for not considering it before.

He saw the streaks of blurred reds and oranges in the west sky as they were absorbed into the blue darkness of the east in their ancient, daily battle. A few airplanes were apparent; the red lights at their extremities showing them silently streak across the sky at an exaggeratedly slow pace. The first flickering star was barely noticeable, and he nostalgically made a wish -- a want for a safe end to what could be the deadliest night in American history.

The Patriot motioned to a waiting cab and its driver shuffled a newspaper aside, inching to the curb expectedly. He entered the car swiftly and leaned forward to speak to the driver, throwing a hundred-dollar bill on the passenger seat.

"LaGuardia. There's an extra hundred if we make it in twenty minutes. I'll pay triple any traffic tickets."

A quick nod put the passenger at ease and after a sudden burst of the accelerator, The Patriot settled into his seat, closed his eyes, and began preparing a mental game plan.

The realization of what al Assad was planning came quickly; the White House State Dinner was a perfect target for any terrorist faction. If they could pull it off, it would be the final 'Fuck you' in a campaign that had already left a bloody trail.

His mind worked wildly on a way to counter the alleged attack as his senses shut off all distractions around him.

Should he call the authorities? Informing them would indeed prevent the strike and be a short-term win, but it could also put unwanted attention on him and wouldn't stop a future attack. Knowing the faction he'd been apart of for so long, he knew every detail had been carefully planned months in advance, and even intervention from the authorities wouldn't stop the assault in the long-term. Al Assad rarely faltered. The attack, whether sooner or later, was imminent if not fated.

He tried to think of the strategy they would employ. Would they hijack the planes like the attacks of 9/11? How could they get inside the cockpit with the door bolted? How many of them would there be? And would they recognize him as an al Assad soldier? Sure he was al Assad, but how could he explain his presence? He could only take down three or four with his bare hands. Any more would be up to God, luck, or both.

Then he entertained an idea so horrific that he hoped it wasn't true. What if the legitimate flight crew *were* the terrorists? What if one or all of them were part of a sleeper cell that had been working years, perhaps decades, for this very day? With the correct credentials and work history, no one would have any idea of their Kamikaze flight until a few minutes before impact. With the cabin door bolted from the inside, only a miracle of intervention could save the souls on board and the several thousand at the White House.

No, he decided. He would be on the plane and stop the strike personally. Was it time for him to fulfill his lifetime mission; finally be the hero? A part of him almost longed for the final chapter, the end of a life that had been so turbulent and unsettling. Ultimate patriotism had brought him into the life he'd led for almost thirty years, but he had aged far beyond that; seen and done things in the name of democracy that were unthinkable.

The taxi screamed around a corner and The Patriot could see La-Guardia coming into sight. A quick show of his watch indicated less than an hour before take-off, which was more than enough time. He was not checking baggage, his identification was impeccable, and he had a first class paid reservation. He closed his eyes and decided to focus on the short-term details, couching the more important items until he was closer to boarding.

Once inside the gate he would lock himself in a bathroom stall, keeping out of sight to psychologically prepare for the hours ahead. When in the air, he would find the lavatory and make a very important phone call.

Special Agent James Gibson opened his eyes, knowing he had been unconscious, but not knowing for how long. The dust hadn't settled and his wounds were still very fresh. From a nearby puddle of his own blood, he deduced he'd been out just a few minutes.

Above and around him, he heard screaming sirens, no doubt coming from a variety of emergency, rescue, and police vehicles racing to the scene. Adding to the chaos were thousands of people, mostly in the streets and dispersing quickly.

Falby was gone.

Gibby immediately noticed the two FBI agents that had accompanied him just moments prior. Looking them over, he knew they were dead, each taking direct hits from the unseen bombs in the close walls. Being between the men had isolated Gibby, and although he was alive, he felt no desire to celebrate. Shaking, he finally stood and began to walk through the smoky corridor, seeking outside air. Once there, like many others, he would seek the answers to countless questions.

His thoughts rushed forward to what had to be done in the next few hours, days, and months. They had no doubt just felt the full force of a terrorist strike from a regime that was supposedly destroyed just hours before. How many more could there be? How many more *would* there be?

Al Assad had brought a war into the United States, creating a front that encompassed the entire country; its horror no doubt finding a home in every American. The only positive was that he was able to tell Falby that Simon had told him of the strike. Although an obvious lie, Gibby had noticed Falby stir. Uncertainty played on the terrorist's face, and Gibby knew that Falby would confront Simon, wherever he was. If that trail could be followed, they would certainly find both terrorists and undoubtedly one would be dead.

The weary FBI man found the blasted door to the outside world and the bodies of many dead agents just beyond the opening, all victims of Falby's escape plan. Gibby removed his jacket, loosened his tie and stretched. He felt as though a truck had hit him, and although blood flowed from wounds over his entire body, he knew they were not life threatening.

He was appalled at the scene, and a strange combination of grief and anger welled inside of him. At the same time, a helpless feeling arose and he felt immobilized, even small, in a world that was spinning out of control.

Then his cell phone rang, an odd reminder that despite the chaos enveloping the area, the world moved on unchecked and undisturbed. He unfolded the small unit, straightened the antenna, and spoke into the receiver as calmly as he could.

"Special Agent James Gibson."

"Listen up Gibby," the familiar voice of The Patriot said.

And Gibby quickly realized that things had just gotten even worse.

Chapter 59

THE PATRIOT BOARDED TCA flight #3311 without incident and found seat 8B, which was the last row in first class on the right. It was an aisle seat, as promised, perfect for moving in an instant's notice. Mobility, he knew, would be the most important counter measure.

He studied the other passengers with heightened senses, his adrenaline running on an all time high. The flight was not full and for that he was thankful. If he was correct and this *was* a Kamikaze high jacked flight, he'd rather it happen with less people on board.

There was a large cross-section of travelers, representing many different cultures and races, further divided by age and gender. But no one fit the typical stereotype of a highjacker. If there were terrorists on board, they certainly had him fooled.

But then an Arab man nervously entered the plane, quickly shuffling down the aisle and systematically moving into the window seat next to his. He seemed to have the plane's seat chart memorized, not having to look for the seat number before sitting down, and this drew suspicion from The Patriot immediately. The man's eyes also focused on The Patriot, as a smile eased across his bearded face.

"Hello Hortence," he whispered, as he passed in front of him. "I didn't know you were going to be on board."

The Patriot looked at the man thoughtfully, showing little emotion and calculating all choices of words. He didn't know the man, nor did he ever remember meeting him. But this was not uncommon. The man was not an al Assad soldier like him, or even Simon or Falby. His was a holy war against the United States; his own personal jihad.

Al Assad itself was divided, with suicide strikes being carried out by true Arab Muslims with an unrivaled hate of western culture. The more elaborate and deadly strikes were conducted by mercenaries like Hortence, Simon, and Falby.

The Patriot waited for the man to sit down, and then leaned closer to him and spoke in a whisper.

"Tonight we make history," Hortence said. "With the sunset of our brotherhood, I thought I would participate in the final act."

The man shook his head so Hortence continued, eager to establish a dialogue.

"How many others are here?"

A flight attendant made her way through the aisle, checking seatbelts and offering drinks, blankets, and pillows. He paused long enough to stop the conversation, and the man turned to look out the window. Hortence could see the man's mouth moving slowly and realized he was in deep prayer, confirming what Hortence thought all along. He was on a plane that would be crashed into the White House.

Looking to the cockpit, Hortence noticed that the door was already locked and secured. There were only three passengers in first class.

The plane pushed from the gate and Hortence thought it took unusually long to get into the number one position for take-off. The passengers were eerily silent, and other than a few random coughs and sneezes, nothing managed to be louder than the dull drone of the powerful engines. Then the intercom speakers came to life.

"Good evening ladies and gentlemen, greetings from the flight deck. This is your captain speaking. We are currently third in line for take-off to Reagan National, where the current weather conditions are partly cloudy skies with a temperature of forty-nine degrees. Our flight time will be fifty-six minutes at a cruising altitude of thirty-four thousand feet. We certainly enjoy having you with us this evening and invite you to sit back, relax, and enjoy the flight. We'll be departing shortly. Flight attendants prepare for departure."

Moments later the plane took off easily and eventually leveled off. Hortence immediately went to the front lavatory. There, he took out his cell phone and dialed James Gibson, telling him of the situation and where it was heading.

He promised the FBI man that he would overpower the plane's crew and divert it into Dulles, but that shooting it down might be the most appropriate strategy. Leaving the impossible decision open, Hortence ended the call, shut off his phone, and took an extra few moments assessing things.

From what he could tell there was only one terrorist on board, but surely one or two of the crew were involved, and that meant the plane may have been high jacked upon take-off.

Complicating things was the possibility of an undercover air marshal, as well as the legitimate flight staff, and over eighty passengers that could give him trouble. With no one knowing the plane's ill-fated mission, *he* would be seen as the aggressor, having to overpower all who stood in his way. Once he gained access to the cockpit, his problems compounded. He'd had general flight training in the Special Forces and certain innate tasks are never forgotten, but a commercial airliner was obviously a different animal altogether.

He exited the lavatory as a strange feeling of confidence came over him. His past flashed by him in a matter of seconds, and he remembered the good things he'd done and what he'd accomplished, albeit unnoticed, for the love of his country. He hoped for a positive outcome, but did not fear failure.

Hortence -- The Patriot -- returned to his seat and began eyeing the cockpit door with discreet enthusiasm.

Chapter 60

HORTENCE EASED into the seat, his hand cradling his chin, his eyes staring pointedly but seeing nothing. His body felt afire and his mind was racing; trying to exact a positive outcome to the dangerous situation he had so eagerly become a part of.

At cruising altitude, the 757 held at a slight upward angle, and Hortence found it easy to lie back in the over-sized, black leather seat. The plane's monotonous drone enveloped him, the pitch rising and falling at random; and he could picture the nose of the plane slicing through the air with delicate ease, getting ever so closer to Washington D.C. and its eventual peril.

From his view in first class, he could see the cockpit door and calculated only a matter of twenty feet of separation. Then, with a casual diagonal glance, he studied a single man several seats away that he thought was a federal air marshal.

Hortence had noticed the man upon entry. Caucasian, young, and military-looking, he appeared very serious and focused. The man had studied the people boarding intensely, and seemed more interested in his immediate environment than relaxing during the short flight. True, Hortence's skills at combat were time-proven and rarely matched, but the air marshal looked very physical and was likely armed with at least one gun. Was he one of the highjackers?

Hortence hoped he didn't have to fight the man but it seemed inevitable. No matter what course of action was taken, the federal agent had to be immobilized. Still, Hortence thought through the circumstances, quickly calculating the odds to a positive outcome.

If the air marshal was party to the terrorist act, he would have to be killed in the process of gaining control of the plane. The alternative was more complex. If the man was truly ignorant to the happenings, then *Hortence* would be seen as the aggressor, and the air marshal would be lawfully obliged to stop *him* and unknowingly enable the terrorist plot.

Hortence knew the airplane would be highjacked but wasn't sure how it could be commandeered. Furthermore, he didn't know how many terrorists were on the doomed flight, so he silently tested several scenarios.

He first thought of the locked cock pit door and how a terrorist could gain access. If someone could immobilize the air marshal and get a weapon, then he or she could possibly, albeit doubtfully, call into the cockpit from the flight attendant station and threaten any number of things to gain entry. Still, the rest of the passengers would have to allow it to happen, which would be dubious considering the lessons of September 11.

The plane turned slightly and Hortence checked his watch. Time was running out. He also decided that the plan he'd just entertained would take time, and with the flight more than half over it was out of the question.

Realization came quickly. The plane *was* highjacked by the flight crew! Either one or all of them he didn't know, but it was highjacked none the less.

Then he thought of the air marshal. He *couldn't* be a terrorist; there would be nothing gained by his presence. If the plane was highjacked by the legitimate flight crew and secretly on a Kamikaze course, with the cabin door locked and the control tower not keen to anything out of the ordinary, there was very little to thwart the plan.

Hortence knew he was sitting next to an al Assad loyalist, but he was perplexed by the man's role. Was he there only as a passive observer, carrying out his own form of jihad? Were any other passengers in the know, and more importantly how many of the flight crew?

If Hortence was correct, at about one thousand feet the plane would make a sweeping deviation from its intended runway at Reagan National, racing toward the White House and covering the short distance in mere moments.

True, Hortence had contacted Gibby, and no doubt the White House was under evacuation, multiple fighter jets would soon intercept the plane -- if they hadn't already -- and the pilot was certainly being ordered to alternative flight coordinates.

But then the airplane slowed and a long mechanical noise extended from its belly. They were beginning their descent!

The pilot's voice came over the intercom, updating the current weather conditions in Washington and promising a landing in less than fifteen minutes. Hortence ignored the message as he stared blankly at the air marshal, not knowing how to proceed but knowing he had to move quickly.

This moment was half a lifetime in the making and he would not waiver. From an elite Special Forces unit in Vietnam, to the jungles of South America and through the deserts of the Middle East, Hortence had secretly and devotedly served his country, forsaking everything else, most certainly his own safety. But now he had to complete one more mission, most certainly his last.

He closed his eyes for a moment and considered his mortality, something he had rarely contemplated. Would his remains be incinerated if the plane were to crash? Or if he died with his body intact, would it be treated like any other "John Doe" without any identification, either being cremated or given a simple burial?

Although he never sought military recognition, he did want a formal military burial. Only then would he truly be at rest. Sure he didn't exist in the eyes of his country, but he *had* invisibly and diligently given as much as the honored dead at Arlington National Cemetery.

But why should he expect to be treated differently in death than in life? He was in effect dead already, completely forgotten by his country. A walking ghost.

Suddenly, a warm feeling eclipsed him, a combination of adrenaline and anxiety, which had almost become innate within him. He turned to the al Assad loyalist to find him staring through the window in a hypnotized gaze.

Hortence glanced around the first class cabin and when satisfied, leaned a few inches off his seat and placed his large hands on the man's neck. Without resistance, he violently snapped it back and forth and felt the neck break, the bones now loose within his grasp.

He let the limp head fall gently against the window, noticing the body tense and then release. He saw the man had relieved himself post-mortem, and Hortence placed a navy blue blanket across his bulk to conceal the wetness. The dead man looked pleasantly asleep and nobody had noticed a thing.

Hortence knew this was just the beginning. He allowed himself a few moments of repose, discreetly regarding his immediate environment and watching for the flight staff.

He again looked to the air marshal just four seats in front and across the aisle. Facing front, his head was tilted to the left, and Hortence pondered the ensuing attack. Although approaching from the rear, he knew it wouldn't be easy. The man looked very strong, and in a sitting position could push off the floor and gain the upper hand. Hortence also knew nothing of the man's training, and non-information was always a vulnerability when initiating a fight.

He silently made his way up the aisle, happy there were no other passengers in the front cabin. He leveled his breathing, quietly sliding to the seat behind the man and hunching over to begin the assault.

Without hesitation and with surgeon-like precision, Hortence's right fist quickly struck the man's nose, retreating only to land another blow to the abdomen. The man contorted as his body shrunk into the seat, and Hortence knew he had broken his nose and knocked the wind from him. Now mostly incapacitated, Hortence swung around to unleash the final blows.

The man made no attempt to defend himself as he frantically tried to speak.

"Please. Please stop!" he blurted.

But Hortence's fist did not recoil. His left hand aggressively held the man's collar as his right hand landed blow after deafening blow. After several connections, Hortence withdrew only to search the man's jacket for weaponry and identification. In a matter of seconds he held two 9 millimeter handguns and the man's wallet.

Hortence loosened his grip and moved to face the man, his eyes studying his credentials, as he pocketed one gun and leveled the other at the bloodied man's mid-section. His instincts were correct; the man's identification showed him to be a federal air marshal.

"What're you doing?" the man hissed, spitting blood, his hands ready to defend another attack.

"Shut up and listen. We don't have much time. I can't go into detail with who I am, but this airplane is highjacked and we've gotta stop it."

The man regained some composure and looked to Hortence skeptically.

"What're you talking about? We're landing in ten minutes!"

"The flight crew themselves are the highjackers, and we will not be landing. We'll be crashing into the White House."

"How do you know this?" the man countered, his eyes leaving Hortence for the first time and looking for the flight staff.

"I can't go into it but it's true."

"Show me some ID," the man said, gaining strength and testing a foothold of authority.

"If I was in on the plot or had my own agenda, do you think I'd be having this conversation with you? Waste all this time?"

The man thought it through, still eyeing Hortence incredulously.

"What're you going to do?"

"Not me. *We* are going to get into the cockpit and retake the plane."

"This is crazy, you expect me to…"

"Take a look out your window," Hortence conceded, waving the gun at the interior wall.

The air marshal looked to his right and slid open the plastic covering, peering through the window.

"I don't see anything."

"Look as far as you can to the rear and into the distance. I'm sure they wouldn't be flanking us for fear of what it would do to the passengers."

The man did as he was told, straining his neck and leaning into the small window. Even in the dark sky, he saw three military jets about a thousand yards out, all maintaining a safe but controlled distance. But they were definitely there.

"Oh my God," he muttered, and then he turned to face his attacker.

"But how do I know they're not here because of *you*?"

Hortence's face pained as he kneeled in one of the vacant seats.

"Don't you think they're in contact with the flight crew, and you'd be privy to this if the pilot was legitimate?"

Seeing the air marshal's acceptance, Hortence continued.

"I'm not the bad guy here and I guess *you are* right. You must take a leap of faith. But look me in the eye, for whatever it's worth. *I swear to you* this is happening and I *will* take that cockpit, with or without your help. I have kept you alive because I want you as a resource, but my generosity has limits and we're running out of time."

The air marshal slowly stood, bloodied but surprisingly composed, as he used the backing of a nearby seat to steady himself. Hortence moved with him, maintaining a comfortable void, still training his weapon on the man and not convinced of his loyalty.

"Just to confirm, if I were the bad guy the pilot would be in conversation with you, correct?"

"That is protocol, yes."

"Good. I'm gonna assume the best then," Hortence said. "You can decide to shoot me or we can deal with the *real* crisis and try to save lives."

Hortence handed the air marshal the wallet and one of the guns he'd taken from him moments earlier. Then, he moved to the front serving station and retrieved a towel.

"Clean yourself up. You look like shit," Hortence said, cracking a small smile and throwing the towel at the man.

"What do you want me to do?" the man asked, taking the towel and wiping his face.

"Do you go by Tom or Thomas?" Hortence asked, remembering the man's credentials.

"Tom."

"Well Tom, we need to get into the cabin and retake the aircraft. We should involve the flight staff so we can make it more legitimate."

Suddenly the curtain opened and quickly closed with a scraping sound, catching the two men by surprise. A flight attendant entered from the rear and approached with vigor.

"Take your seats, gentlemen!" she said with controlled authority. "We are beginning our descent."

The two looked at each other uneasily, each knowing how trite her words were.

"Are you okay?" she gasped, looking at Tom's bloodied face.

The air marshal quickly moved the towel over his face, wiping away some of the blood from his fresh wounds. Then he motioned for Hortence and the flight attendant to join him near the front of the plane.

Once there, he lowered his voice to a whisper and showed her his identification. Hortence thought it fitting Tom should speak to her, seeing as he had federal authority and the necessary credentials.

"There's no right way to say this ma'am, but I'm a federal air marshal and this plane is highjacked."

The words hit her hard. She backed into the wall and unfolded a staff seat, sitting dumbfounded. Then she put her hands to her face.

"No!" she cried. "Where are they?"

"In the cockpit."

"How?"

"The perps are the pilots themselves, but they have no idea that we know."

The two men studied the woman as her face played a revelry of emotions.

Then the plane swooped down, losing altitude with a subtle right turn. Understanding the slight movement to be a prelude to a not-so-distant landing, Hortence was suddenly direct as he turned to Tom.

"How many rounds do you have?"

"Fifteen in the clip, two other clips right here," he responded, patting his left jacket pocket.

Hortence checked his own clip, happy to see all fifteen.

"Do you know the cabin door code?" Hortence asked the flight attendant.

"No, but I'm sure I can talk them into unlocking it."

The men looked at each other and shrugged, finding no better alternative. She eased to the door and put her ear against it. Both Tom and Hortence crouched in strike formation.

Straightening herself, she cleared her throat before gently rapping on the door.

"Captain? It's Tara. I need my purse in the compartment. I hate to ask but it's an emergency. You know, a female thing."

There was nothing but silence as the plane continued its descent.

"Captain?" she began again. "I'm really sorry."

A few moments passed without feedback, but then the door cracked and a purse was tossed out.

Immediately, Hortence kicked the door and rushed the small cockpit. The pilot glared at him, but didn't seem to be surprised at the dramatic entry. He even seemed to be expecting it!

Hortence took in the scene immediately. To his left was a member of the flight staff slumped over dead, a stale gunshot wound in his forehead. To his right, another man sat in a chair unmoving, certainly dead of the same fate. Straight ahead was the blackening sky; the ground changing quickly as the plane swept over the brownish green landscape. He could see they were about four thousand feet off the ground.

Then Hortence's eyes settled on the pilot, who held a handgun leveled directly at him. The military man knew it to be a .40 caliber Smith & Wesson, but what concerned him more was the silencer that was attached to the long barrel and the man's steady, unwavering grip of the weapon. Hortence was directly in its sight and less than four feet away. Then he heard the slight gasps of Tom and Tara as the awful scene was revealed.

Hortence saw a slight movement of the pilot's hand and heard the gentle chirp of the weapon. He immediately fell to the floor, feeling a sudden hotness in his chest. Then he heard two more shots and the short-lived cries of his two new friends.

His last thoughts were of the people he had failed, the thousands that had unknowingly depended on him. His hands clutched his chest at the source of the unfamiliar pain, his eyes became fixated, and his lips pursed as if trying to speak. Feeling numb and suddenly cold, his breathing relaxed and darkness consumed him. In a bent position, his face eventually set in a peaceful smile as he closed his eyes.

Chapter 61

ALTHOUGH BLOODIED and beaten from the attack on Madison Square Garden minutes prior, Special Agent James Gibson was effective in reaching Reagan National's tower, Andrew's Air Force Base, and the Secret Service. Moving away from the loud sirens and confusion, he found a custodial closet and had made the calls.

The White House was under evacuation, several fully-loaded F/A-18 Hornets were launched from Andrew's Air Force Base, and the authorities had established a dialogue with the pilot.

But news of the pilot's alleged intentions had come too late, as the aircraft was only minutes from touchdown. What added to the confusion was that it showed no sign of compromise, its flight path vectors completely normal, if not routine. Even the dialogue between the pilot, Approach Control and the tower within the Terminal Control Area thus far had been nothing short of textbook.

Still, the authorities had given the aircraft direct vectors and had a visual on the airplane and the flanking military jets.

With emergency procedures in place, the FBI began to dissect the situation, starting with the credibility of the information. Although Gibby believed The Patriot's story, he had to admit that he'd only met him once and that the man technically did not exist. Furthermore,

Steve McCallister introduced the two in an unofficial meeting, and with McCallister dead, Gibby couldn't substantiate anything.

With time working against them and the airplane showing no hint of abnormal flight plan behavior, the decision was made to allow the plane to land with an impressive military escort. It was already well within Washington D.C. air space and the traffic flow was full into Dulles and Baltimore Washington International. Several fighter jets had met the plane and all other air traffic was ordered to hold at the outer perimeter.

Sitting on the floor, with his back against a wall, Gibby's thoughts were of The Patriot. He cursed the man for waiting so long to call, but worried for his safety and for the others in the air and on the ground.

He felt sick because he knew this was not a false alarm, but a well-planned strike that a simple military escort could not prevent. Surely they would have the plane targeted with the anti-aircraft weaponry on the White House grounds, but even if they were to shoot it down, there was only a matter of seconds to spare before impact, and there would still be substantial casualties.

Feeling helpless to change the events unfolding above D.C., and dulled from the attack on Madison Square Garden, Special Agent James Gibson closed his eyes, and for the first time in a long while he prayed.

Hortence awoke suddenly with little body movement and barely open eyes. Despite feeling weary from the loss of blood, the plane's landing gear had come down, awakening the few senses he had left.

He lay on the floor facing the pilot, who was speaking into a headset, calmly rattling off heading and altitude changes to Approach Control. The plane was systematically maneuvering lower, and Hortence guessed they were mere moments away from landing. Or crashing.

He felt the cold wetness on his chest, a combination of sweat and blood, and shivered at its discovery. He could feel at least two bodies -- probably Tom and Tara -- lying on top of his still legs, but he dared not confirm it. The pilot must have locked the cabin door and piled the bodies on top of each other in the cramped compartment.

He tried to move his foot to no avail, either from the weight of the dead or his body's own malfunctions from the gunshot wound. He blinked a few times, causing his watering eyes to form warm, stinging tears that ran down his face. More focused now, he managed to move his right hand, which was curled directly in front of his face and covered in his own dried blood.

The pilot resumed his talk with Approach Control.

"Reagan National at 11 o'clock, ten miles contact tower at 119.1."

"Roger that," he said, and he tuned to the designated radio frequency.

"Reagan Tower. This is TCA 3311. Eight mile final for runway zero one."

The plane continued to drop steadily and Hortence determined that they were probably less than two thousand feet from the ground.

Despite the dementia he felt, he recalled the last few moments and his duty. With borrowed energy, he moved, slowly at first, until he was on all fours. Thankfully, the steady noise from the engines camouflaged his movements, and the conversation with the watchful tower held the pilot's full attention.

Then, without warning, and with a sudden burst of acceleration, the plane veered to the right. Hortence was immediately fully extended as he was held against the side wall. The two unrestrained bodies followed as other random and unsecured clutter was thrown his way. Screams rose from the rear of the plane and simultaneous crashes rose above the now roaring engines.

The pilot threw his headset to the side as he recovered from the fifteen degree bank. The aircraft swooped lower, gathering momentum.

With the plane level, Hortence was now standing against the wall. He saw the Potomac River below and the Washington Monument and capital dome to the right. In the distance, the universally low, white buildings of Washington D.C. covered the landscape.

The plane jerked to the right, and Hortence knew a missile had just struck the aircraft. Many of the instrument panel lights came to life, but the plane continued its course, relatively unmolested. Another jolt, this one more pronounced, caused the plane to suddenly lose altitude and go into a free fall. Hortence was thrown to the floor hard, alarms began to sound on the console, and several oxygen masks fell from the ceiling.

He was able to rebalance and immediately leapt toward the pilot, placing him in a headlock and landing several short punches. He then grabbed at the plane's yolk, instinctively jerking it back as he moved the throttle forward to allow for a climb.

But the plane proved to be unreactive as they continued their uncontrolled descent. The plane hit the Potomac River evenly and forcefully, sending it skyward before hitting the ground near the Washington Monument.

The landing gear collapsed upon the second touchdown and the engines hit the ground hard, ripping three of them from the wings. The plane glided erratically, tearing up land with ease and carving a long black etch in its wake. The scene was impossible, the view surreal, as the ninety ton aircraft bullied through Constitution Avenue, casting aside several cars in its undecided route.

Bystanders, out for an evening walk on the grassy fields, ran from its path, only to watch it take its unlikely course. Eventually it came to rest on Pennsylvania Avenue, just short of the White House fencing. It was turned sideways and the nose was buried in the ground.

Its trail covered almost a mile of the grassy area between the Potomac River and the White House. Several of the craft's spent parts were left on the ground, as random pools of fire burned in the path, evidencing the magnitude of the event.

Smoke was billowing from the rear of the craft, and other than broken windows, a bent undercarriage, and open holes in the craft's rear, the airplane was relatively intact. One of the four engines still thundered, drowning out the screams of the passengers, many of whom were blankly looking through the unnatural holes along the battered fuselage.

In the front cabin, Hortence leaned against the inner cockpit wall and took his last breath. The last sound he heard was the first of several Fire and Emergency vehicles closing in around him.

Chapter 62

FALBY'S FIRST TASK was to get out of New York without leaving a trail for the authorities. This had been accomplished with relative ease, after hot-wiring a car, dumping it at a bus terminal in New Jersey, and picking up the rental he'd left there a few days before. He just needed to get to Chicago. Once there, he would begin writing another chilling chapter in American history.

Throughout the all-night drive, he became determined, if not obsessed, to understand how things had gone so wrong. His imagination was wild with scenarios; each fueled by the monotony of the road and his own adrenaline from the events of the evening.

Sure he always planned for alternatives, but to have them played out so explosively was discomforting. He had been in the belly of the mammoth, concrete arena, surrounded by the enemy, and had escaped virtually unscathed. The FBI agent *had* been able to get off a shot to his shoulder, but the wound was clean, and his belt had alleviated most of the bleeding.

As his body shifted with the road, his upper arm stung and pulsed, but he didn't mind. Pain was useful to Falby, a private motivator that kept him alert and energized. It also served as a very real reminder of what he had to do. He stayed in the right lane at the designated speed limit and concentrated on his immediate future.

Had Simon compromised his mission? Was he a traitor? How did the FBI *really* know about his plans in New York? During Falby's phone call with Almedi Hahn Sahn, just before the man met his fate, the great leader had questioned Simon's loyalty.

Falby was on his way to meet Simon, so the first two questions would be easily answered. The third would take more time, but *would* be uncovered. He would personally hunt down the FBI agents that interfered with his plans. It would become his mission in life. The thought of laying low, allowing them to acclimate back to their lives, and then striking was thrilling, and Falby unknowingly gripped the steering wheel tighter as a strange smile played on his face.

He knew his attack on Madison Square Garden had been partially successful, but wasn't sure to the extent. Understanding the details was second to a successful escape to Chicago. There, he would regroup, deal with Simon, tend to his injury, and plan his next move.

He had listened to the car radio, changing stations regularly to gather as much information as possible. What was the death toll? What was the extent of the damage? Was there any talk of the people responsible? Of him?

Conflicting reports were evident, and he soon realized that the commentators were as confused as he was. Some claimed that nearly all of the people had been evacuated. Another suggested that several suspects were in custody. Others remained tight-lipped about the entire matter, their information no doubt being controlled by the FBI. Then he heard the breaking news of a commercial airliner being shot down over Washington D.C., and the time passed easily as the reports flooded in.

After being awake for thirty-six hours, Falby paid cash at a small roadside motel and after parking the car out of view, he allowed himself to rest.

Despite the intensity of the past twelve hours, his thirst for the breaking news, and the urgent need for his arrival in Chicago, he slept undisturbed for three hours, awaking somewhat refreshed, but still disheveled. A quick shower cleaned his wound and injected him with energy. Upon thorough inspection, he saw that the bullet had merely grazed him, leaving a somewhat clean wound that he'd stitched himself.

At two p.m., he entered Chicago through the Dan Ryan. He dumped the car on a side street and took a cab to the Hotel Intercontinental on Michigan Avenue.

It was time for him to deal with Simon.

———————

The small motel sat humbly off the Pennsylvania Turnpike, just west of Pittsburgh, as if discarded like the litter on the road itself. It was old, broken down, and dirty. Absolutely perfect for a man on the move.

One of its occupants had arrived at night, facing near exhaustion and needing a place to regroup. The dilapidated motel was as good as any he'd seen; places like this were so common they were often above suspicion.

A small television was tuned to CNN and he was reading the last of several local and national newspapers he'd purchased earlier. Each chronicled the events of the week with different angles, the cumulative effect of which was very telling. He casually sipped a bottle of water, internalizing everything and debating his next course of action.

Worldwide media attention was split between the Madison Square Garden attack, U.S. air strikes on al Assad camps, and the crash of flight #3311 in D.C. There was talk of little else.

The man watched the television intently. He knew that much of it was wrong and easily deciphered fact from what was designed for public consumption, but he showed interest in it all just the same.

He was one of a handful of men that knew a lot more than he should, and surviving long enough to act on the coveted information was the task at hand. But there were an unknown number of players, most of whom he did not know.

It had been preliminarily reported that over five hundred people had died at Madison Square Garden, including nineteen in law enforcement. Information had not yet been released on the specifics, but eyewitnesses attested that trampling and Sarin gas were obvious contributors.

Several small explosions were reported moments after the gas was released and a shoot-out with suspected terrorists was rumored. Scores of people remained hospitalized, and many of them were not expected to pull through.

What *was* widely reported, though, were the crucial minutes prior to the explosions. Unknown sources had detected something wrong and an evacuation had begun well before game time. All but a few thousand had exited, which radically decreased casualties.

"Still," a FBI spokesman had commented, "One American life lost in the wake of terror is too many, and we will not rest until those responsible are brought to justice."

The entire arena and a two-block perimeter had been cordoned off, with several hundred federal and local law enforcement personnel working around the clock. The media was held at bay, rehashing what everyone already knew: al Assad had struck the arena, American lives were lost, and there were no suspects in custody. A vigil of several thousand had gathered almost immediately and had been sustained since.

A couple hours prior, the United States had struck at the heart of al Assad, leveling many suspected terrorist camps in several countries.

In the press briefings since, the president assured the American people that U.S. retaliation had been successful, wiping out more than ninety percent of the faction's resources and crucial personnel.

The president conceded that there were an unknown number of al Assad sympathizers, and that the tentacles of the faction operated throughout the world, but he promised to expose and eliminate terror.

"The United States and its allies will win this new war," he emphatically declared. "Those who stand against us, impede our progress, or are in league with terror will realize a very grave consequence."

The Pentagon had released several de-classified tapes of U.S. air strikes against several alleged terrorist camps, showing all being leveled. Prairie Cutter bombs were dropped in scores and videos of them were shown constantly.

The crash of flight #3311 was the latest tragedy, with twenty-three on board and thirteen on the ground perishing in the forced landing. It was confirmed that the intended target of the high jacked plane was the White House and a veteran pilot was the lone conspirator. A background check revealed random oddities, but a video tape he'd left at his residence made his intentions very clear.

The latest terrorist attacks had triggered a rehashing of older stories about al Assad. There was a focus on the possibility of future strikes, and the United States' expanded call for democracy and exertion of control. Politicians, the media, and the American people were examining foreign policy, and the Constitution was under heavy scrutiny.

The man carefully sipped the last of his bottled water as he scanned the parking lot for the third time in the hour. He knew he had not been followed, but his senses remained on high alert.

Technically, in his present state he didn't even exist.

The man knew that somewhere in the vast network of intelligence, deep inside the Department of Defense, there was knowledge of the Patriot operation, and perhaps he was the focus of a top-secret conversation at this very moment.

In the beginning there had been twenty 'Patriots' and he'd known them all; following their movements as they had certainly tracked his. They had been the best of the best, picked for their elite skills from various Special Forces units to simply disappear and fight a new, invisible war to benefit a country they had to disinherit.

But with the events of the past week, he *knew* he was the very last of that breed of modern, clandestine warriors -- the only remaining glimpse of the Patriot operation.

With Hortence dead, *he* was the *last* of The Patriots.

Still, there were loose ends. The man knew there was one more terrorist action in Chicago and at least two al Assad soldiers still at large. He knew he had to proceed with extreme caution, his years of training would certainly not go without trial.

With his few possessions packed into a small duffel bag, the man made his way to the parking lot after a quick sweep behind dark sunglasses. He then got into a rental car and turned west, on the move once more.

The last surviving Patriot headed for Chicago.

Chapter 63

THE LAST PATRIOT arrived in Chicago late in the afternoon, on borrowed time and with a daunting task. The long drive did little to calm his nerves or dull his senses; as he focused on what he knew, and more importantly what he didn't.

He was one of a small number who had limited knowledge of a pending terrorist action in Chicago, having received the information from Hortence, a fellow Patriot, just before the man's death on flight #3311. The intelligence was also passed on to the CIA.

But although it was speculated that the strike would be in the next couple of days and perpetrated by Simon, the specifics were not known, at least to him, and The Patriot hoped that the proper authorities were acting on more information than he was.

Arriving at the Wyndam hotel in the early afternoon, The Patriot was quick to check in and get settled. Time was something he didn't have and sleep would be a distant luxury; something he couldn't even entertain.

He immediately left for a short walk to a consignment shop he had located earlier, and was soon back at the hotel organizing his various purchases. With a quick garment change and careful application of make-up, he looked the part of a much older homeless man. If he had time, he could have been more elaborate, but this would do for now, he decided. He had to hit the streets immediately, and this persona would be as good as any to try to locate and stop America's current number one threat.

He knew that Simon was in Chicago and poised to deliver a terrorist strike, but he could only guess where the killer was. Knowing the man's ego and sense of style, The Patriot focused on the more modern and comfortable hotels on Michigan Avenue, but he couldn't discount the Gold Coast.

Using a side door, he exited the hotel and practiced a slight limp, heading toward Michigan Avenue and the Magnificent Mile. The sights and sounds of the street hit him hard, as the occasional wind blew an array of smells his way. All of the elements reminded him of the city's extensiveness and fueled his uncertainties about finding Simon, but he still moved on.

Although his ultimate goal was to locate and stop Simon, he didn't feel it necessary to *physically* locate him. Instead, he was looking for a possible FBI or CIA stakeout, in hopes that they had already located the terrorist and were monitoring his moves. If he could find the surveillance team, the killer's locale would be revealed, and it was certainly easier to find several agents, albeit undercover, than a terrorist hiding in a room somewhere in the city. At this point, he knew Simon wouldn't dare venture outside. He was too smart and there was too much to lose.

The Last Patriot walked robustly, even with the limp, trying not to arouse suspicion, while taking in everything around him. Approaching Michigan Avenue, he was amazed at the number of people and vehicular traffic, and was again confronted with the huge task that was his. He was looking for a handful of invisible agents in a city that saw nearly three million people on any given day!

The buildings seemed to rise higher than he would have imagined, and the people quickly passed, each purposefully going about their day. Working against the many stares of the pedestrians, many with looks of disgust, he made his way through the crowd, occasionally stopping to topically peruse the contents of a trash can or to ask for spare change. Maintaining anonymity was a must. After all, he was not only hiding from the terrorists themselves, but the very people that were tracking them as well. Several hours passed and he decided to rest at a large concrete square near the Wrigley building. He would wait until nighttime, when fewer people would be out and an organized stakeout, if it existed, could be more readily identified.

For now though, he continued looking for any sign of an organized watch, searching for well-built, military-looking males, silently sitting or standing by themselves, who were focused on everything except the normal sights of the city. He knew most would be wearing jackets to hide expansive weaponry, and all would be connected by the latest in communications.

The Last Patriot knew the tricks of the trade, and the skills of the agents would certainly match his own. They could be as transparent as they wanted to be.

But he was looking for a mistake. Everyone made them and he was aware that the grunt work associated with stakeouts was often given to rookies.

Sitting on his haunches before plopping down, he settled his back against a concrete slab and shut his eyes for a brief moment. Though the evening wind now carried a slight chill, he was still sweating from hours of walking and dared not remove his hat or coat. Instead, he bobbed his head, feigning exhaustion or even drunkenness to the average passerby.

And that's when he saw it, if only for a brief moment.

The man, just fifty feet to his left was looking through a pair of binoculars, covered slightly with a newspaper, panning the hotel across the street. He was wearing a jacket that was too heavy for the weather of the evening, and upon closer inspection was also speaking into his lapel.

The Patriot had stumbled into the middle of a stakeout, hopefully *the* stakeout, and he had to get out. He knew he'd been noticed as soon as he'd entered the agents' immediate environment, and detection was something he didn't need. The man was looking at the Hotel Intercontinental and The Patriot smiled at the revelation.

He quickly stood, pretending to dust himself off as he slowly walked away. Before he left the area, though, he looked to the sky to notice the placement of the sun and then to the storefronts on Michigan Avenue. He also looked at his compass. Seeing what he expected, he continued a measured walk. But even with his head down, he saw three more agents lying in wait.

He recognized two of them, and one was Manford Gillespie of the NSA.

Chapter 64

THE KNOCK ON THE DOOR was unexpected, startling Simon and stalling his reflexes. He wasn't expecting anyone and room service had already come and gone.

His eyes were immediately on the door, a quick assessment unfolding in his mind. He was sure he hadn't been followed, but his confidence waned in the ensuing silence as empty seconds ticked by.

He thought of escape, but being on the twenty-first floor, the door was the only exit, unless he could barrel through the reinforced, double-paned window that edged a three-hundred foot drop.

He considered his immediate safety. The door was locked and chained, not that it mattered. As he regained his thoughts, he instinctively fingered his 9 millimeter. The weapon comforted him and his confidence began to mount. He was armed to the hilt and ready to take down as many of *them* as possible.

Still, he maintained his position in the chair, cradling his gun and waiting for the door to be kicked in. But nothing happened. Had he imagined the sound?

When the knock came again, this time more forceful and deliberate, it echoed through the room, another reminder of his vulnerability. This time, he didn't hesitate. He was on his feet, gun in hand, purposefully walking to the door and to *whatever* was on the other side.

Simon had left New York in a hurry and had been back in downtown Chicago, staying in a suite at the Hotel Intercontinental. From this room, he was to make the final preparations for his final mission, an assault that could prove to be the largest civilian death toll on American soil. And it was less than a day away.

From his perspective, things had gone smoothly in every regard. His assignment was completely on schedule, with the last of the details exacted a week prior. Since then, he'd worked in Alabama, New York, and Chicago, stewing over his latest run in with Falby, and digesting the news of the annihilation of al Assad camps half way around the world.

He had been surprised by the attack at Madison Square Garden, having no prior knowledge of the strike, but knowing full well it was Falby's handiwork. The man's signature was all over it!

Simon watched the television in awe, switching between news networks and absorbing the latest reports as they came in. He saw the amateur footage of people running from the arena in the immediate aftermath of the blast, and the on-sight, unrehearsed interviews of eyewitness accounts. He watched as ambulances took hundreds of people away and EMT's worked on others right in the street. The scene was appalling, and he felt emotionally attached and almost angry, as he watched from a civilian's perspective.

In the hours afterward, there was more formal, edited footage of body bags being removed from The Garden, news conferences from the authorities, and doctor and family interviews. Biochemists were answering questions on every news channel and giving official opinions to a stunned America that couldn't get enough.

Since the recent attacks in New York and Washington D.C., and the elimination of the al Assad camps, Simon had been glued to CNN like the rest of the world; turning away only for a few hours of sleep or to order room service. Other times, he would simply smoke a cigarette and watch the Sears Tower, memorizing every angle, from street level to its large twin antennae. Simon had thought of little else over the past several months.

Still, Simon had to concentrate on his own duties. Though his room was relatively small and his better judgment kept him locked inside, he spent his time easily, mostly in deep thought about his mission and his uncertain future just a day away. His alignment with al Assad was clearly severed; his life a blank canvas that only he could paint.

The Hotel Intercontinental was in the heart of the Chicago skyline, and as such, he was afforded a number of views. With complete anonymity, he voyeuristically spied on the immediate world, often spending hours each day with a brandy in hand, patiently smoking a cigarette in quiet deliberation.

He watched the small matchbox-like cars on Michigan Avenue move in slow silence, and he followed large groups of pedestrian traffic as they went about their daily drone on the sidewalks far below.

But his favorite view was of Lake Michigan. He lost himself in thought as he studied the blurred horizon in the distance; where the water seemed to rise to greet the sky in their ambiguous gather. Simon had become enamored with the lake's vastness and seemingly endless breadth. Was his future as open?

Over the past several months, working as an electrical engineer and contractor, he and men from the local union had been tasked with the routine maintenance and overhaul of the electrical systems of the Sears Tower.

Under contract and with valid identification, he had full access to nearly every inch of the building, specifically its hollowed vertical corridors that were the elevator shafts. He was cleared to come and go with large pieces of machinery and materials at all hours of the day.

His labors, he knew, had gone unnoticed, camouflaged by a magnificent skill of the trade and the blessing of a legitimate engineering contract. He was part of a larger team; honest workers who diligently worked eight-hour shifts, collected their meager pay, and more importantly didn't ask questions. Simon had been hired as a site manager six-month's prior and even collected a respectable wage.

Over a two-month period, Simon had been able to place over six tons of explosives inside the elevator shafts of the Sears Tower. The manufactured TNT hugged the inside walls and was masked with gray spray paint; the same color as the cinder blocked walls they adorned. Even if detected, each was heavily booby-trapped; so much so that it would take a skilled bomb technician of Simon's caliber several days to defuse.

He had prided himself in every detail of his work. Each bomb was tied to detonators with multiple frequencies and a two-mile range, and all were controlled by a single, hand-held transmitter the size of a palm pilot. If somehow it was destroyed, lost, or stolen, he could call in the detonation from any cell phone, thanks to the blasting caps he used.

If so inclined, he could detonate all of the bombs at the same time, or follow any pattern of his choice. He had long studied the layered structure of the building, ultimately deciding to detonate east to west and top to bottom to exact the most force possible. He couldn't know for sure if the structure would tumble, but he knew he would destroy at least forty floors, and several thousand worked there every day.

He reached the door, peeked through the hole, and his mind relaxed while his heart beat a little faster. Simon allowed the man to enter without a word, his gun cocked and ready for use, depending on his visitor's intentions.

Simon kept his side arm steadily on the man's back. He knew he would have to kill him in the future, but now was hardly the time. Clearing his throat, Simon was the first to speak.

"What are you doing here, Falby?" Simon scowled. "Shouldn't you be dead or something?"

Chapter 65

FALBY'S CONFRONTATION with Simon was unrehearsed at best, but he knew the exchange could have one of two endings.

If Simon had compromised the mission, Falby would kill him without hesitation. If he was still loyal to the cause, together they would carry out the final attack against the United States and *then* Falby would kill him.

The meeting would be short but intense, tested by loyalty and burdened by past conflicts. Falby hated Simon and he was sure the feeling was mutual. He also knew that Simon, though admittedly sloppy, was very dangerous and was likely planning to exact the same fate upon him.

When Falby entered the room, he was struck by the vigilance of his compatriot. Simon looked polished and alert, completely at opposite with Falby, who had suffered a tumultuous few days. Falby -- the lone operator of a substantial terrorist strike in New York -- had been in and out of disguises, on the run, shot in the left shoulder, and had slept about seven hours in the last three days.

If Falby was to move on Simon, he didn't have the benefit of turf or awareness. This registered with Falby immediately, and he let his guard down to ease the obvious tension. Simon spoke first.

"What are you doing here Falby? Shouldn't you be dead or something?"

Falby refuted the comment by walking past the larger man, casually regarding the layout of the room, and sitting in the nearest chair. Falby crossed his legs and eventually looked at Simon, searching the man's face for any trace of emotion. Aggression, compassion, or anger. Anything that would hint at his motives.

But all he saw was Simon's usual dark features and confident manner. His long black hair was in a ponytail, he maintained a clean-shaven face, and stared at his unwanted visitor with cat-like, penetrating eyes.

Simon was complete muscle and much taller than Falby. He wore a black silk button down shirt that hung well on his large frame, and a silver studded black leather belt made the transition into dark blue jeans. His boots were made of snakeskin and were also garnished with silver studs.

Falby's sitting position enhanced the difference in size between the two, and the image was not lost on the smaller man. Did Simon know that he was here to kill him? Was Simon planning the same for Falby?

It wasn't easy to read Simon, and Falby was again reminded of how potentially dangerous a situation he was in. On more than one occasion, Falby had circumvented Simon and undermined the man's character. Their last two exchanges had been charged with hate; the conversations abrasive and cut short by Falby either walking away or hanging up on Simon.

Falby had also insulted Simon by tasking him to kill McCallister by pairing him with an incapable partner. He knew this, though he would never admit it. Although exposed, Falby remained stone-faced and unmoved.

"Just need a place to crash in Chicago, is all," he said in his thick German accent. "...thought I'd stop by and have a drink. We are, after all, the only material trace of al Assad."

"*You're* all that's left Falby, not me," Simon said, pointing his gun at the television. "That old religion is dead and buried. I'm just doing this shit for fun."

Silence filled the room. True they were the only real remainder of al Assad, though neither man subscribed to the fallen group's religion or political motives. Each affiliated to al Assad for different reasons and both men searched the other's intentions at the moment.

Simon knew Falby was a sociopath, though the man wasn't insane. Falby knew *exactly* what he was doing and killed for the absolute thrill of it. A mass serial killer of sorts. Falby's rush came from innovative and very high profile ways of killing. The man was methodic and careful, exacting his many talents with complete precision and lack of emotion. Simon had studied the man and found him to be the most skilled operator he knew. An absolute professional.

Conversely, Simon was a lost soul and far more concerned with self-preservation than anyone or anything else. Unlike Falby, he wouldn't choose to go down in a blaze of glory or die a blurred death of honor. He lived for the moment but yearned for a future he had yet to discover. True, his work for al Assad was thrilling in every regard, and like Falby he was a skilled operator. But when the umbilical cord was cut, his perspectives had changed dramatically.

The United States government had trained Simon to kill, and after Vietnam the man found it hard to think or do anything but that. The legitimate world held nothing for him, and he severed all ties with the United States by simply walking away and living in Cambodia for several years. Al Assad had found him, challenged him, and held his allegiance for almost three decades. But now they were gone.

"Tomorrow we'll finish the game," Falby said.

Simon was taken back by the statement. Only he and a dead man should have known of his mission, but now the information flowed so freely from Falby. Who else knew of his plans for the Sears Tower? Suddenly, he felt undermined and small. Had al Assad been playing him like a pawn the whole time?

"What do you know about tomorrow?" Simon asked.

Falby embellished his conversation with Almedi Hahn Sahn, of the leader's remarks questioning Simon's loyalty, moments before he ate a missile. He reminded Simon that he'd allowed an al Assad infiltrator --Yamir -- to send information to the CIA, that he'd talked too much to the general's great grandson in Alabama, and that he'd failed to kill Steve McCallister.

When Falby finished, he looked at Simon squarely, who glared back as he moved closer to his unwanted visitor. Falby continued to sit in the chair, although he knew he was exposed and easily attackable.

If an altercation were to erupt, it would be now, and Falby almost welcomed it. It had to happen sooner or later. Only one of them, they *both* knew, would survive past tomorrow.

"Don't you *ever* question me, you son-of-a-bitch," Simon hissed. "I have *never* faltered in my efforts."

Another eerie silence hung in the stale air and Falby studied the wall while maintaining a peripheral on Simon. Satisfied with his response, Falby grinned at his nemesis and the situation eased.

"Well then, we'll do it together. I understand that you are to deliver the punch at 1 p.m. Let's meet here at noon. I like blowing things up as much as the next guy."

Simon was surprised for a moment and uncertainty played on his features. Two things crossed his mind simultaneously and he relaxed a bit, knowing that he would soon be rid of Falby and on his own.

First, he knew that the planned hour of detonation was to be at eleven in the morning. Secondly, he was to be almost a mile from the building, sitting in a car pointing south and out of the city. Falby, it seemed, was given erroneous information and Simon decided to play along.

"I'll see you then," Simon said, pointedly. But then the killer moved directly toward Falby, staring down at him with immeasurable disdain. "Now get the *fuck* out," he added.

Falby frowned and glared at Simon, but decided not to engage him. The time was not right. With spirited moves, Falby was up and around the larger man. He palmed the doorknob, offered Simon a knowing smile, and was soon heading down the hall.

Simon sat on the bed, reflecting on the short exchange. He glanced out the window and at the Sears Tower, proudly standing mere blocks away. Beyond it, to his left, was Lake Michigan and again Simon thought of his future. He smiled at Falby's mis-information and shook his head at the fool's words.

But then he became wide-eyed as a detail came to light.

How did Falby know where Simon was staying in Chicago? Not even the late Almedi Hahn Sahn knew that, and Simon's many fake identifications and personas had never been shared with anyone.

What kind of game was Falby playing now?

Chapter 66

FALBY AWOKE alert and purposeful. He was at the Marriott, directly across from the Hotel Intercontinental, and couldn't wait to play out the morning's events.

During the hot shower, he was careful to avoid direct water pressure on his shoulder. He kept his left arm elevated and again admired the quality stitch work he'd done the night before.

The FBI man's bullet had grazed him just deep enough to require stitches, and Falby had been careful to make them as perfect as possible. The end product, he decided, was nothing short of artwork. In his line of work, keeping any identifiable marks to a minimum could only help his cause. The lack of a local anesthetic had been difficult, but the pain only cemented his resolve to carry through with al Assad's mission.

He enjoyed a very strong Americana coffee from The Bean, as he sat in the overdone, marbled lobby, savoring the moment. Scanning his complimentary *USA Today*, he discounted the news stories about the highjacked plane crash in D.C., choosing instead to read about his work at Madison Square Garden two night's prior. The article was cosmetic and rehashed what was already well-known, but he read it intently just the same. Today would make that seem like nothing.

At 10 a.m., he walked up the lobby stairs and exited onto Michigan Avenue, pausing a few moments to take in the immediate area. Melting into the crowd, he walked past Kenneth Cole and Nordstrom's, parallel to the loud traffic on the busy street.

He wore a White Sox cap, non-descript navy windbreaker, jeans, and loafers, and carried a light-weight backpack of supplies. Mirrored sunglasses further hid him from view, as he strolled with both hands in his pockets, sunning himself. Despite the slight throbbing in his shoulder and the complexity of his morning agenda, he was completely at ease and focused. After a few blocks, he hailed a cab and settled into the large back seat of the aged sedan.

"West Erie and Orleans," he said, flatly.

"No problem," a pleasant female voice countered, and the cab slipped away from the curb.

"The name's Mary Lou," she said, and Falby confirmed it with the license that stuck to the console.

"I'm Eddie. From Seattle," Falby lied.

"First time in the Windy City?"

"Yes ma'am," the killer said, continuing the dialogue with uncommon interest.

"Let me give you a piece of trivia then. Do you know why they call Chicago the Windy City?"

"I would assume because of the winds off Lake Michigan?"

"Nah. But don't feel bad because that's what everyone says. It's because of the long-winded politicians that used to give speeches here."

"Wow. I didn't know that," Falby responded.

The cab driver nodded in silence, but soon began to ramble about the weather, before discussing the Chicago Bears latest loss. Falby listened carefully, offering affirmations when appropriate, but kept his words to a minimum. He was actually enjoying the exchange with the woman and found himself in a jovial, friendly mood.

Still, he never took his hand off the glock, which he faithfully carried just inside his jacket pocket.

The sunlight beamed through the hotel window with sharp, straight edges; inching further into the room as the sun gained strength and climbed higher in the sky.

Simon had been awake since early dawn, watching the digits on the clock turn as each anxious minute passed. Today would be a pinnacle high for him and his career. The day he had planned for had finally arrived, but a rare emptiness consumed him and he couldn't place its source or shake the feeling. He decided to rise and begin the day, hoping to lose the uneasiness in the activity.

By mid-morning, he had completed his meditation and stretches, showered, and shaved. After dressing and packing his belongings, he sat on the bed, once more reviewing the mission he had been planning for almost a year.

From here it was just a matter of getting to the intended location, blowing the Sears Tower, and driving the rental car out of the city. If he encountered Falby, he decided he would kill him without hesitation, but he didn't plan on seeing the man any time soon. Falby had the time wrong and wasn't completely in the know about his mission. Simon's *last* mission.

At 10:30 a.m. Simon checked out through the television menu and made his way from the hotel and into one of several waiting taxis.

"The corner of Wells and Ontario, please," he ordered.

The cab pulled away, and on the five-minute ride, Simon removed and studied the detonating device that would change many a life on this fateful day.

The Patriot awoke after only a few hours of sleep and made a quick trip to a consignment shop, this time for a well-used mountain bike, a pair of spandex pants, some cleaning supplies, sunglasses, and a biker's helmet.

Within moments, and now sporting a goatee, the Patriot emerged as a bike messenger; complete with a worn backpack stuffed with newspaper and his 9 millimeter. Wrap-around Ray-Bans hid most of his upper face, and a backward baseball hat seemed to reverse the years in moments.

He headed back to the Hotel Intercontinental, again not knowing when Simon would make his move, but having no other choice. Today could very well be the intended day. If not, surely it was close at hand. He just hoped the CIA agents shadowing Simon were more informed and able than he was.

At the sidewalk where he was the night before, the Patriot slowed and hopped off the bike, his hidden eyes scanning the immediate area. He quickly saw what was probably six undercover CIA agents, all watching the Hotel Intercontinental with occasional but unmistakable glances. This had to be it!

He removed the backpack from his shoulders and rummaged through it for several moments, hopefully looking the part of a carefree bike messenger, killing time before his first delivery.

He flipped the bike on its handlebars so that the tires were waist high. Then, with newspaper and a spray bottle, he began to meticulously clean all of the wheel spokes and chrome. The storefront next to him, just as he suspected the night before, was perfect for spying on the agents. The glass was a dull green in color and thick in width. This, combined with the placement of the morning sun, offered a virtual mirror of what was happening on the street and beyond.

Working on the bike with his back turned, he was able to watch two of the agents without turning toward them. And monitoring two was almost as good as seeing them all, as they worked and moved as a team.

The only problem was time. How long could he credibly remain there before arousing suspicion? He was, after all, in the middle of a well-spun web, dealing with fellow professionals, and watching one of the deadliest and capable men in the world. Everyone would be on edge and everything would be noticed and analyzed.

Stretching his legs, The Patriot left to buy a bottle of water from a nearby vendor, and that's when he saw Simon leave the hotel and hop into a cab.

Before the car moved from the curb, The Patriot was on his bike and crossing the street to head north on Michigan Avenue. He hoped the authorities were on his tail as well, but he had no time to validate it.

The cab took a left on Orleans, and The Patriot did as well, knowing that he was completely exposed.

Fortunately, the car had to stop at many of the traffic lights along Orleans, and his bicycle was able to keep a steady pace, allowing him to keep the cab in his sight at all times. After about two miles, the taxi paused at a curb. Simon quickly emerged and looked around cautiously. Then he moved to a parked car, opened the door to peer inside, and walked to the corner of Wells and Orleans, where he looked at the Sears Tower and checked his watch.

Two blocks away, The Patriot threw his bike down and crouched behind a brick wall that hugged a convenience store. He removed his helmet and sunglasses and checked his Sig Saur; stuffing two extra fifteen-round clips into each side pocket.

Looking down Wells Street through binoculars, he had a perfect view of Simon and the Sears Tower in the distance. At a proximity of about two-hundred feet, The Patriot knew he could hit the terrorist, but a guaranteed kill shot was most likely out of the question. Still, he had Simon in his sights and was ready to take him down when a woman with a baby carriage approached and a conversation ensued, spoiling any chance of a clean shot. The Patriot hoped that the agents were on top of the situation. Where were they? The target was the Sears Tower, he was sure of it!

Then he watched as Simon pulled out a cell phone and had a brief conversation with someone. The Patriot again took aim and was about to squeeze the trigger when several things happened at once.

It all began when a man appeared, seemingly from no where, and vigorously walked directly toward Simon.

Chapter 67

SIMON STOOD on *the* designated corner. He had picked the site long ago for several reasons, and he was thankful for all of them. Although within the city limits, there was plenty of available parking, a perfect view of the Sears Tower, and it was just off the I-90/I-94 ramps out of the city. His escape route.

About twenty blocks from the Magnificent Mile and an equal distance from Chicago's Financial District, he stood and took in the scene. Gino's Pizzeria, Carson's Ribs, and Ed Debevics Restaurant were on the corners, along with a small and unattended off-road parking lot. All of the food businesses were closed at this hour, even for a workday, and the only activity was the steady vehicular traffic.

He had already checked on his rental car in the southwest lot, an inconspicuous two-door economy that he'd rented the day before.

Satisfied that everything was as it should be, he waited for the chosen time of 11 a.m., when he would detonate and quite possibly level the Sears Tower. The autumn sun had burned any evidence of cloud exposure, and Simon had a spectacular view of the target down Wells Street. A quick glance of the watch revealed it to be 10:44 a.m.

Still, he hadn't been able to shake the awful feeling inside him. Doubts had been entering his mind all week. Thoughts of his past and future flooded his mind, battling for consideration. What exactly would he gain from this? Was he doing it because he was programmed to? Was he really the monster he always thought he was?

He heard the closing footsteps behind him and inwardly cursed himself for leaving himself so exposed. He had momentarily lost self-awareness and someone had walked within yards of him undetected.

Quickly turning, and palming a concealed gun in his jacket, his eyes met those of a young mother walking a baby carriage. She stopped at the same corner and waited for the north/south traffic to break.

"Hello," she offered Simon with a smile. "Beautiful day, isn't it?"

"Uh yes, it is," Simon managed. "One more nice day before the seasons change."

The women nodded and waited for several cars to go by, and the unlikely pair stood on the corner as the sounds of traffic rose and fell.

"This is Abby's first walk in the big city," she said, and she bent to look into her daughter's eyes. "She's two-month's old today, aren't you sweetie?"

"Congratulations," Simon offered, awkwardly.

He looked at the small baby, taking time to notice how tiny and frail she was. He immediately felt a connection as a strange feeling overwhelmed him. Her entire future, like his, was unwritten, and suddenly the inner turmoil he'd been feeling was released. He didn't want to be Simon anymore! He didn't want to kill another innocent ever again. He realized that his only goal was to get out of Chicago and start life anew, and in a moment of clarity he finally understood that *he* held the key, not a disbanded terrorist faction or his promised allegiance.

The traffic lightened and the woman continued her slow walk after a slight wave. As Simon watched her go, he noticed the Sears Tower in the distance, with its shiny dark exterior looking like a black ice sculpture as it reflected the bright sun.

He knew that he couldn't carry out what he had long planned. He took out his cell phone and called 911.

"911 operator, what is your emergency," a rehearsed voice said.

Simon hesitated one last time before answering. This was it.

"Listen very closely. I will talk slowly and without interruption so the proper authorities can listen later and act accordingly."

"Go on," the softened voice responded.

"My name is Simon. The FBI will know *exactly* who I am so I'll get to the point. There is a *tonnage* of explosives inside *each* of the elevator shafts between the thirty third and seventy-third floors of the Sears Tower. They are ready to detonate, and I was moments from doing so, but have decided against it. In a few moments I will destroy the transmitter and make it impossible to discharge. The devices are booby-trapped, but expert bomb technicians can dismantle them with time. I have used mercury switches, anti-lift devices, optical sensing switches, and push-pull switches. The electrical circuit *must* remain open."

Simon stopped and let out a large breath as silence hung on the line.

"Sir?"

"Until today I was part of al Assad. There's one more of us left and his name is Falby. I know I will be hunted, but he is more of a threat. He's the last of al Assad and he's in Chicago."

Simon disconnected the call and scanned the area, as the uneasiness in his stomach began to dissipate. He took out the detonator, glanced at the Sears Tower, and separated the small device into three harmless pieces. All of them were easily crushed under his heavy boot and he started a slow walk.

Once again, he didn't hear the footsteps that were closing in from behind.

———————————

At 10:40 a.m., Falby was motionless, lying on the cool concrete in a parking lot near the corner of Wells and Ontario. His back was against a brick wall and most of his body underneath a parked car. From his limited perspective he spied on the immediate area, as he palmed his 9 millimeter and impatiently waited for Simon to arrive.

After Simon blew the Sears Tower, Falby would kill him, settling an old vendetta that had been eating away at him. Meeting with Simon the night before had just been a tease; a message that Falby was in town and was watching his every move. Falby was the better man and he wanted Simon to know it before Falby sent him to hell.

But for now he waited, wishing the minutes could pass faster, as the long awaited eleven o'clock hour inched closer. The hour of sweet revenge.

As if on cue, Simon arrived by cab, coming within yards of Falby as he checked on a car, and then standing on the corner speaking with a woman pedestrian.

Falby watched the man closely, wondering why he was hesitating in detonating the explosives. Peering out from behind the car, Falby heard Simon's call to 911 and saw him subsequently destroy the detonator.

Realizing that Simon was not carrying through with the mission, a feeling of nausea flooded Falby and he unraveled. He emerged from behind the car and quickly approached Simon, tightening his grip on his exposed gun.

He was directly behind Simon, as they both crossed Ontario Street and walked along Wells.

Chapter 68

SIMON QUICKLY TURNED, but even he knew it was too late. He faced his killer, a glimpse of recognition in his eyes; and although failure was on his mind, fear was something he could not embody.

With the gun pointed inches from Simon's face, Falby pulled the trigger. The explosion consumed the immediate area as time seemed to stand still. Simon fell dead, his body hitting hard against the pavement. Bright red blood flowed freely.

Standing above the body, Falby pumped two more rounds into the man's head, but before he could recover from the moment, a flurry of gunfire erupted and several government agents ran from well-veiled places.

Falby felt the bullets on his chest, and although the Kevlar vest proved effective, each delivered a staggering blow. He moved with their momentum for a few moments before breaking from the line of fire and running to the side door of a nearby building. The heavy door slammed shut with conviction and he entered the darkness with confidence, happy to leave the scene behind and quite certain of his future.

He carefully opened his backpack and removed several plastic explosives and two remote detonators. One red and one green.

Then, he quickly moved up the stairs, following the path he had re-hearsed earlier.

The Chameleon always made contingency plans.

Immediately after the first shot sounded, The Patriot had been on his bike, heading in the opposite direction. He had seen Simon die, watched the agents open fire on their target, and saw Falby's hasty retreat into a building. He knew the feds were closing in and the terrorist's apprehension would be slow but imminent.

Still, he decided to circle the area and reenter from another di-rection. Surely he could become one of the many spectators that would happen upon the scene. He knew that Falby had a history of escape, even in the tightest of spots, and as such The Patriot was determined to stay until the man was in custody or dead.

Several police cars, their sirens blaring, sped down the street as The Patriot moved against the fray. A strange smile formed at the corners of his mouth at the realization that his fight was almost over. The heart of al Assad had been destroyed and the two remaining soldiers had just been taken care of. Certainly there was more work to be done and evidence of treason to be assembled against high ranking officials, but soon *he* would finish his life-long mission to the United States. Soon he could rejoin what *he'd* left behind.

Coming up on Wells Street from the north, he joined several people at a makeshift barricade, and assuming the role of the unin-formed, he asked the questions that were on everyone's minds. No one knew anything, but a body lay motionless in the street.

Several emergency vehicles arrived with screeching tires, as EMT's ran to the closest grouping of authority. Their large vehicles were parked at odd angles, as their lights flashed an ominous red against the pavement and buildings, adding to an already tense mo-ment.

The Patriot watched as several agents ran in immediate pursuit of Falby. They crouched in their classic navy suits as they slid along the building's wall, arms extended at right angles, guns held tightly. Approaching the door, the point man raised his left hand, indicat-ing a countdown. When finished, with a fist in the air, he quickly yanked the door open and three agents rushed inside in standard close-combat configuration.

Uncomfortable seconds passed and then several explosions sounded, followed by spurts of gunfire. An eerie silence fell upon the crowd as all eyes focused on the door, waiting for the next horrific scene to unfold.

The door flew open, releasing a billowing mass of gray smoke. Two agents emerged, bloodied and dazed. They stumbled a few feet and then collapsed into the arms of others.

As a crowd gathered around the fallen men, an even bigger explosion shook the building, blowing out every window. Those standing in the immediate area were forcefully sent to the ground as debris of all types rained down. Smoke poured from every opening and pockets of orange flames licked at the air.

Easy groans collaborated with pleas for help as a general whimper rose from the small grouping of police, federal agents, and EMT's. Others, able to walk but dulled by the happenings, seemed to move in slow motion as they ambled to uncertain destinations.

From across the street and at a generous distance, The Patriot and the gathering crowd had not been thrown to the ground. Rather, they had instinctively knelt low, save a few who ran for more distant shelter. Now they slowly stood, silently regarding each other and in awe of the elaborate destruction.

The Patriot watched as Manford Gillespie emerged from a nearby car and formed a disorganized huddle between fellow agents and local police. He barked instructions loudly and despite the commotion, his voice boomed loudly against the noise.

His message was one of containment. Nobody would go back into the building. Fire and ambulatory support were on the way. Helicopters were en route and the entire area was surrounded. Every agent was to report in to his or her supervisor immediately.

Chapter 69

INSIDE, Falby had reached the top of the stairs and opened a window. With one leg on the roof of the adjacent building and the other still inside, he'd waited for the agents that were sure to enter.

When he heard the door open, he jumped onto the roof and ran, counting to ten before pressing the green detonator in his left hand. Green was for go. He felt the roof buckle as the stairwell exploded behind him. Soon after, he heard gunfire -- panic fire, he gathered -- as the agents shot randomly up the stairwell to where they *thought* the terrorist was.

Without the backpack, Falby made steady strides and covered the length of the rooftop easily, even as he crouched. He came to the end and studied the red detonator before pressing another button. This time a more powerful blast erupted and once again the force shook the rooftop on which he stood.

Jumping about ten feet from the roof, he landed in an alley on the balls of his feet and executed a quick roll to lessen the impact. He was soon jogging east. On both sides he saw the rears of several small homes and businesses, but more importantly, no people.

Approaching Wincott Avenue, he slowed and planted his right shoulder against a brick wall, carefully peering into the street. He saw two federal agents. Both were speaking into walkie-talkies, completely engrossed in conversation with what Falby guessed was someone at the scene he'd just left behind. One held a large cup of coffee and Falby was thankful for it. Any distraction that could hinder a counterattack was always welcome.

Attaching a silencer to his 9 millimeter, Falby quickly planned his next move, formulating a course of action and reviewing it in his mind. He knew very well that success was the sum of opportunity and planning, and that the tiny, seemingly unimportant intricacies could mean the difference between life and death. This time was no different. He slowed his breathing, closed his eyes and suddenly rushed toward the agents, just a hundred feet away.

One of them saw Falby immediately and dropped to one knee, reaching for his gun. Falby leveled his weapon, aiming at this smaller target first and fired several shots, dropping the man. Hearing nothing but a panicked groan from his comrade, the other agent turned too late, still holding his coffee. Within moments he was on the ground as well.

Satisfied, Falby removed a single car key and opened the door to the Ford Capris he'd parked there the night before. Driving slowly, he adjusted the rear-view mirror as the radio came to life. He properly signaled as he turned on Ashland Avenue, heading toward the Financial District and eventually out of the Windy City.

With Simon dead and the authorities on his trail, he knew he would have to go underground, most likely to the islands. There, he would regroup, catch a nice tan, and plan his next move.

That, he knew, would be eight months away and would eventually take him to Chile.

———————————

The Patriot watched the sad scene in awe, wondering how it could have gone so awry. The authorities were just as confused as everyone else was. They furiously went about their duties, running here and there, speaking into walkie-talkies and cell phones, trying to contain a rogue situation.

Didn't they know that their activity was just cosmetic? They would never catch Falby. The Chameleon had changed his colors while everyone watched and had simply disappeared. The Patriot cursed himself for not taking the shot when he could have.

But what troubled him wasn't the present but the immediate past. It was obvious that the CIA knew where Simon was for at least two days and they hadn't moved on him. They also had specific knowledge of his morning agenda and hadn't done anything.

Questions swam through The Patriot's mind as theories began to emerge. Why didn't they pick Simon up at the hotel? Why didn't they apprehend Simon *and* Falby when they were completely in the open? Why did they fire upon Falby only *after* he killed Simon? And where was the FBI?

These questions would lead to very telling answers, he knew, and he directed his eyes away to avoid any distraction, isolating each query.

He understood the CIA's motive in part. With Simon contained to his room and Falby at large, they had essentially used Simon as bait, knowing that Falby would come. While the terrorist's individual agendas were unclear, their utter disdain for each other was obvious, and was sure to bring them together at some point. Why risk lives trying to apprehend Simon, when Falby would do it for them and show himself in the process?

But then there was the most important consideration. What was Simon's ultimate plan? The Patriot was sure it was the Sears Tower and from what he could tell, the building hadn't even been evacuated! How were the authorities so sure that Simon wouldn't have detonated the bombs? The Patriot guessed that there was a sniper's rifle on the man's head the entire time. But what about Falby's? Had the sniper missed?

Also, why hadn't they tried to prevent Falby from killing Simon? His apprehension could lead to more information about possible sleeper cells of al Assad, and with the subsequent would-be kill shots to Falby, the CIA clearly didn't want Falby in custody.

"Dead men don't talk," The Patriot whispered to himself, as he drew the first of many conclusions.

The Patriot knew the director of the CIA had a limited alignment with al Assad, and the man's motivations suddenly became clearer. He was obviously trying to eliminate any evidence of his treason, and Falby it now seemed, was the only remnant that could link the two.

Also, without the FBI, the director could better control things. Even though the entire situation was domestic and the FBI had absolute jurisdiction, these rules could be blurred by the fact that al Assad and the men in question had links to international terror. The group had also killed one of the CIA's own, Steve McCallister, and that certainly expanded their authority.

The Patriot grabbed his bicycle and mounted it slowly, leaving the area in much less of a hurry than he'd arrived.

He passed a grouping of CIA agents, and moved close enough to hear the breaking news just three blocks east. Two more of their own were dead, the victims of multiple gunshot wounds. One of the fallen men had drawn his weapon but had not fired.

The conclusion was obvious. Falby was at large, and although the authorities would surely pursue him, they would never catch him.

But The Patriot *did* know one place where Falby would eventually emerge, and he had eight months to prepare and make arrangements for the trip to Chile.

Chapter 70

THE LIGHT RAIN made polite and deliberate thumping sounds on the black umbrella; a drone that resonated against the thick fog that blanketed Arlington National Cemetery. For Director Donald Willard of the CIA, the weather -- with its enveloping grayness and chilly undertones -- mirrored exactly how he felt.

In the months after al Assad had begun their jihad against the United States, a cold and uncomfortable sensation had gathered deep within the CIA director; a bitterness he couldn't shake or ignore.

It had been three days since the attack on Madison Square Garden and the high jacking of flight #3311 over Washington D.C.; and today a select group would bear witness to the burial of Steven D. McCallister, a man the director had betrayed and ordered dead days before.

A tent had been erected to cover the eight mourners from the rain. The director stood just outside the temporary shelter and its harbored chairs, none of them full. He was the first to arrive for the funeral at the famous military cemetery.

Taking several small steps, seeking neither direction nor destination, he casually read the epitaphs on several of the perfectly lined, bright white tombstones, as he strolled in the gray fog and constant drizzle.

Soon, he could no longer see the tent and was alone amongst the countless rows of honored dead. With the fog encompassing the immediate area, the feeling was surreal, as if walking on clouds or in heaven. But this only amplified his feelings of betrayal to his nation and friend.

Wasn't he a hero in his own right? Hadn't he exposed a terrorist network that could have launched a more aggressive and unchecked campaign in the future? Sure he was part of the evil that had attacked his country, but he *did* eventually shut the terrorist faction down. Couldn't he be considered a loyal son to his country, even if his methods were outside the lines? Men could label him a traitor, but he knew his country was better for what he had done.

Still though, a dull sense of nervousness had saturated his inner being. He regretted the deaths of the innocent, especially Steve, and he *did* fear getting caught. The thought of it had invaded his consciousness since the very beginning.

And it wasn't over yet. Although the infrastructure of al Assad had been destroyed, the feds had yet to locate and eliminate Falby, the only remaining al Assad loyalist that could link the director to his betrayal. The NSA had also failed to track Falby's movements, but the director *did* have a direct feed to every source available to track the progress.

If the director's actions fell under scrutiny and he was tried in court, he would likely be put to death. But at least his motives would be found to be pure. While al Assad fed on hate and revenge, he had a much nobler directive: to increase awareness and military funding, and counter underground militant extremists. Unfortunately, American lives had to be lost to bring them to light.

He had been in the business of war for almost fifty years, and even if the liberals in D.C. didn't see it, he knew that the United States had to maintain, if not aggressively build upon their military strength to stay the most powerful nation. The thought of entertaining a shrinking military budget just wouldn't do. No, he reassured himself silently, this was for the best. He had stopped them his way, even though it appeared as though he was a traitor to his country.

Arriving back in the tent, he quietly regarded the other people who had arrived: FBI agent James Gibson, Manford Gillespie of the

NSA, and the Secretary of Defense. Two of the other men he did not know. A lone woman sat unmoving, her eyes focused on the casket in a trance. The director had invited Armor, Steve's favorite secretary, out of necessity. She didn't accept Steve's death and wanted to be at his funeral. She wouldn't take no for an answer.

This was a private ceremony and closed to the public for several reasons, mainly due to the secret work of the deceased and the attendance by the president, Secretary of Defense, and perhaps Director Willard himself.

But the director was baffled at the president's attendance. He could recall several heated, very real confrontations between Steve and the president. Steve had always attacked the administration's foreign policy and dealings in national security, and the president repeatedly questioned Steve's tactics, however successful they were. The top brass had always commented on how different the two men were, despite the fact that they both sought the same resolve.

Also, being a closed ceremony and technically not even on his official itinerary, the president wasn't going to score any points with the press or further any public relations agenda. No photographs would be taken here.

Perplexed at the president's motivations, the director turned his attention elsewhere. *Most* of the attendees were *not* mourners, rather there only to extend full military honors to the deceased, in the rain and in full regalia, without the benefit of umbrellas. None of them though, seemed to be effected by the chilly downpour.

Several uniformed soldiers stood to the left of the coffin, still as statues, arms at right angles, each steadfastly holding a rifle. An army corporal stood in silence behind them, a bugle in his left hand. To his right, a minister waited patiently under an umbrella. Six other uniformed men stood in the distance, their white-gloved hands at their sides.

The scene was absolutely spectacular to witness.

Always a reserved man, the director cringed at the thought of being the beneficiary of such colorful and elaborate arrangements. Being the center of such splendor would certainly be uncomfortable for the undead, but he knew that his service to his country would warrant it, possibly even drawing media attention. Then again, he could also be executed and buried in the simplest of wooden boxes outside of a penitentiary. There he could go without the simple luxury of a tombstone. He smiled at the irony.

The coffin was a dark shade of mahogany, resting on a large pedestal and surrounded by rows of fresh, colorful flowers, sent by Steve's staff. Their sweet smell had made it over to the director several times in the last few moments, another silent reminder of his betrayal.

Then the director's train of thought was broken as he heard and then saw the outlines of several motorcycled police noisily making their way up the roadway that snaked through the bright green, well-manicured lawn. A black stretch limousine slipped through the fog, bearing the familiar flags and seal of the presidency of the United States of America.

The car stopped several hundred feet from the group, and with rehearsed synchronicity, every door opened and several Secret Service agents emerged with identical poker faces. The president was handed an umbrella as he walked toward the others in long, brisk strides, with more than fifteen agents in tow. He offered a smile at the director before taking a seat next to the Secretary of Defense.

The chaplain considered the crowd in a moment's glance, before addressing the coffin in silent reflection. Then the proceedings began.

"We are here today," he began in a low voice, "to pay our final respects from a grateful nation, to one of its fallen sons; a man who gave his life so that the freedoms and liberties of America could readily be enjoyed by others. Steven Donald McCallister was a man of honor. He was loyal to the people he served and faithful to his one love, the United States of America. He will be missed by us all."

The director listened to the pastor's words, swaying between exhaustion and emotion. He became physically uncomfortable, inwardly blaming the folding metal chair, but knowing it was the manifestation of inner turmoil. Several minutes passed as he thought of happier times, and he became deeply saddened at Steve's peril.

Then gunshots were fired, and the boom shook the immediate area, forcing everyone to tense. Two subsequent volleys sounded, a total of twenty-one in all, and six men in different, but equally impressive uniforms made their way to the coffin. Undaunted by the now steadfast rain, they took their time in perfectly folding the American flag, before handing it to a waiting general.

The general made his way to the president, who stood, and the two men saluted each other for a long moment. Steve had no living relatives and it was decided that the flag should go to the president of the United States, because Steve personified America's son.

The president accepted the flag and stood solemnly. The bugler slowly played Taps and all heads immediately bowed at the sad purr of the mourner's hymn; a staple at every official military burial since 1891.

All eyes were on the commander in chief, as he shuffled the flag to a secret service agent and slowly made his way to Steve's coffin, refusing several umbrellas along the way.

The rain sustained itself in a relentless fall and occasional wind gusts threw it sideways, drenching the president within seconds. He slowly removed a picture frame from clear wrapping and carefully placed the Presidential Memorial Certificate at the base of the casket.

Taking two steps back, the president of the United States saluted the coffin for several moments. Then his chin fell to his chest and he closed his eyes in silent prayer. When finished, he stepped back respectfully, turned on a quick heel, and led his entourage to the waiting motorcade.

Armor was next to approach the coffin. Hers was a less majestic display. Wrapping her thick arms around the top and weeping uncontrollably, she had to be consoled by the minister and eventually moved away from the area.

The others slowly made their way past the coffin, each placing a red rose at its base before dispersing, and the burial of Steven D. McCallister came to an end.

Afterward, Manford Gillespie approached Director Willard and the two men walked deeper into the cemetery, away from the withdrawing group. Manford was the first to speak.

"What's the latest on damage control?"

"All of the Patriots are accounted for and al Assad is gone. We're safe."

"I don't believe in *ever* being safe, Donald." Manford countered, and the use of the director's first name added a touch of unappreciated hostility.

"I'm telling you that McCallister is dead. Al Assad is no more. We've achieved our directive and America will be better for it," the director said.

"What about Falby? He can still tie us to this."

"He'll be taken care of. It's only a matter of hours, I can assure you."

"Your men are hunting him?" Manford inquired.

"You could say that," the director lied, and a confident smirk played on his chubby face. "He won't get far."

"I want him found and eliminated. Understood?"

"Don't worry, my best men are on it. And I don't appreciate receiving orders from a man half my age who has never seen combat!"

The comment hung in the air for a moment and Manford became pensive, considering his words carefully. With his own ties to the Department of Defense, Manford Gillespie probably knew more about Falby than anyone else. With the endless resources of the government at his disposal, and top secret clearance in the areas where it mattered most, he had independently tried to track the man for days. But like the CIA and FBI, his efforts had fallen impotent.

Manford didn't like feeling so exposed and he certainly didn't like the director's false sense of security. He knew Falby and his capabilities, and it scared him. The much younger NSA officer squared himself against Director Willard, placing his hands in his trench coat pockets as he did.

"Then let me ask you something, Donald. What are you going to do if Falby decides to hunt you?"

The director's face went white as Manford walked away and eventually out of view. Completely alone, hidden by fog and burdened by guilt, Donald Willard began walking to his car, again reading the names on the many tombstones along the way.

He became visibly shaken, his breathing labored. He reached his car after considerable effort and plopped his large body into the driver's seat. But he didn't start the engine, deciding instead to relax and listen to the rain pound the roof of the car.

Then he openly wept.

Chapter 71

Eight Months Later
June
Hall Mount, Vermont

THE PLASTIC LAWN CHAIR, once shiny white in color, was now dulled and scratched from years of use and exposure. Pete leaned back, testing the strength of its legs, as he rested his feet on the wooden railing of his deck, just like most evenings.

The summer rain had stopped sometime near early dawn, but evidence of the downpour was still apparent; in the smell of the wind that cut through the humidity, and in the bright green leaves that hung lower from water weight. The light fog and waning sunlight made the nearby lake visible -- albeit by the slow dance of the thinner trees -- and the voice of the forest came alive in the distant, random cackles of all types of birds as they sounded from unseen places.

Pete always enjoyed his slow times on the deck, sipping beer and smoking his only cigarette of the day. The scenery, peering down through the woods from his high place was inspiring, and the surrounding forest offered incomparable solitude.

But the recent events had made Pete lethargic, and he'd been introverted and distant for several months, even to Jillian. His household duties, which he'd always taken pride in, had been neglected.

He noticed the uneven and paint-chipped surface of the deck, and realized that this was the first year he hadn't sanded and sealed it. Now gray and porous, the uneven boards forced small puddles of water around him. Fallen acorns and other offerings from high trees had found homes in the jagged cracks separating the boards.

A low scratching sound announced a squirrel several feet away and Pete watched as the small animal scurried up a tree, only to stop at the end of a small limb, its nose in the air, whiskers twitching at a new scent. Life seemed suspended, and it was another happy reminder of why he and Jillian had built their lives here.

Located in western Vermont, Hall Mount was a sleepy township that hugged Lake Champlain. Antique shops and family-owned restaurants lined the cobblestone main street, a gazebo and fountain ornamented the town square, and a frisbee was always in the air at the nearby park. Milk was still delivered door to door by the local dairy and everyone ate breakfast at Mable's diner at least once a week.

The town seemed to stall time and the feeling was not lost on the year-round residents, each seeking a slower life.

Visitors came from busier places to enjoy the fabulous hiking, fishing, camping, and unequaled scenery the area had to offer. But the roads had a way of twisting away from the popular action, and one could easily live undisturbed in the peaceful landscape.

Pete swigged the first taste of his Labatt's Blue, and after releasing a short belch, took a satisfying drag of his Marlboro. The alcohol and nicotine hit him immediately and the anxiety of the day began to leave him.

He turned to his left and studied the large American flag that jutted proudly over the deck's edge. He had raised it in the days after Steve's death as a patriotic gesture, but it had become just another reminder of the vulnerability he felt inside.

He and Jillian were living in what the media called "A New America," which they defined as a new perspective on things. Gone were the days of blind naiveté; of going about the day in the traditional manner and retiring without a thought of what freedom really cost.

Throughout the country, American flags and support banners were everywhere. Nationalism was at an all time high. Every sporting event, speech, holiday, and organized affair held a patriotic flavor. Still, it seemed that the terrorist acts of late had dulled the American people, especially the children, who were forced to grow up a lot faster than previous generations. There seemed to be a sense of buried anxiety in everyone.

A terrorist faction had infiltrated the United States and committed several deadly actions. Everyday citizens -- mothers, fathers, sons, and daughters -- people of all race, color, and creed, had been killed by terror; and although al Assad had been disbanded, if not destroyed, the horror in their wake would not be soon forgotten.

A New America.

Pete couldn't help think about the ordeal that he and Jillian had been through, how close they had come to the action. Al Assad had kidnapped and interrogated him, cut off his right pinky finger in the process, and Jillian had spent time on the road, running from an invisible something. His two best friends, Blake and Steve had been murdered.

Pete and Jillian had spent a week's time at CIA headquarters to recover, and they had enjoyed extended protection at their Vermont home. But things hadn't been the same. There had been no closure.

His thoughts turned to his annual getaway with his deceased friends, as he entertained an empty smile. Those few days in Switzerland the prior year had been perfect in every way. The restaurants, bars, and café's had been wonderful, the conversations energizing, and the short excursions into the countryside memorable. They acted like they were all ten years old again, bickering about things that just didn't matter.

Pete's smile widened at the thought, and he took another pull from his beer.

As usual, Blake had bragged about his life in California, telling outrageous but entertaining stories that stretched the limits of reality. Steve had been quiet and serious, but always seemed to say the right thing with precision timing. But Pete couldn't shake the feeling that Steve was holding back. Something serious had been on his mind.

His two best friends, and now they were gone.

Pete remembered his CIA friend being so adamant about the three of them going to Chile for their next meeting. "No matter what happens," he had said, "I *will* be there." But his friends had been killed, and however emphatic Steve had been, death had a way of changing things.

After Steve's murder, Pete had confided in Jillian about their would-be rendezvous in Chile. He knew that it went against Steve's wishes of utmost secrecy, but Pete didn't see that it mattered now. That meeting was supposed to be in two days.

Still he wondered what his friend had meant. Steve had always been the serious type and had always meant what he said. Did Pete owe it to him to journey to Chile, to another continent, as he had promised almost a year prior?

The sweetest voice caught Pete off guard and his shoulders jerked at the interruption. Turning, he saw his wife, her soft brown eyes looking him over and searching for his mindset and a way in. It was rare for her to intrude on his deck-time, but he welcomed the company.

She wore dark blue jeans and an oversized light blue shirt. She stood in homemade moccasins as she bounced on the balls of her feet, expectantly.

"Hi honey," she offered. "What are you thinking about?"

Pete contemplated an answer. He stared at her and then back to the dense forest, considering the view. After several moments, he finally spoke.

"I guess it's the time of year. Steve, Blake, and I should be packing for Chile. But I'm the only one left."

Jillian was behind him in a matter of seconds. Her small hands massaged the back of his neck before moving to his chest. Her arms held him and they fell into an eventual hug. He smelled her sweet perfume and took in her essence. He missed times like this and hated that the recent past had come between them. Then she spoke the words that had been on his mind all year.

"Pete," she started. "I think we should go to Chile. I think you need to follow through on the promise you made in Switzerland. Even if the trip is for nothing, at least we'll be together and you'll have closure."

Pete flashed a smile before she finished speaking.

"But the meeting is in two days," he said.

"Then I better make some calls."

Chapter 72

TWO MORNINGS LATER, Pete and Jillian arrived in central Chile, having first taken the red eye from Boston to Miami; and then the eight-hour flight into Balmaceda Airport. But the flights were only the first leg of their journey. Their final destination, a small town near Puerto Natales in southern Chile, was still more than five hours away by car.

The couple was exhausted, and as the plane finally came to a stop and they rose to stretch, each tried to gather momentum for the long day ahead. Jillian had outfitted them both in comfortable workout attire, but even in first class the space was limiting and the re-circulated air seemed to affect them in a strange way. Pete's skin felt gray, his mind numb, and a metallic taste had formed in his mouth. Each had tried to sleep en route, but unexpected turbulence and random cabin noises made any sleep very light and not altogether relaxing.

Pete had very little time to plan the trip to Chile, and it was the next several hours -- the drive through the country -- that concerned him the most. He had contemplated chartering a small plane to cover the distance in a fraction of the time it took to drive, but he wasn't comfortable with the idea. He had little faith in the mechanics of smaller aircraft and he couldn't trust anyone he'd never met, especially after living through the past year. He sensed that the fewer people involved in their movement through Chile, the better.

What little research he had time for told him that the roads in southern Chile varied from very poor to average. Some stretches of highway were said to be nicely paved for several miles, only to become fractured between towns, occasionally ending in hardened, sun-beaten earth and riddled with unpredictable terrain.

The infrastructure between the airport and their destination was clearly not homogeneous, and Pete had mentally separated the five-hour ride into several short-term points, consisting of the scattered towns and villages in between. He had also been warned of potential bandits and thieves that invisibly populated the sometimes-vast distances between locales, preying on the unaware and naive. Still, he decided that proceeding by car was the safest way to go.

But the physical travel was only part of Pete's concern. He and Jillian were willfully venturing into a foreign land that neither had ever seen, to meet two men who had supposedly been dead for almost a year. Brought by a burning intrigue to unravel the mystery of their deaths, he was possibly placing their own lives in danger and forfeiting their safety to the very people who had killed over a thousand Americans in the very recent past.

On the deck in Vermont, the purpose of the trip had seemed like such a good idea, almost a natural revelation. But now, as they moved to the aircraft exit, the reality hit hard. What *were* they doing here?

Jillian sensed Pete's uncertainties and with perfect timing, took his larger hand in hers, giving it a light squeeze.

"Steve said he would be here," she said, flatly. "He said that no matter what happened he'd meet you, and he's never let you down before."

Jillian cocked her head slightly, an old nervous habit, and her long dark hair fell along her shoulders. He listened to her words, studying the face he had loved for so many years, and he was again reminded just how precious she was to him. Still, he couldn't pretend everything was fine.

"Death can change things, Jillian."

"If no one's there, we have each other *and* the truth," Jillian countered, automatically.

Pete didn't want to debate the issue with others so close, and decided to end the exchange on a lighter note.

"Okay babe. You're right," he said

As they descended the aircraft stairs directly onto the tarmac, the sunlight hit them hard. Pete followed the source and regarded the sun for several moments. It seemed different to him. The last time he'd seen it was over the lake in Vermont, and here it was again, looking much larger than he'd ever remembered, its placement looking a bit off considering the time of day. Then he remembered that although it was June, it was early winter in Chile, and he sucked in the crisp, clear air.

He continued to cradle Jillian's hand as they walked, anticipation conquering fatigue. The airport was surprisingly modern and well kept, and when their luggage appeared quickly and they easily found the rental car counter, Pete began to feel more at ease. This could be an exciting vacation for them both, a bonding experience that could deepen and renew their relationship. Maybe some time together was exactly what they needed.

Soon they were in a semi-new Ford sedan driving south on Highway 7. Taking advantage of the cool day, they opened the windows, allowing the wind to blow a well-needed regiment of adrenaline at them as they picked up speed and acclimated to the road.

Within the hour, they entered Coyhaique and ate lunch at a small café. Jillian studied the map, trying to better route the trip. Pete gulped strong coffee, staring into the distance in deep thought.

The proposed meeting that was nine months in the making was at 7 p.m., almost six hours away.

Chapter 73

FALBY HAD BEEN LAYING on the building's roof for several hours, patiently waiting for any one of his targets to literally step into place. His shiny black Remington Bushmaster -- easily the best sniper rifle in the world -- was more than four feet in length and at the ready. With his lean body stretched out beside it, the sleek weapon seemed a natural extension of him.

Without so much as a twitch, the killer's eyes darted to the digital clock, not two feet away. It was 6:47 p.m. and any action would be in the next several minutes. This is what he had waited for; had been anticipating since learning of the meeting when shadowing Steve McCallister in Switzerland the year before.

He had followed the CIA man's movements for years, just as Steve and a team of several others at Langley had no doubt *tried* to follow him. The two had been playing a dangerous game of cat and mouse -- a delicate and deliberate dance that Falby secretly enjoyed -- and although their paths had only crossed once, they undoubtedly knew more of each other than anyone could imagine.

But through all of their worldly travels and exploits, Falby knew the one place and time where Steve would be. If the man was even alive.

So the killer waited.

Falby smiled at the thought of their only encounter, even though Steve had no way of knowing it was Falby he was sitting next to. At a cafe in Lucerne the previous year, Falby had taken the look of an old Swiss man and engaged Steve and his friends in conversation for the briefest of moments, arguing about German occupation of Switzerland in World War II.

But Falby was more concerned with the present. Supposedly, Steve would be meeting his two best friends, Blake Edwards and Pete Swaggerty. These men were initially believed to have knowledge of al Assad, but time had proven them innocent, and Falby didn't regard them as any real threat. They were accidentally tossed into something they couldn't possibly understand, and if they made an appearance, would play audience to the end of the game. That was if the meeting happened at all. Steve and Blake *were* supposedly dead.

Determining if Steve McCallister was alive was almost worth the wait, and if he were alive, killing the man who had helped stop al Assad would be worth *everything*. The ultimate trophy!

The killer was also very curious and looked forward to talking with his nemesis. There was so much to ask the man! How had the authorities come so close to him? Had there been betrayal inside al Assad?

These questions didn't really matter now, he knew. The faction had been destroyed, save the unorganized bands of insurgents and reckless dissidents with their wild disregard. And with Hortence and Simon gone, along with the countless others who had perished, certainly he was the last of any *real* presence.

He thought he saw McCallister in Chicago, if only for a brief moment. A bike messenger had been at the scene, but the man's clothing and helmet had masked any determining features. And being on the run, Falby had only the shortest of time to observe him. It was just one more query to make.

During the past several months, Falby had plenty to think about as he battled boredom. Pensive by nature, his murderous path was always fun to reflect on. Sometimes he would sit in the sun and relive the action he so dearly missed. But the scene he'd left was too hot and his picture had been broadcast everywhere. Even with his many disguises, he knew the trap would eventually close. His dedication to detail, though, would force any capture or ultimate showdown to be on his terms. The thought of an uncalculated happening just wouldn't do.

After Chicago he had easily traveled to Baltimore -- one of four escape routes he'd planned for -- and then to Aruba via a commercial cruise. There, he had stayed for nearly six months in a rented vacation home on Wheeler road near the California Lighthouse. Three weeks earlier, he was in Venezuela and heading southwest by car to his current location.

After the adrenaline rushes in San Francisco, New York and Chicago, he was ready for one last strike. He hadn't killed in nine months and was dulled by inaction. But if his instincts held true, the evening would not disappoint. If Steve was alive and made an appearance, he knew that one of them would certainly die tonight.

As he surveyed the area once more, he saw no change from his arrival under darkness the previous night. There were only seven structures over four stories high, and he was on the roof of the second tallest, hidden against the backdrop of a high wall. The only door to the roof was wired with explosives, and tiny mirrors in front of him provided a total view of the rear, where motion sensors kept an invisible and untiring watch.

The setting sun continued to warm his back, but he knew the temperatures would soon drop to the forties within the next few hours. But even as discomfort set in, his only thoughts were of the clock and any movement at the target building, not two hundred yards away.

The light wind that swept over him picked up small pebbles on the rooftop, throwing them against the brick without consistency, but causing a rhythm that the killer had become accustomed to. Other than patience, Falby knew that a sniper's most important skill was his ability to acclimate to his immediate surroundings; and having been on the roof for nearly eighteen hours, Falby felt he was an extension of the building below and the atmosphere above.

Then a trail of dust rose from the northern part of town. Through binoculars he made out a medium sized sedan, obviously a rental, with two occupants that he knew to be Pete and Jillian Swaggerty, and right on time.

As he palmed his rifle and anticipation grew within, a rare smile formed and eventually broke into a toothy grin. The meeting was on, or at least one third of those invited were present.

The vehicle entered the small town, slowing as it passed the first grouping of buildings. It finally stopped at the Hotel Miramar, the designated meeting place, and Pete and Jillian cautiously emerged.

Through the rifle's scope, Falby tracked their movement and made adjustments, accounting for the current wind conditions, distance, and approximate 22 degree drop.

———————

Pete got out of the car and stared at the faded sign of the Hotel Miramar, disbelieving that anyone was even in the building, especially his two friends who were supposedly dead.

But Steve was so adamant about meeting on the third floor of this specific building at this exact time and date.

"What do you think kiddo?" Jillian asked, nonchalantly. "At least the place exists. That's a start, right?"

Pete didn't answer, choosing instead to scan the immediate area, searching for anything out of the ordinary. But what *was* normal? He'd never been here before.

Other than a few locals milling about, the town appeared run down, dilapidated and almost abandoned. It was a random clutter of wooden and cement-like structures, with a jaggedly paved road snaking in between. In the distance mountains rose, and there were miles of orange and brown clay or sand in the vastness in between.

"What time is it, Jillian?"

"Looks like we've got about ten minutes. Should we hit the tourist information center and inquire about the night life?" she joked.

Her quips always lightened the mood and Pete moved toward the building, reaching for her hand.

"Let's do it," he managed, firmly.

As they entered, floorboards creaked and the building seemed to shift. The foyer was simple and unkempt. The place could've easily been a nice inn some time ago, but the musty smell indicated its vacancy and affirmed Pete's suspicions that the whole trip was probably for nothing. *Why were they here?*

Still, they climbed the winding wooden staircase, finally arriving outside the only room on the third floor. Pete would soon understand information that had taken so many lives.

He studied his right hand. His pinky finger was gone, severed while being held captive in Philadelphia, and although completely healed, the scar would never go away.

With Jillian waiting at his side, Pete cupped the doorknob, feeling it conform to his sweaty palm. As he opened the door, butterflies swarmed in his stomach.

He closed his eyes and stepped into an uncertain future.

Chapter 74

THE DOOR FLEW OPEN, but before Pete could register a response, he and Jillian were whisked into the room by two very large, grim-faced men. They were dressed similarly, both in relaxed pants and sport shirts that hugged bulging muscles. Each wore a shoulder harness that showed impressive weaponry, and upon closer inspection Pete noticed they wore headsets with tiny microphones; the apparatus tightly hugging their thick necks.

The door was quickly closed, the couple unhanded; but the men stayed at their side, standing indifferently and awaiting their next directive.

Pete surveyed the room, too quickly to settle on any one person, but he counted about fifteen others and all eyes were on them.

"What's going on?" Pete asked nervously, to no one in particular.

A familiar voice sounded and he looked to the source.

"Pete!" the voice called, and a hurried body rushed him.

Recognition flashed in Pete's eyes as Blake came over. The long-lost friends embraced, not wanting to let go as they rocked in the center of the room, oblivious to the many others watching.

"Is Steve alive? Is he here?" Pete asked, expectantly.

"Yes and yes," Blake said, facing Pete and eyeing Jillian. "Everything's gonna be okay, you'll see."

Moments passed and Pete noticed the excitement from their entrance begin to wane, as the operatives in the room returned to their duties. Sensing safety, an unintended sigh escaped him and his heartbeat returned to normal. Pete turned to Jillian, holding her hand while squaring himself against her.

"We did it. We're safe," he smiled.

The couple hugged, and Pete couldn't remember an embrace so charged with energy or passion. Then Pete noticed a small, balding man, the only one in the room wearing a suit and tie. He was approaching quickly with outstretched arms.

"Hello Mr. and Mrs. Swaggerty," he began carefully, shaking their hands. "I'm Special Agent James Gibson of the FBI and I have no doubt you are very confused."

He allowed a moment before speaking again. "Steve is here but currently unavailable. He will *hopefully* be along very soon to explain everything."

"Where is he?" Pete blurted, automatically.

Several cackles sounded from various walkie-talkies, and all attention was at the windows on the west wall.

Gibby motioned for Pete and Jillian to be calm, as Blake put a beefy arm around his old friend. Then they all watched Gibby speak into a head set.

"Unit one, what do you see?"

A loud voice boomed in the room, sounding from the many communication devices. "McCallister is about to engage the suspect. Jamming devices are in play. Stand by."

Steve McCallister -- The Last Patriot -- scaled the ladder in no time, stopping just shy of the ledge to check the spotters, just one hundred feet to his left, before continuing his ascent. With the acknowledgement he needed and in a sudden burst of energy, he jumped onto the roof, immediately seeing the target about fifty feet away.

Intelligence had provided details of where Falby had placed explosives, and since his attacks at Madison Square Garden and in Chicago, the feds had trained on several scenarios that the terrorist could employ, given the opportunity to engage him. This scene was very close to one they'd been keen to, and Steve had eagerly volunteered to confront Falby.

With his Sig Saur leveled and his legs steadily carrying him toward the target, Steve's eyes darted in all directions, ready for anything. But Falby did not move or even flinch at the obvious intruder moving behind him.

"Release your weapon and put your hands on your back, interlocking your fingers!" Steve shouted.

Falby showed his hands and with cat-like speed, turned over and kneeled before the CIA man. Seeing no threat, Steve allowed the motion but paid very close attention to the many wires that were attached to the man's waist.

"I've been awaiting you, Steve," Falby started. "You know you look good for a dead man? It's good to see you before I return you to the grave."

"Interlock your fingers high above your head or I *will* shoot."

Falby snickered at Steve. "You know I can't allow that. And quit being rude! Besides, I have questions."

Steve inched closer; his Sig Saur still locked on Falby and his finger halfway into the two-pound pull. There was no way the killer could even flinch without drawing fire from Steve, who now stood just to his left at an elevated position. It was obvious Falby was in trouble, though his confidence suggested the contrary.

Steve would permit a dialogue. If anything it would kill time and allow more opportunity for back up to arrive. Still, Steve eyed Falby closely and was ready to drop him at the slightest move.

"How'd you get so close to me at The Garden in New York City?" Falby asked.

"Tax records," Steve said quickly, as he maneuvered to within five feet. "Got Capone too."

It was clear Falby didn't like the obvious lie or being toyed with. The man scowled at Steve, realizing that any questions would be dealt with in a similar manner.

"Were you in Chicago?" he tried again.

"You and I have plenty of time to talk, I promise you that. Now slowly raise your *fucking* hands and move your body forward, lying on your stomach."

An excruciating moment passed and the two stared at each other, exacting the looks of hardened men. While Falby's glare held hatred and disdain, Steve's icy blue eyes were a wall that communicated a simple message. *Everything* stopped here; there would be no negotiation. Zero tolerance.

Steve sensed the breaking point and spoke slowly and confidently.

"Your detonators are no good Falby. We've jammed every frequency. And before you do anything rash, let me tell you about my invisible friends, all professional snipers flown in just for you. They're located every hundred or so yards, going in every direction and at multiple angles. If you make one wrong move or even scratch your nuts, you're going down."

Falby casually glanced past Steve to the buildings in the distance as he cursed himself for being so careless.

"You know I don't fear death, Steve."

"Who said anything about death?" Steve said, as he lowered his weapon and removed a pair of handcuffs and a tazer gun. "We want you alive."

A mass of air escaped Falby, taking with it any sense of confidence or perceived advantage. And for the first time he was confused. *This is not how it's supposed to happen,* he thought as he felt his future slip away.

"I can't go down like this. I'm better than that and you know it."

"That's what they all say, Falby. But it's time to go. It's over."

Before Steve could get behind the kneeling man, Falby sprung up with a quickness Steve could not have expected. Falby reached into his shirt as he ran to the edge of the roof in an obvious suicide attempt.

But before he could even reach for his useless detonators or take his own life from the fall, bullets ripped through his body. The man fell to the ground, arms and legs outstretched, blood absorbing into the porous pebbled rooftop.

Steve was on him in a matter of seconds. He handcuffed Falby and flipped him over easily, removing three detonators from various pockets. He administered CPR on the unconscious man, blood pouring from the bullet holes and his mouth with every sequence.

Soon others were on the roof and medics assumed the job of saving the life of the deadliest terrorist in the world. Steve stood and watched the scene, his clothing soaked from Falby's many wounds. He lifted a walkie-talkie to his bloodied lips.

"We're clear."

Chapter 75

A HALF HOUR LATER, Steve entered the Hotel Miramar, running up the stairs with the gait of an excited boy. He had already changed his clothing, now wearing faded blue jeans and a navy blue windbreaker.

He entered the room and everyone applauded. Still, the only three that approached him were Blake, Pete, and Jillian. They celebrated with a group hug, which brought more cheers and whistling.

"All right Steve," Blake finally said. "We're all here just like you asked us almost a year ago. Now what do you want?"

They erupted in nervous laughter as Pete regarded his two best friends, who were dead to him just an hour before. Finally, logic dictated a flurry of inquiries and Steve looked to his friends, ready for the questions.

"I know that look, Pete. Ask away," Steve said.

Pete smirked. "'Why?' seems to be an appropriate, all-encompassing query at this point. Wouldn't you say?"

Steve managed a thin smile as he contemplated a response.

"About eighteen months ago, our intelligence agencies, working in tandem with Interpol, MI-6, and other unofficial sources, became aware of the specific intentions of the terrorist faction al Assad. This is of course the same group responsible for the recent attacks on our country."

"We had been monitoring them for years and up until recently, their mainstay had consisted of small strikes in parts of the globe that didn't really effect our infrastructure. But they were growing."

"I was heading the intel on them and when we met in Switzerland, I was in the thick of everything. They were on to me personally, and our little vacation couldn't have happened at a worse time. That's why they put hits on you both. They thought I may have shared information with you, which would have been an obvious breach of duty and impossible. But we got to you first, faking Blake's death, and hampering their efforts with Pete."

The three stared at Steve as he spoke, each wide-eyed and unsure of what to say.

"Where have you guys been?" Pete asked.

"Blake's been in a safe house, being a pain in the ass to every agent that's covered him, and I've been on the move planning for today. I knew al Assad was listening and I needed to create a time and place where I could potentially tie things up and have them follow me."

"Who was the burned body in Blake's car? Who's in that cemetery plot?" Pete persisted.

"I won't go into detail about the body in Blake's car, but the casket at the funeral was empty."

"So we were bait?" Jillian asked, obviously upset.

"You were not bait, Jillian," Steve said, compassionately. "Your lives were never in any *real* danger. Someone was with you at all times."

"What about this, then?" Pete asked, showing him his right hand, his missing pinky finger.

"Pete," Steve began. "I'm very sorry about that. We *did* have a man on the inside monitoring things, but it happened too quickly. He's the man that facilitated your escape. His name was Hortence and he also helped me fake my death."

Pete nodded, softening a little. "If he saved my life, I owe him my thanks. Is he here?"

"He's dead," Steve said, pointedly. "And *many* people owe him their thanks. People who will never even know what could've been. He was a *very* good and honorable man."

Then Steve's face relaxed as he pulled two envelopes from his pocket. "Look guys, this is for you. Inside, you'll find an itinerary for two weeks in Australia, this time with guests. I think it's about time for a *real* rendezvous and a little relaxation. It's set for a few weeks out."

They silently accepted the envelopes.

"See. I told you guys we were going to Australia," Blake laughed.

"Excuse me, everyone," Gibby interrupted. "But I have to steal Steve away for a de-briefing. These men are charged with your travel back to the States."

The same men from before swiftly appeared, and it was apparent the trio was expected to leave with them immediately. Gibby put an arm around Steve and they started walking.

Steve looked over his shoulder and smiled. "I'll see everyone in Australia in a few weeks. Everything's in the envelopes."

And he was gone.

Chapter 76

THEY CALLED IT "GHOSTING" and nobody did it better.

If the CIA wanted someone held outside normal justice procedure -- away from the press and any form of organized defense -- they would simply make them disappear. No one would know of their plight or even where to look, save a handful of hardened men. The CIA's finest.

These unfortunates were the ghosts of the system, housed in small facilities throughout the world and moved often to spoil any sense of normalcy or comfort. Interrogations were slow, methodic, and brutal; every rotation designed to extract as much information as possible. In the world of intelligence, things moved lightning fast and this method, though not commonplace, was well rehearsed and exacted several times each year on the most dangerous operators.

The courts had proven themselves a waste of time and resources, allowing murderers undeserved freedoms and a foreseeable future. These "ghosts" had no such hope and technically didn't even exist. No one ever made it out of the system alive and most hoped for a quick and uneventful death.

Falby was now part of that system and was awaiting transport to a place known only to a few.

It was almost midnight and the group of five stood at the end of the makeshift airstrip waiting for the plane to arrive. They were well into the Chilean desert and the night had fallen like a blanket, causing near blackout conditions and snuffing any evidence of the sunny day. Now it was colder, a steady breeze testing a chill in the air.

Steve had been charged with this final detail before he and his team would fly non-stop to D.C. Back to the life he had left nine months before. He looked to the horizon, barely seeing the separation of land and sky. Several red blinking lights were apparent though, and Steve knew it to be the transport team that would take Falby away.

He glanced at his clipboard, illuminating it with a small flashlight to review the outbound flights. He saw that at 9:20 p.m., Pete, Jillian, Blake, Gibby, and several others left for Andrews Air Force Base, near D.C. Then there was this incoming flight, and ultimately the last flight that would carry him and his team. Within the hour, they would *all* be gone and the desert wind would brush away any evidence of their efforts.

Steve glanced at Falby. The fallen man had recently topped the FBI's most wanted list. Now he was tied to a gurney with IV's running through him, an equal amount of medical staff and armed personnel occupied by his every move. Unconscious, the man still wore handcuffs and leg shackles. He was still very much alive and they weren't taking any chances.

The sleek jet landed easily, stopping about one hundred feet from where the group was standing. Steve walked toward it as the engines slowed and eventually stopped. The interior lights came to life and the stairs fell out, landing flatly against the hard ground.

Two beefy men exited, regarded Steve with a nod and stood firm. Then an older man appeared, sucked in the desert air, and walked directly to Steve.

"So where's my ghost?" he asked, turning his attention to Falby.

Chapter 77

TWO AFTERNOONS LATER, Steve led an impressive entourage of six military police, all dressed in army fatigues and carrying M-16's, as they walked purposely into the atrium of the Central Intelligence Agency at Langley. Steve had made several well-placed calls earlier in the day to head off any possible delay.

The ornate lobby was just as Steve had remembered; the expansive granite flooring casting a hardness and rigidity that one couldn't deny, the overall décor imposing and impressive. This was truly a place of power and there was no denying the designer's intentions in conveying it.

Several stared, but not because he was a former CIA team leader, but rather a man that was supposedly dead, buried, and already memorialized at Arlington National Cemetery. Steve and the MP's kept an even stride as they walked past the security desk and into the narrow, inner workings of the building.

On the seventh floor, the men turned left at the elevators and into the long hallway that ended at Director Donald Willard's office.

Steve had walked the hall many times and fought the urge to turn right and into his old office. Instead he quickened his pace, his eyes focused on the large mahogany door that became larger as he drew near.

Steve curled a hand around the brass doorknob and nodded for the MP's to wait in the hall. He entered swiftly, smiling as he moved toward Kimberly, the director's personal secretary. Startled by the intrusion, she looked up, but before her astonishment could force a word, he spoke.

"Hi Kim. I need a word with Donald. Could you please see the gentlemen outside?"

Speechless and clearly confused, the woman made her way to the hall, while Steve proceeded forward, opening another door and entering the main suite. He regarded the extensive room before focusing on the bulky man behind the desk.

"Steve!" the man shouted. "Is that you?"

Steve moved closer. "It's me, old man."

"How? I mean, where have you been? We thought you were dead!"

"I've come for you, Donald," Steve said flatly, clearly in no mood to waste time. "I know all about your treason."

The director froze, the silence instilling as much pressure as the words that seemed to hang in the air.

"Steve, I don't know what you think..."

"Don't even try it!" Steve shouted. "I *know* everything!"

The director carefully removed his glasses and placed both hands on his head. He nervously finger-brushed his gray hair, as his mind searched several emotions. When he finally looked at Steve, tears were in his eyes and he openly wept.

"I knew you were coming for me Steve. I *did* think you were dead, but I *swear* your ghost was haunting me. As you can see, I'm a few days away from a breakdown and probably just a couple of years from the grave. I guess it's better this way."

"Just tell me why, Doc."

"I don't have to tell you that the defense budget is pitiful."

"And what does that have to do with al Assad?"

"I thought that if we allowed small, short-term terrorist actions, it would lead to more funding. We need to remain a world power and the defense budget needs to be top priority."

"But they were innocent civil..."

"Spare me your Boy Scout crap, Steve!" the director shouted, gaining his composure. "Nobody's innocent, and it's because of men like *us* that they're even enjoying their freedoms. Civilians don't give a shit about us or those who have died giving them the liberties they ignore everyday. They have the luxury of not knowing what freedom truly costs."

"But we *have* that privilege," Steve countered. "And it carries a responsibility greater than all of us."

"Steve, we are…"

"It got out of control didn't it?" Steve interrupted, seeking another direction.

A moment passed and when the director spoke again, he was despondent.

"There were supposed to be only *two* terrorist strikes and then we were going to eliminate the threat. I was going to turn on them sooner than they planned, but they proved too elusive and we couldn't get a bead on them. So the terror continued. Then you got close to the truth and had to be eliminated. I didn't want you dead Steve, please believe me. You were like a son to me."

Steve decided not to engage his mentor. Instead, he slowly walked the room, perusing the many pictures that dated the director's experience and influence in Washington. There was a wall completely dedicated to him and the former presidents, and in every picture going back forty years, there was Donald Willard smiling next to the commander in chief.

Another wall hosted photos of the action the man had seen, showing Donald in the Korean War, Vietnam, and other armed skirmishes that Steve couldn't place. In every picture, his eyes showed the fire of a man that was destined to go far, his stare holding a detachment that only a man of action could show.

The director approached Steve from behind and laid a heavy hand on his friend's shoulder.

"I know it's over, Steve, but I can't say it wasn't worth it."

Steve stood his ground, acknowledging the director but still staring into the man's past.

"How did you know?" the older man asked, softly.

"When I was leaving Switzerland last year, you knew precisely where I was and what direction I was heading. Hours earlier, I had called off the only men who could've known that information. The only other ways were by satellite or by human intelligence, likely provided by al Assad. It was a hunch but the ensuing surveillance provided the rest. I also checked the satellite positioning for that day, and they couldn't have tracked me."

The director nodded, almost in admiration and Steve continued.

"When I first met Manford Gillespie and he spoke of The Patriot operation, I knew he was a traitor too."

The director was confused now. "What did Manford say that gave *him* away?"

"He spoke of things that only a Patriot would know."

"But how do *you* know of the 'Patriot Operation'?"

"Because we were all given the same orders. And before we separated we enacted additional safety measures, swearing absolute secrecy and always promising to maintain the integrity of the unit. We swore to recite certain intel if captured and pressed, and there were code words that only *we* knew."

"Manford's information came from a captured and likely tortured source. A Patriot *had* to have given it up. It proved him or someone close to him a traitor."

The director was now wide-eyed. "What do you mean '*we*' were given...?"

"Because I'm a Patriot, Donald. I was the silent member that monitored everything. They are all dead or unaccounted for except for me. I *am* the Last Patriot."

The director took a step back, in obvious awe of what he was being told. Steve could tell his mind was racing, assembling the pieces and stunned at its discovery. The man's life was unraveling and it came to him in an abrupt and painful moment of enlightenment.

Suddenly the director groaned and grabbed his chest. He was forced to the floor, his bulk crashing hard. Steve knelt beside him, easily identifying the signs of cardiac arrest. The man was already sweating profusely and taking in large gulps of air, his eyes moving wildly as he tried to regain focus.

Steve unbuttoned the director's shirt and loosened his tie. He pushed him on his back and pressed his open palms against the older man's large chest, beginning CPR.

"Please stop," Donald gasped, taking Steve's arm. "Are you really a Patriot?" he whispered.

"Yes I am."

"Maybe in time…" Donald said between hurried breaths. "… They'll see me as one too?"

Steve looked down at his old friend, his mind contemplating the emotions of love and hate.

"Yeah," Steve nodded, grim-faced. "Maybe."

"Steve?" the director murmured.

"I'm here Doc," and Steve found himself instinctively holding his friend's hand.

The director's breaths now came in borrowed gasps. "I know I have no right to ask, but please don't tell my family. And bury me with my old unit at Arlington. Will you promise me that?"

Steve laid his hand on the man's chubby red face as he cradled the director's head. The man had caused so much pain in the past year, but now he looked so pitiful and terrified; like a small child that had done an obvious wrong. Steve thought of the man's family and the many functions he'd attended with them. Then he reflected on the military history of the Willard family and the proud lineage of service the director's forefathers had given. Steve knew he had a duty to expose the truth, but he immediately thought of what it could do to the people's faith in national security. He studied his mentor, searching the dying man's eyes for common ground.

"Nobody will know, and you'll be buried at Arlington with honors. I promise."

Understanding flashed in Donald Willard's eyes. His breathing became erratic, eventually leveled, and then stopped altogether. Steve continued to look into the director's eyes as his glassy stare settled into permanency.

Standing above the dead man, Steve calmly opened his phone and punched in a familiar number.

"This is Gibby," a voice said.

"I'm done here. What's happening at NSA?"

"Manford Gillespie just committed suicide."

Chapter 78

THE DAYS PASSED without event, merging together easily and forging a natural separation from the pains of the past year. With guarded optimism, Steve returned to his duties at Langley -- back to tracking terrorists abroad -- and temporarily assuming the role of acting director of the CIA.

He embraced his charge just as he had before, with unmatched vigor and a commitment to detail. If any inefficiencies or shortcomings had evolved since his departure, they were quick to disappear as he settled back into the rhythm of thirteen-hour workdays.

And although the brutal schedule had confined him in the past, he was determined not to allow it to in the future. For he'd become increasingly more reflective and more aware of his place in the world. A change had emerged deep within him and he'd realized an emptiness that he knew only a woman could fill.

Specifically, his mind was on Dana Carpenter, the reporter from the *Washington Times* he'd met almost a year prior. Although his job required unwavering attention and a near-emotionless posture, he dwelled on her constantly. Whether he was driving his car, walking the halls, or taking advantage of small moments between meetings, any stray thought was of Dana.

He reconnected with her the day Director Willard died and they'd spent the last four nights together. She had been hesitant about his long absence and the limited information he'd shared about it, but the ensuing conversations were relaxed and there was never an empty moment. When they were together, they surrendered to immaturity and to each other, as they explored a possible future together.

And now she was beside him as they traveled east on Route 66 in Arlington, Virginia, before 7 a.m. on a clear Saturday morning.

He glanced at her, offering a smile as he casually palmed her bare knee with his hand.

"Trying to get a little, so early in the morning?" she asked, playfully.

"You know us military guys. I figured your defenses would be down."

She brushed her hair aside and smiled, natural beauty oozing from every pore. He was really falling for her and had never felt so vulnerable or happy in his entire life!

The traffic was non-existent and they moved quickly, entering Arlington National Cemetery and driving past visitor parking. A Marine waved them in, as another opened the black wrought iron gates.

Steve took time to notice the six gold stars that decorated the upper part of the imposing gateway; the regal, gold clad emblem that made up its center. 'Navy Department. USA.'

Steve slowly maneuvered the car on the smaller roadway, until he came to the designated area, deep within the manicured interior.

They exited the car and her beauty struck him once more. She wore a white sundress with a matching ribbon in her hair, understated jewelry, and white sandals. Her blonde hair fell just below the neck, accenting her perfect frame. She bounced as she walked and her smile suggested a glow that was larger than life.

He was in full military dress -- his formal blues -- jacket neatly pressed and wearing every medal he had ever received. Placing his hat on his head, he reached for Dana with a white-gloved hand, and with equal stepping they tested the plush greenery of the cemetery lawn.

Dana spoke first. "So are you going to tell me why we're here so early on a Saturday morning?"

"I have to take care of one more thing before putting the year behind me."

"But you've already saved the world, caught the bad guys, and got the girl. What else is there to do?"

Steve smiled briefly. "It's something that I don't want the general public to see. That's why we're here so early."

"But I represent the public. Freedom of the press, remember?" she smirked.

"You're not 'The Press' right now."

"Then what am I?" she teased.

"A pain in my ass."

They erupted in laughter before settling into smiles. Then Steve moved forward and looked at the rows of tombstones that stretched over the grassy fields and into the considerable distance. Looking north east, the landscape dipped downhill, as if the military cemetery was bowing to Washington D.C. in idled, permanent respect.

Dana looked at him, noticing a detachment from who he was only moments before.

"What's the matter?" she called out.

When he turned, he was serious and thoughtful.

"Dana," he paused. "I didn't tell you *why* it's so important for me to be here today, but you *must* believe that it's *very, very* important. Perhaps the most important commitment I've ever made."

Dana nodded and Steve led the way to a row of tombstones. She instinctively walked behind him, silently reading the epitaphs as she moved.

Steve stopped at a specific grave and knelt, moving his fingers over the fresh carvings in the white stone. He removed the Purple Heart from his chest, studied it by rolling it between his fingers, and then placed it on the tombstone, observing it with esteemed reverence.

He spoke so Dana couldn't hear.

"You got your wish, Hortence," he whispered. "You are finally at home and at peace with the brave men and women who have died for this country. The *president* of the United States came to your funeral, though I was regrettably absent. He even saluted you. *Please know that you are memorialized and remembered. You are a true hero -- a 'Patriot' -- who completed his mission and saved lives. And I thank you.*"

Steve stood and backed away, raising his right hand into a fast salute and standing for several moments in a concentrated stare. His eyes were fixed on the tombstone.

When finished, he looked to Dana, who was watching at a respectful distance.

"Hortence Garcia," she read aloud. "He must have been an amazing man."

Steve managed a thin smile and then spoke slowly, his words thick with emotion.

"He sacrificed *everything he had* to selflessly save others he'd never met. He was also a very good friend of mine."

Dana nodded. "Can I ask a stupid question, being the inquisitive reporter that I am?"

"Go ahead."

"Why does the stone look so new but the grave has obviously been here a while?"

Steve was taken back and it showed immediately. He looked to the distance as he considered a reply.

"You're right. The stone was placed here just yesterday, though the body has been here for over eight months. You're very good, I have to remember that."

He chose his next words carefully as Dana studied him.

"Dana," he began. "This is where I was *supposedly* buried with full military honors. This man died after I faked my death. In fact he helped me do it. He is an unknown, but he deserved to be buried here perhaps more than anyone, so I put him here in my stead. Up until yesterday my name was here."

Dana was unsure of what to say and it appeared that Steve was unwilling to talk any further. She reached for his hand and they began to walk.

"Thank you for bringing me here Steve," she offered. "I'm honored. I really am."

"I promise that our next date will be a lot more fun."

"I can't wait," she said enthusiastically, leaning her head on his arm.

"Actually, how about accompanying me to Australia in a couple of weeks?" Steve asked.

"Are you serious? What's in Australia?"

"Just meeting some old friends. You'll love 'em."

"Australia sounds more than a date though," she kidded.

"Consider it a long date. But I promise we'll go to a carnival and I'll win you a stuffed koala bear."

They continued a slow walk, each contemplating the other. When they were almost to the car, Steve turned to her.

"Dana, you get to pick the stories you report, right?"

"Of course, but my staff editor gets the final say."

He nodded and then spoke thoughtfully.

"I need to ask you a favor and it could also make your career. I'd like the *world* to know about a man named Hortence Garcia and *everything* he did for his country."

And she was all ears.

Acknowledgements

Thank you to everyone that has been so supportive of this project over the last several years. I have really appreciated and taken to heart, all of your warm wishes and words of encouragement along the way.

A special thank you to all the readers who read the pre-final manuscripts and offered very important advice, opinions, and critiques: Kimberly Hilliard, Dave Kushner, June Sharkey, Jennifer Plant, Steve Hilliard, Bill Hooper, Barbara Hilliard, Donald Hilliard, Mike Miller, Kathy Rouse, James Uhles, Lorri Reed, Kenneth L. Reed, Dana Cate, Diana Landergren, Maura LaGreca, and Lisa Keenan.

Thanks also to everyone who offered their expertise throughout the story. Without you, I could never have built bombs, created Sarin gas, flown a plane, broken into heavily-alarmed mansions, known so much about firearms, and moved around the globe with such accuracy and ease. All of the mistakes are mine. Thank you to the following amazing people: Chester & Chris Craig, Tom Middaugh, Patrick Scolla, Warren Zander, Linda Wiedmer, Wayne Hooper, Michael Bruciak, Donald Hilliard, Larry Cate, and Craig Bober.

And finally, a very warm thank you to all of my friends at AuthorHouse, for helping my dreams come true!

Printed in the United States
40467LVS00004B/310-405

9 781420 896350